MARY STEPHENS CORBISHLEY MBE
1905 – 1995

A Biography of her Life

and

History of her Oral School

for Deaf children

At

Mill Hall, Cuckfield

To: Lisanne

Kind regards.

Ian M Stewart

June 2016.

Ian M. Stewart

To:

all ex-pupils, ex-teachers
and friends who knew Corby
and her succeeding Principals
at Cuckfield House
and Mill Hall Oral Schools

Mary S. Corbishley, M.B.E. *circa* 1955
©*Photograph on loan by Jean Landriani*

CONTENTS

CONTENTS *(Continued)*

INTRODUCTION & AUTHOR'S THOUGHTS

On March 10th 2007 I had the pleasure of joining the members of the Mill Hall Old Pupils' Association for their Reunion luncheon in Rottingdean, Sussex, to mark the 70th Anniversary of the School's founder, Mary Corbishley's sudden departure from Dene Hollow Oral School for the Deaf in Burgess Hill of the same county, to set up her own Oral School for Deaf children. In response to my speech – as the author of this book – we all rose to drink our toast in celebration of that historic Thanksgiving Day of 10th March 1937 and for Mary Corbishley, our Principal, with gratitude and warm memories of our happy days.

Mill Hall Old Pupils' Reunion in Rottingdean, Sussex to celebrate the School's 70th Anniversary of its founding. In the background is what used to be The Creamery where Mill Hall pupils had their annual Thanksgiving Day tea and ice-cream.
©IanMStewart 2007

Two reasons why I have written this book are, firstly, the time is opportune for the profile of the School's founder be raised to illustrate her beliefs, aims, achievements and a lasting legacy in her Oral School for Deaf children in Cuckfield, Sussex and, secondly, the need for her biography is prompted by a paragraph in her autobiography *Corby* which is eloquent in itself:

> "The successes written about in this book [*Corby*] are intended to give all glory to the Lord. Human success is probably better spoken of by others, certainly not by oneself." (*p. 52*)

How modest and self-effacing Mary Corbishley was!

"She loved deaf children." "She loved God and Jesus Christ." These two virtues were the main attributes and life mainstay of Mary Corbishley, which helped her achieve success in establishing her School for the oral education and spiritual guidance of deaf children who came her way.

Many books have been written about schools for deaf children, but none about Cuckfield House and Mill Hall Oral Schools. It is my privilege, or perhaps modest honour as a former pupil (1942-46), to take on the challenge of writing this book about her School for others to read and enjoy – and to reflect. However, despite the current proliferation of writing and publishing books – successfully or not – there is a serious purpose to this book which is to demonstrate hopes and inspirations of oral education for deaf children.

Mary Corbishley's *Corby*, published in 1980, provided an excellent starting point and a fundamental basis for this book. *Corby,* unfortunately, is rather a maelstrom of events, dates and years not clearly set out, thus prompting a need for their re-arrangement into a chronological order. I have not endeavoured to imitate her book, nor have I attempted to question or justify her views, beliefs, decisions and actions. This book is intended to enable you, the reader, to form your own judgement of her as a woman whose life revolved around her deaf children whom she loved.

I visited Mary Corbishley almost annually at both Mill Hall and her retirement cottage, Orchard Cottage, in the school grounds, and finally at her nursing home in Lindfield where she died in November 1995. I recall her declining health from when she was young, strong, fearless, indomitable and upright up to the final stages of her life which left her bed-ridden – but she was serene to the end and gave me an unmistakeable impression that she was ready for her afterlife with the Lord. The last time I saw her, she uttered to me – and to her God – her last words: "*Thy Will be done*", meaning her life work had come to an end. Little did I realise she was soon about to depart from life on earth. The "Will" she expressed was meant to relate to her life-long duty in imparting through oral education her Christian principles and teachings for the spiritual development of her deaf children. She was 90.

During many conversations I had with her, she drew on memories of her life and happenings, and would show delight at some of the amusing happenings she experienced, and expressed regret and sadness at some of the incidents which occurred at Cuckfield House and Mill Hall. She told me stories of her struggles and fears during wartime (with flying bombs dropping around her school), her pride in her pupils' achievements and successes, her love for Mill Hall – the pinnacle of her life-long dream – and her loyal friends and supporters whom she loved and for whom she expressed her deep gratitude for their unstinting support for and faith in her.

There is no place in this book for the political hot potato which is the controversy over oralism versus British Sign Language and their respective pros and cons. This is a totally separate matter deserving of a book to be written in an impartial manner by someone who really understands what the argument is all about. Too many views which have been expressed are based on bias, fear and prejudice with no fair "on both sides of the coin" attitude. Hence my decision to exclude this issue from the book which is intended to be biographical, historical and educational, and hopefully non-politically written.

Several articles and books have been written on – what is believed to be – the suppression of sign language, starting with the 1880 Milan Conference, enjoyed by the Deaf so much that oralism has been seen in a bad light with all its inherent failures. One must understand that even in the hearing speaking world spoken language acquisition does fail as well as succeed all round. So do both sign language and oralism. There is no perfect means of communication between the two peoples of entirely different cultures of the Deaf and the Hearing any more than there is between hearing speaking peoples from different countries and cultures.

It is neither here nor there that we should criticise other people's different communications, but we should attempt to understand and accept or embrace the underlying principles of communicative languages. I invite every reader of this book to approach the subject of oralism, *unprejudiced and uncritical*, as of right of those who received oral education from Mary Corbishley, her teaching staff and her succeeding Heads and their teachers at Cuckfield House and Mill Hall.

The term "Deaf and Dumb" used in this book is purposefully enclosed in inverted commas to indicate my disapproval and utter non-acceptance of the way Deaf pupils and adults had been labelled by the ignorant and prejudiced hearing society for centuries. Where I have quoted verbatim this term *sans* inverted commas in strict reference to the original source, this is merely to demonstrate the attitudes then shown to us, the Deaf pupils, regardless of our injured feelings. Incidentally, we have hearing people who have lost their power of speech through accident, birth, war or illness; why are they not termed "Hearing and Dumb"?

For a long length of time the Victorian legacy of being labelled "Deaf and Dumb", mentally retarded or, worse still, mentally defective or deficient (MD) was suffered by the deaf, and Mary Corbishley battled long and hard against this labelling and continually challenged the assumption that deaf children (and adults) were ineducable, leading to loss of rightful education and opportunities in gainful employment post-school. She was a true defender of every deaf child's God-given right to a normal education in a supportive environment prior to entry into the hearing world.

The reason for quoting from various sources is to depict the original thoughts of those who knew or came in contact with Mary Corbishley, whether they be views, opinions, praise or even criticism. She had her own perception of the secular world and God throughout her life which she would make clear in a no-nonsense straightforward "look-in-the-eye" manner. I, as the author, do not accept responsibility for their differing views, opinions and the like and would ask the readers, researchers and the interested to use their own judgement of such issues expressed.

This book has been written in plain good English to hopefully match and suit differing reading skills of both the Deaf and the hearing, whether they be former pupils, friends, teachers, parents, educationalists and the general public. Also, I neither employed nor asked for advice or assistance a ghostwriter to assist me with this book as I assert that this book is my entire creation 100% written and typed by my own efforts – unaided.

In these days (2007) of multi-culturism, -lingualism and -faiths, political correctness, feminism, racism, equal rights and equality and other newly-introduced philosophies and ideologies of modern society, I have striven to maintain good plain Standard English as of my right under the Human Rights Act 1998. Any reader who shows zero tolerance of my such right is asked to overcome his or her negativity and acquire a better understanding and tolerance of the legal ruling that we all have our rights as defined in the Act. This means no-one has any right to change, amend, dispute or reject any of my English writings, however much he or she may dislike, object to or disagree with them.

Bearing in mind the multi-faith cultures, inclusivity and diversity in 2007, I stress that this book is a biography of Mary Corbishley and her Christian faith in her God and must be understood as such, purely *not* reflecting on other faiths, nor does it promote Christianity alone.

I have been fortunate that I was able to make good use of modern electronic communication technology as I relied so much on e-mails and occasional websites for my research work and for obtaining responses from many contributors, librarians and archivists, which meant an enormous amount of time saved compared with surface- and air-mails requiring several days of writing, posting, waiting and receiving. In this way I "travelled" by internet thousands of miles across the globe to Canada, France, New Zealand, South Africa and the USA, and many faraway places in the UK. This, however, is not a criticism of our splendid General Post Office workers who have safely delivered many invaluable and irreplaceable historical and archival materials to my home address in a small seaside village, for which I wish to record my grateful thanks.

I have written the book in a non-committal and hopefully impartial manner as I was fortunate to be taught orally at Cuckfield House School, which helped me learn, observe and appreciate the differing communications between all kinds of peoples from different cultures and faiths as well as their differing views and opinions on, particularly, deaf children's education; this has helped me to write this book with an open mind.

Although this biography would ideally end with Mary Corbishley's passing in 1995, it became essential to add Chapter VI to illustrate the history of Mill Hall Oral School's last 21 years of 1975-96 before it was finally closed down and relocated from Cuckfield to Newbury.

As someone – an author – once remarked, "Researching and writing is a lonely life", it is true that the author tends to become a recluse locked away from the living world if he or she needs the book to be researched, written, edited, typed and completed in manuscript form for the printers. In common with other authors and biographers – budding or experienced – it has not been an easy time for me as I had to divide my time between the seclusion of my writing interspersed with researching, interviewing many people and much travelling and the need for survival involving cooking, shopping for food, household chores, ironing, sorting out home problems and keeping the garden in trim condition as well as part-time teaching English for Work to Deaf adults.

I therefore wish to apologise for seemingly neglecting my relatives and friends – which I haven't – but beg for their understanding of my solitude and hermit-like existence imposed by this task.

Note: Upon useful advice gratefully received, I wish to state that, after much careful researching for two years starting in September 2005, using and checking printed and written evidence, archival records and the like and careful correlation of facts, I have used the dates and years throughout this book, which I believe to be correct at the time of writing and printing. I therefore do not hold myself responsible for any unfortunate inaccuracies, errors or misinterpretations in such dates and years, should they be found to be different from what is expected of them to be.

©Ian M. Stewart
October 2007; updated December 2009

ACKNOWLEDGEMENTS

During my research work I received an enormous amount of feedback and contributions – large and small – from former pupils, parents, teachers, friends and members of the Corbishley family who have given me so much encouragement and help as well as an incentive to take up the challenge. I was very much heartened by their positive enthusiasm and support for which I cannot thank them enough. Their names are acknowledged with grateful thanks below (in alphabetical order):

Former pupils: (née names in brackets)
Ann Allen (Down); Susan Armour (Munt); Andrew Avery; Angela Barker (Batten); Sally Barkes (Woodhouse); Annabelle Bolingbroke-Crabb (B-Kent); Jean Carter (Warburg); Angela Charles-Edwards (Bodenham); Jill Conquest (Jenner); Julia Crummy; Rosalind Dalladay (Momber); Sandra David (Israel); Ian Depledge; Carol Fraser-Evans (Sanderson); Andrew Godber; Jennifer Greenfield (Bray); Rosemary Hackforth (Gilbey); Joanna Healey; Rachel Heron (Peacock); Sarah Holtby (Hutchinson); Lesley Hunter (Walker); David Kimbell; Jean Landiani (Baldry); Alison Leach; Michael Long; Diana Messer (Whitby); Mary Monk; Elizabeth Mortimer; Eric Nielson; Chiamaka Olejeme; Catherine Penrice (Hutchison); Sarah Redshaw (Allan); Malcolm Reid; Susan Rennie (Cox); Carol J. Robinson (Carter); Anne Riseley (Bower); Robert Riseley; Ebrahim Saleh; Funda Saleh (Gürel); Veronica Savory (Armstrong); Alison Sedon (Saunders-Davies); Elizabeth Seneff; Angela Spielsinger; Tracy Spielsinger; Terry Sutton (Prickett); Deirdre Taylor (Millin); Hilary Warner (Yarnton); Wendy Weeks (Mears); Lynda Wood (Fox)

Other contributors: (Principals, teachers, parents, friends, members of the Corbishley family, ex-Dene Hollow pupils and others)
Jenny Baker (Mill Hall staff); Anthony Boyce (British Deaf History Society); Malcolm Bown (Principal 1984-1993); David Couch (teacher); Mrs L. L. Evans (friend); Andrew Gibbons (Bricklehampton); Howard Gregory (friend from Bournemouth); Joanna Hannah (Dene Hollow); Avril Hardman (teacher); Gillian Jackson (Mill Hall staff); Barry Laflin (friend); Elaine Lavery (British Deaf History Society); Mrs Connie Mager (teacher); Cicely Melvin (Spurs Club); David Mortimer (Mill Hall); Jeanne Murphy (Dene Hollow); Margaret Parry (Dene Hollow); members of the Corbishley family; Bob Priestley (friend); Tilak Ratnanather (Woodford School, Essex); Martin Redshaw (ex-

Mill Hall girl's husband); Andrew Revell (Cuckfield House); Lewis Roberts (London evacuee); RSG-Moody International Ltd (Cuckfield House); Sybil Sanders (Dene Hollow); Paul Simpson (Principal 1994-96); Michael Sutton (South Africa); Andrew Symonds (friend); Mrs Phyllis Treganowan (Secretary); David Vaughan (Mill Hall); David Warner (teacher); Mrs Helga Webster (Principal 1974-84); Norman Whitty (Dene Hollow); Maureen Wood (teacher); Naomi Woodcock (Dene Hollow)

Librarians, administrators, curators and archivists:
My grateful thanks are extended to the librarians, administrators, curators and archivists of libraries, societies, associations, educational bodies, institutes, museums and other organisations, who assisted me with the research:
Aldershot Library, Surrey; Almonry Museum, Evesham, Worcestershire; Baptist Historical Society; Brighton History Centre, Brighton, Sussex; the British Association of Teachers of the Deaf (BATOD); Canterbury Cathedral Archives, Kent; Chipping Campden Library, Gloucestershire; the Commonwealth War Graves Commission; Companies House, Cardiff, Glamorgan; Cuckfield Baptist Chapel, Cuckfield, Sussex; Cuckfield Museum, Cuckfield, Sussex; East Sussex Record Office, Lewes, Sussex; Elizabeth Elliott of the Central Institute for the Deaf, St. Louis, Missouri, the USA; Family Record Centre, Islington, London (relocated to Kew Garden, London) ; Richard Goulden (Spurs Club archivist); Hassocks and District Round Table 779 (incorporating Haywards Heath 95); Jubilee Library, Brighton, Sussex; Land Registry, Portsmouth, Hampshire; National Archives, Kew, London; Newbury Reference Library, Newbury, Berkshire; Peter Reece of Fulton School for the Deaf, Durban, Mozambique; St. Dunstan's Centre for blind ex-Service men and women, Ovingdean, Sussex; the Rectory Office, Elmley Castle, Worcestershire; the Royal National Institute for Deaf People (RNID) Library at the University of Central London; the Royal Sussex Regiment (WSRO); the University of Birmingham Library of Special Collections, Birmingham; Wandsworth Public Library (Local History), London; West Sussex Record Office, Chichester, West Sussex; Worcestershire Record Office, Worcester, Worcestershire

Special thanks are also extended to:
Mare Hare Primary School (Mill Hall), Greenham Common, Berkshire, Mill Hall Old Pupils Association and the National Deaf Children's Society (NDCS), London for allowing me access to their archives and records; Mary Hare Alumni Association for posting my appeal on their website; Anthony Bailey, photographer, Newick for his assistance with the CD for the book; Catherine Holland, Oxford for proofreading

ACRONYMS

BATOD – British Association of Teachers of the Deaf, formerly National College of Teachers of the Deaf (NCTD), Rochester, Medway, Kent
BDHS – British Deaf History Society, Warrington, Cheshire
BHC – Brighton History Centre, Brighton, East Sussex
BJL – Brighton Jubilee Library, Brighton, East Sussex
CADHAS – Campden & District Historical & Archaeological Society, Gloucestershire
CCL – Chipping Campden Library, Chipping Campden, Gloucestershire
ESRO – East Sussex Record Office, Lewes, East Sussex
FRC – Family Records Centre at National Archive, Kew, London
MHGS – Mary Hare Grammar School, renamed Mare Hare School, Newbury, Berkshire
Mill Hall OPA – Mill Hall Old Pupils' Association*
NA – National Archive, Kew, London
NDCS – National Deaf Children's Society, London, formerly Deaf Children's Society (DCS), London
RNID – Royal National Institute for Deaf People, London, formerly National Institute for the Deaf (NID), London
UBL – University of Birmingham Library, Birmingham, West Midlands
UCL – University of Central London (RNID Library), London
WRO – Worcestershire Record Office and History Centre (County Hall), Worcester, Worcestershire
WSRO – West Sussex Record Office, Chichester, West Sussex

++++00++++

*Mill Hall Old Pupils' Association was formed in 1973 with Mary Corbishley as Chairwoman and later President. The Association Committee organises annual reunions, family get-togethers and weekends at various venues and occasional outings and buffet-dances.

MARY S. CORBISHLEY
1905 – 1995

CHAPTER 1
1905 – 1928

Birth in Bricklehampton – Farm life –
Scarlet Fever – Isolation hospital – Chipping Camden
Grammar School – First job in London

Mary Stephens Corbishley was born on 24th July 1905 to a farming family in Bricklehampton, Worcestershire. She was the youngest of six children, two boys and four girls, born to a tenant-farmer, Geoffrey and his wife, Elizabeth Anne. One of the sons had died at the young age of one in 1900. She was baptised at St. Michael and All Saints Parish Church in Bricklehampton on 26th August of the same year. The church was Church of England (C. of E.)

Her family lived and worked on a farm, Court Farm, adjoining the parish church and ran orchards of what were likely to be apples and pears grown for cider and perry. According to the Land Tax Assessment 1898-1916 for Bricklehampton (WRO), Geoffrey Corbishley as occupier-farmer rented Court Farm and its two orchards, described as "Lower and Upper Orchards", alongside Elmley Glebe land nearby. Court Farm was owned by a William Henry Bagnall, a wealthy landowner from Cheltenham, Gloucestershire. Geoffrey also rented "buildings and land" in Comberton Parva (now called Little Comberton) owned by the Rev. E. S. Lowndes, as well as "house buildings and land" in Bishampton owned by Duc d'Orleans, a French landowner believed to be living in exile in London.

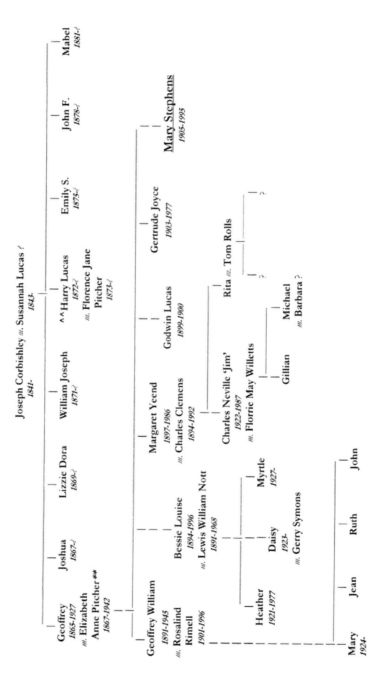

CORBISHLEY FAMILY TREE

©Compiled/created by Ian M. Stewart 2007

BRICKLEHAMPTON

Court Farm on the left, where she was born. Lynchgate on the right.
©Ian M. Stewart 2006, with owner's kind permission

St Michael's Church where she was
baptised and her parents, sister Joyce
and brother Lucas were buried.
©Ian M. Stewart 2006

Mary Corbishley at age of 5
with her Mother (*clip from
large family group photograph*)
©Mill Hall OPA archives

BRICKLEHAMPTON (*Continued*)

Distant view of village below Bredon Hill
©*Ian M. Stewart 2006*

Approach to the village
©*Ian M. Stewart 2006*

BRICKLEHAMPTON *(Continued)*

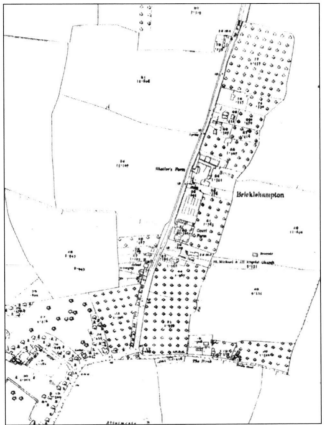

Reproduced from 1923 Ordnance Survey map with kind permission of
the Ordnance Survey. *©Crown copyright. All rights reserved.* (NA)

In 1905 Bricklehampton, part of Elmley Castle chapelry, was a small
hamlet with a population of approximately 190 in the heart of the famed Vale of
Evesham abounding with hop, apple and pear orchards and comprised a long
open country lane with two or three farms, 35 cottages, a blacksmith's forge and
an imposing Italianate Bricklehampton Hall, the owners of which also owned
some of the surrounding lands. It has been claimed that the name
Bricklehampton is the longest solidly written place name with fourteen letters of
the alphabet in any English-speaking country without repeating a letter of the
alphabet.

There was a C. of E. school opposite the parish church, a minute's walk
from Court Farm. The school was opened in 1855 and became a public

elementary school under the Education Act of 1870, but it was closed on 31st May 1922 by order of the Local Education Authority (Worcestershire County Council Education Committee) under the Education Act, 1921.

The countryside around Bricklehampton is a large flat plain with enclosed fields and isolated farms widely scattered over the area, and is overlooked by Bredon Hill to the south and the wide open end of the Vale of Evesham to the north.

As described in the *Encyclopaedia Britannica, 1911 Edition,* the Vale of Evesham, also known as the Avon valley, was devoted to orchards and market gardening, with red marls and rich loams both excellent for market gardens and tillage. Orchards were extensive with large tracts of woodlands. The equable and healthy climate was very favourable for the cultivation of fruit, vegetables and hops. The principal grain crops were wheat and oats, alongside other crops such as turnips, potatoes and beans.

Geoffrey Corbishley originally came from Hulme Walfield in Cheshire where his family ran a prosperous farm believed to be mainly of potatoes for the local garden markets. His father, Joseph, was known locally as "Tater Jo". Joseph, who was born in Horton, Staffordshire, married Susannah Lucas from Hulme Walfield in *circa.* 1864 and they had eight children, of whom Geoffrey was the eldest.

According to the *Encyclopaedia Britannica, 1911 Edition,* Cheshire was 4/5th cultivated for large quantities of oats and for, mainly, potatoes which were the most important green crop. The climate was temperate and rather damp. Agriculture became the main industry after shipbuilding on the river Mersey and cotton manufacture because of new improved farming equipment and methods which were taken up by enterprising farmers.

Joseph Corbishley was unable to find another local farm available in Cheshire for his son, Geoffrey, so he sent the son further afield and Geoffrey as a result left home for Worcestershire where he secured employment probably on a farm in Comberton Parva. At the age of 24, he met and married Elizabeth Anne, a daughter of William Godwin Yeend (Sen.) Pitcher, a prosperous tenant-farmer and subsequently, landowner of Nash's Farm in Comberton Parva, a few miles north-west of Bricklehampton, on 16th April 1890 at St Peter's Church in that village. The Rev. E. S. Lowndes, the rector and landowner, officiated at the wedding ceremony.

Elizabeth Anne was the eldest of eleven children, five sons and six daughters, born to the Pitcher family. Their mother, Mary Stephens, having married into the Pitcher family in 1866, came from the Yeend family of Comberton Parva; however, their maternal grandfather, Joseph Harper Yeend, was a ship chandler/merchant in Gloucester, Gloucestershire. It seems likely that Mary Stephens Corbishley was named after her grandmother to retain the family name as was customary in those days of the Victorians and Edwardians. Mary Stephens Yeend was living in Tooting Graveney, South London at the time of her marriage to William G. Y. (Sen.) Pitcher who probably travelled by steam train (with the Great Western Railway), stagecoach or, even, horse and trap from Worcestershire to seek her hand to which her father, Joseph Harper, gave his consent, and he, Joseph Harper, was present at their marriage at the parish church of Tooting on 10th July 1866.

After marriage, Geoffrey and Elizabeth set up home at Court Farm in Bricklehampton. He also farmed in Bishampton, five miles north and on another farm, Old Fallow, in Comberton Parva, a couple of miles away. From 1889 to 1893, according to the Minute Book for Bricklehampton Parish Church, Geoffrey served on the Committee as overseer and surveyor of the highways as well as chairman. He was responsible for the upkeep of the highways in the vicinity. He was also what was then described "qualified" as Guardian of the Poor, a role he carried out additionally for Pershore. Under the administration of Pershore Union established by the Poor Law Amendment Act 1834, his role involved checking on and giving succour to the poor, the ill and the unemployed. In 1907 and 1911, during harvest festivals, he and his wife gave lunches for school children who were invited to partake of the special "Bread" distributed at their home, Court Farm; the "big loaf" was donated to the Church by one of the local residents. (*Bricklehampton School Log Book* – WRO)

Father on his new steam plough-tractor *c.* 1910. He hired the tractor out to local farmers. ©*Photograph by Corbishley family*

PITCHER FAMILY TREE

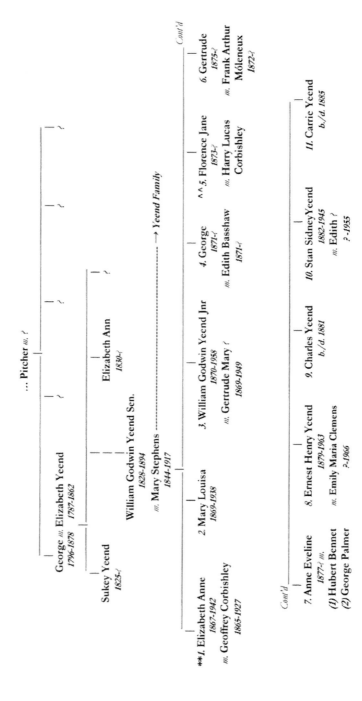

YEEND FAMILY TREE

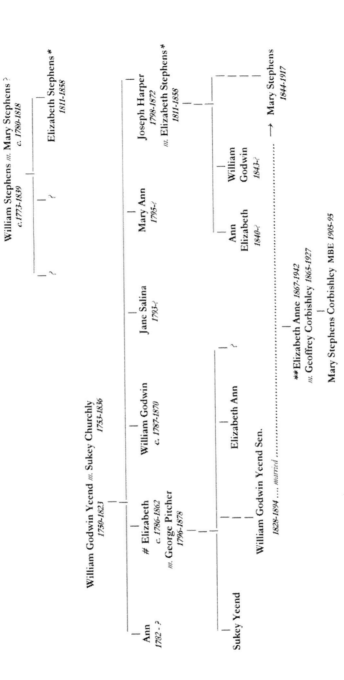

William Godwin Yeend *m.* **Sukey Churchly**
1750-1823 / 1753-1836

William Stephens *m.* **Mary Stephens** ?
c.1773-1839 / c.1780-1818

Ann
1782 - ?

 # Elizabeth
c.1786-1862
m. **George Pitcher**
1796-1878

William Godwin
c.1787-1870

Elizabeth Stephens *
1811-1858

?

?

Jane Salina
1793-?

Mary Ann
1795-?

Joseph Harper
1798-1872
m. **Elizabeth Stephens ***
1811-1858

Elizabeth Ann

William Godwin Yeend Sen.
1828-1894 .... *married* ....

?

Ann Elizabeth
1840-?

William Godwin
1843-?

→ **Mary Stephens**
1844-1917

Sukey Yeend

****Elizabeth Anne** *1867-1942*
m. **Geoffrey Corbishley** *1865-1927*

Mary Stephens Corbishley MBE *1905-95*

9

When Mary Corbishley was four and a half years of age, in November 1910 she contracted scarlet fever and spent several weeks over Christmas and into the early months of the new year at an Isolation Hospital in Three Springs Road, Pershore. Her father was one of the governors there. The Isolation Hospital was believed to be under the same management as that of Pershore Cottage Hospital, the aims of which, according to the Cottage Hospital Rules, were to receive "persons from Pershore and the neighbouring parishes suffering from accidents and diseases requiring active medical or surgical treatment." The Annual Report of the Pershore Cottage Hospital for the Year ending 31st October 1911 recorded: "under circumstances which no amount of foresight or care could prevent, Scarlet Fever has twice introduced itself into the Hospital during the year … the cases were promptly removed to the Isolation Hospital…" (WRO)

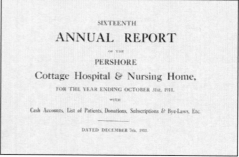

Pershore Cottage Hospital   Extract from Annual Report
©Sixteenth Annual Report of Pershore Cottage Hospital (WRO)

There were also some entries referring to the scarlet fever epidemic in Bricklehampton School's Log Book (quoted *verbatim*): *December 20th 1909* – "Sanitary Inspector visited and enquired causes of sickness and owing to one case of Scarlet Fever in the village": *January 10th 1910* – "School re-opened (after Christmas hols) and duties resumed. Attendance irregular on account of sickness (Scarlet Fever epidemic)": *April 8th 1910* – "36.1 on books average attendance. 31.1 and 86 per cent. This shows the lowest per cent during the year on account of Epidemic of Scarlet Fever." It appears that the epidemic was giving cause for serious concern to the local community. Mary Corbishley was unfortunate in being one of a very few local residents to have succumbed to this debilitating disease which was to affect her health and education later in her life and leave an indelible mark on her psyche.

Owing to her delicate health weakened by scarlet fever, she with her older sister, Joyce, grew up in a nursery at their home with a governess – probably one of her aunts – who taught them domestic skills including sewing which she disliked. However, her mother ensured that she was being taught to read well and develop good general knowledge by her governess at home. It appears from official records that she might not have attended the public elementary school, merely a few yards from her home, although the Elementary Education Acts, 1870 and 1876 laid down that every child of five upwards was obliged to receive formal education. The School Rolls of 1911-1917 did not appear to register her name which probably explained her non-attendance at the school. However, there was provision in Section 74 of the 1870 Elementary Education Act to the effect that a child being prevented from attending school by sickness or any unavoidable illness would be exempt by virtue of such sickness or illness being "a reasonable cause for not requiring his/her parents to send him/her to school."

In Bricklehampton, in common with other country villages, local life was very much to the fore in a village community of farmers, farmhands and other labourers attending the church which was a focal point. Church and Christianity were the two strong influences in Mary Corbishley's young life. Additionally, there was a very strong family community of the Corbishleys, Yeends, Pitchers and Stephens all living within easy reach of each other, and there were a few inter-family marriages, too.

Mary Corbishley suffered other usual childhood illnesses except mumps which she claimed she never had, and several attacks of rheumatic fever, despite enjoying the healthy farm life in the open air, one of which was to curtail her grammar school education.

Street of Bricklehampton with local school at the centre.
©*Ian M.Stewart 2006*

The World War One broke out in August 1914 and lasted until November 1918. Mary Corbishley and her family moved out of Court Farm sometime during the years of 1911-1915 to live on Old Fallow Farm where her eldest brother, Geoffrey William, farmed. He later inherited the farm as a descendent of the family. Interestingly, the author was informed by the present owner of Court Farm that in 1911 a George William Stephens bought the farm; the Land Tax Assessment, 1898-1916 (WRO), registered the change of occupiers of Court Farm in 1915-16 when George Stephens moved in to occupy it.

Growing crops was an essential occupation for the nation's survival and self-sufficiency; despite her weakened health, she at a young age lent a hand with the work on the land and even milked cows. In a war effort she joined the Women's Land Army set up to undertake general field work as well as dairy work, and was awarded with "a green armband with a scarlet crown upon it for my services to the Land Army." (*Corby, page 17*) Her armband was moth-eaten after such a long time and was discarded.

Although she lacked an elementary school leaving certificate, she was, nevertheless, enrolled as a boarder at Chipping Campden Grammar School in Chipping Campden in 1918 when she was thirteen. The Grammar School, one of the best known oldest schools in the country, was founded in the 1400s as a free school for the children of Chipping Campden with the help of an endowment by local benefactors. It later became a Grammar School. Fronting the High Street, it was an imposing three-storey building constructed of Cotswold stone, and comprised classrooms, boarding accommodation and a master's residence, and had a playground to the rear. The school was closed in 1927 and relocated to new premises elsewhere in the same town. The picture on *page 14* features what Mary Corbishley's class could have been like with neat rows of desks, boys in smart suits, stiff collars and ties and with tidy hair styles, and the girls in blouses and dark-coloured skirts (and presumably dark stockings).

Her headmaster, Walter Matthew Cox, was described as "dynamic" and his inspirational leadership led to the Grammar School regaining its former good reputation which had been dissipated under his predecessor, and his efforts resulted in his having to cope with the over-crowding and over-subscribing.

The Grammar School was co-educational with girl-boarders staying at a hostel opposite. Mary Corbishley received tuition in such subjects as Scripture, English, Geography and Arithmetic [*sic*]. She found the last-named subject a bit beyond her ability as she tried to grapple with anything arithmetical further than day-to-day practical use. She admitted in *Corby*: "…but Arithmetic – I was and still am hopeless beyond practical level." *(p. 17)* She played in the School Hockey Eleven, a tough game for which her farm life had stood her in good stead.

Sketch of Chipping Campden Grammar School. *Reproduced from* John Horne's *A Short Account of the Chipping Campden Grammar School (pub. 1879)* (CCL)

Former Grammar School in 2006 ©*Ian M. Stewart 2006*

Chipping Campden Grammar School pupils (undated). *Reproduced from*
©David Viner's *The North Cotswolds in Old Photographs, pub. 1988* (CCL)
Permission applied for.

School room in the Old Grammar School.
Photograph reproduced from John Horne's *Chipping Campden
From the Grass Roots,* Booklet pub. 1982 (CCL)

Unfortunately, her time at the Grammar School was cut short; after having spent only four terms, she went down with another attack of rheumatic fever which meant she was withdrawn from the Grammar School before completion of her education there. Even, when she had recovered from the illness at the age of 15, she was advised by her Headmaster, Mr Cox, not to return to the grammar school, much to her great disappointment. But she said in *Corby*: "… how adamant he was (in telling me) that when I found my niche I should be a success but it would probably be *something quite unorthodox, which would capture my imagination and my heart.*" (*p. 19*)

How extraordinarily perceptive of the Headmaster it was to have predicted her future so true. Her autobiography is dedicated to this gentleman among many others. In addition to that unfortunate time, it is likely that her mother, to whom the Headmaster had spoken, was suffering from financial straits and might have found the school fees too expensive. Her father probably agreed, although he might have not been involved in the discussions with the Headmaster.

Mr Cox had supported Mary Corbishley during her terms at the Grammar School and assessed her skills and qualities in his *letter of reference dated 15th December 1925* (typed copy *verbatim*): "I have known Miss Mary Corbishley and her family for the past seven years and cannot speak too highly of her. She is particularly good with young people, soon wins their affection, and is tactful in handling them. Domesticated, useful in any emergency and ready to adapt herself, Miss Corbishley may be relied upon to carry out conscientiously any duties with which she may be entrusted. I am quite sure she will be found absolutely reliable and very loyal to her employers."

In September 1920 she was a bridesmaid at the age of 15 to her elder sister, Margaret Yeend, who married Charles Clemens, a coal merchant and widower from Pershore at St Peter's Church in the parish of Comberton Parva. In the wedding photograph on the next page Mary Corbishley is on the right of the bridegroom with the Rev. Lowndes on her right. Her mother can just be seen on the extreme right of the group; the other bridesmaid was her eldest sister, Bessie Louise.

When Mary Corbishley's brother, Geoffrey William, got married in 1923, her parents and sister, Gertrude Joyce, moved out of Old Fallow Farm to a rented Edwardian terrace house in Bridge Street, Pershore. The author was told that Mary Corbishley might never have actually lived there, but she subsequently made several visits during school holidays and for Christmas and occasional family celebrations.

Wedding of her elder sister, Margaret Yeend, 1920
Mary Corbishley is second from the left
©Photograph by Corbishley family

Mary Corbishley's parents' home in Pershore.
©Ian M. Stewart 2006, with owner's kind permission

Misfortune and hard times had already befallen the Corbishley family, so Mary Corbishley in order not to impose on her struggling parents went to Kenilworth to live with a family as a babyminder. She gained invaluable experience from nursing a sick baby and realised that her earlier experiences of many illnesses had befitted her for the job as she learnt the importance of emotional stability in a close relationship and so nursed the sick baby to a full recovery. This undoubtedly sowed the first seeds of her future caring for and of babies and young children, subsequently of her teaching and nurturing deaf children from an early age.

Shortly after that baby-minding job, still in her teens, she moved to live with her uncle and aunt and their four children in the same town, Kenilworth. They all caught diphtheria; she was once again sent to an isolation ward. Although she was prevented from completing her grammar school education, she had developed a strong belief in herself, sustained by her beloved Mother's deeply religious teachings. This alone helped her to face her unknown future, when she came to decide to leave home for her first job in London in 1925.

She might have been weakened by scarlet fever and rheumatic fever when young but had inherited a strong character from her father who toiled on his farms all his life before giving it all up and moving to Pershore where he died on 4th June 1927 at the age of 62 and was buried at St Michael and All Saints in Bricklehampton. She was 21. Her mother continued to live in Bridge Street until she died on 29th December 1942 at the age of 75 and was buried next to her husband's grave at the same church. Mary Corbishley was already running her Oral School at Cuckfield House in Cuckfield, Sussex, and upon a telephone call from her sister, travelled through war-stricken and heavily-bombed London to Pershore where she spent her last Christmas Day with her Mother. Afterwards, she returned to her dark, cold and empty school …

When she had fully recovered from diphtheria, Mary Corbishley applied for a job through an advertisement as a housekeeper (or, perhaps, governess as it is not clearly established) which she succeeded in obtaining. Her new employer was an influential and well-to-do lady with two houses and six children living in Hampstead, north London. So in late 1925, at the age of 20 armed with the letter of reference from her Headmaster, she set forth on uncharted waters from Pershore to London, likely not knowing what the future would hold for her, but with hope and resolve in her heart and faith in God whom she had always believed in since her early childhood.

Upon arrival in Hampstead, she soon found herself busy trying to cope with co-ordinating by telephone – a fairly new invention – between the family home and her new employer's London office. The nature of work of her lady employer is neither known nor described in her autobiography. Her employer paid her well and offered her warm and comfortable accommodation. She recalled in *Corby*: "I still remember the warmth, even in winter, the toilets. Each had a tiny gas flame burning day and night, presumably to prevent freezing." (*p.33*)

Little did she realise what kind of world she was about to enter and experience – a total cultural change, for her employer was very entertaining and highly respected and cultural with many influential guests, authors, judges, musicians and others from the academic and art worlds. She felt as though she was "still the uneducated twenty-year-old" girl in the midst of such highly sophisticated, cultured, artistic and academic company; she must have felt like a proper country bumpkin.

Despite feeling somewhat daunted by the new unfamiliar world, she was experiencing much excitement with theatre-going and dinners, which were fashionable as she was caught up in the Roaring 1920s in London. How she must have struggled to keep up with the fast moving new culture, totally different from her previous earthy and quiet country life with farms, small villages and local communities. In London her happiness was further enhanced by romance which she enjoyed with a man, John, and which brought her "ultimate joy" of true love. However, being a country girl at heart, she had enjoyed male company on the farm and had learnt to accept the inevitability of not achieving the love she hoped for at this stage, believing in self-discipline and deeper growth of love. She said in her autobiography: "May I state with the poet – *'Tis better to have loved and lost than never to have loved at all.*" (*p.30*) That was quoted from Lord Tennyson's poem *In Memorium XXVII – on Love*:

> *'I hold it true, whate'er befall;*
> *I feel it, when I sorrow most;*
> *'Tis better to have loved and lost*
> *Than never to have loved at all.'*

This observation summed up her feelings about the importance of lasting deep true love, and her self-prediction of never finding fulfilment of love in marriage.

The new happy life in Hampstead had taught her to become more organised and skilful in the catering side of the house, which was to prove handy and invaluable later in her career. Not only that, but also someone remarked that she should take up teaching the boys in the family, which was another skill she felt she had not yet acquired as she had never previously taught. She travelled with her employer's family between London and Brighton in Sussex where they had a flat. On one occasion she met a cleaner-woman who was the first-ever person to call her *"Miss Corby"* as she found her name too difficult to pronounce. This sobriquet was to remain with Mary Corbishley to the end and she always loved being addressed thus by her pupils present at her school and ex-pupils after school and by her friends, staff and teachers in an affectionate manner.

Mary Corbishley in 1926
©Mill Hall OPA archives

But in 1926 – barely a year later – she was once again struck down by rheumatic fever and was sent home to Mother's in Pershore. She was bitterly disappointed with the recurrence which meant her new cultural life in London was untimely cut short and wondered how much longer she was going to survive. So she resorted to her Bible and found solace in it. Though weakened and resentful, she resolved after having read the Lord's Prayer that "there is a

Kingdom, not of this world." She challenged God: "You give me the power and the Lord's shall be all the glory. Amen." She declared in *Corby* (pub. 1980): "*That was my birth in the Spirit (John 3:1-21) and it is as clear today as it was then.*" (*p.25*)

It is apparent that this experience was the defining moment of her life, which was to fortify and sustain her throughout the difficult times of establishing and running her school for deaf children at both Cuckfield House and Mill Hall.

She soon recovered and was able to dress herself and move about to the astonishment of those who had grave concern and doubts about her health. Her health and physique improved with renewed strength in her belief in the Bible, her only source of spiritual guidance and resolve. However, as she became idle with no prospects of work or direction for her future, she spent a lot of her free time reading and studying the Bible. Soon she suffered from appendicitis, resulting in further hospitalisation following her operation.

In a letter of May 2006 to the author, Mary Corbishley's niece from Exeter, Devon recalled: "In 1927 [Aunt] Mary came to live with us at our cottage in Tonbridge, Kent when my younger sister was born in July of that year. … I recall having great fun with her playing bands with wooden spoons and saucepan lids, pretending to be in a boat but really in a large tin washing bowl … not sure when she left us but think it may have been in the Winter of 1927 … when she was with us she had a very good male friend called Barney – tall and good-looking – he visited us, he was a tea planter & wanted Mary to go with him to I believe South Africa … believe they were engaged but Mary would not go. She so loved her Mother & felt she could not leave her. Mary was always interested in outdoors, the country and farming."

One does not need to speculate much but would wonder what would have happened had she agreed to go with her fiancé to South Africa. She would probably never have set up a school for deaf children at Cuckfield House and Mill Hall. During the last years of her life she in retrospection would most certainly have believed that God *had* intervened, such was her faith in Him so strong and steadfast. [Ed: The new Union of South Africa was established in May 1910 whereby the Cape of Good Hope, Natal, the Transvaal and Orange River Colony were united under South Africa Government based in Pretoria. Historically, tea plantations were set up mainly in the coastal zone north of Durban in Natal since 1880 when tea cultivation became an established industry.] It could likely be that this tea planter, Barney, might have acquired an entrepreneurial spirit and was seeking a wife to accompany him to the outlying areas of the then British Empire and probably thought Mary Corbishley with her farming background and experience would be ideal for the role.

Photograph of Mary Corbishley believed to be taken in *c.* 1927
©Mill Hall OPA archives

It seems likely that it was soon after this happy joy-filled episode in Tonbridge that, following a family problem causing great tension, Mary Corbishley made a sudden and unexplained decision to leave home in Pershore for the last time in 1928 to seek better fortunes in another world elsewhere, fortified again by her Bible. She believed this unhappy time with her engagement and family problems was a good experience of preparing herself to overcome self-pity and to determine upon a great sacrifice of herself for the good of others with the help of her God:

'Look around for others, even deeper in distress, act on their behalf and lift them up …' (Corby, p.33)

CHAPTER II
1928 – 1937

Teaching work in Sussex – Teacher training at
Dene Hollow Oral School, Burgess Hill –
Left Dene Hollow – Thanksgiving Day

Mary Corbishley travelled to Brighton in Sussex in 1928 to find work so that she could start earning to support her Mother by sending her some money. She had already been offered a spare basement room in Brighton by the cleaner-woman whom she met at the flat owned by her previous Hampstead employer; she took up the offer and resided there. The location of that basement room is not known.

Her first job, in answer to an advertisement in the *Evening Argus*, a local paper, was as a nurse to the grandchildren of a Jewish hotel proprietor and she had to rely on her common sense when it came to nursing, of which she had little previous experience. She always remembered this kind, compassionate and understanding grandfather who explained to her the orthodox Jewish faith. He, moreover, loved her laughter and joy in his hotel.

Then she was introduced to another Jewish family at the hotel and was taken back to London where she was to suffer the extreme opposite - a very stern atmosphere with little laughter. In the end after having felt exploited on religious grounds, she was moved one Sunday to put her foot down and insisted that that day was *her* "Sabbath" and gave him an unmistakable look which spoke more than she actually said. She resigned the next day and returned once more to her Brighton basement.

She took up various odd jobs providing her with enough income for her needs. One daily job involved endlessly preparing and cooking spinach for a lady living in a luxury flat near Seven Dials (*Corby, p. 28*).

In Brighton, as it was a seaside resort, jobs were neither plentiful nor forthcoming in the winter months and once again Mary Corbishley experienced near poverty with only 5s. (25p in 2007). Feeling perhaps a bit downhearted, she found a job advertised in a local paper for a child-minder to a ten-week-old American girl living near Worthing. She got the job purely on the strength of a single phone call to the girl's mother who remarked on her good English which would be ideal for reading to the baby. She spent the Christmas period with the American family, enjoying the warm hospitality and harmonious atmosphere. She enjoyed reading to the baby because thankfully to herself no arithmetics was involved.

When after Christmas the four-week contract was up, she again wondered about the next step as the American family was returning home to the United States. She received an unexpected phone call from a local doctor whom she did not know but who had heard about her through word of mouth. She went for an interview with the doctor who was getting married again in the following March and was seeking a nanny for his five-and-a-half-year-old girl, for which she accepted a retaining fee.

At this momentous time in 1929 Mary Corbishley was about to embark unexpectedly on a new journey which was to last for the rest of her life and career as a teacher of young deaf children. This five-and-a-half-year-old girl in Worthing had been diagnosed with deafness – a new problem very little understood by doctors then, and it was her first ever encounter with a deaf child at a private home where the child's nursery was to become her school-room. Mary Corbishley recalled her Headmaster, Matthew Cox from Chipping Campden Grammar School, predicting back in 1920 her future success: *"a niche which would be quite unorthodox and would capture her imagination and heart."*

Recognising that she was to become a school teacher in the Lord's service, she rose to the challenge of educating her first deaf child by giving nursery lessons and the beginnings of lipreading. For the last-named skill, she trained herself by watching her own natural lip movements in the mirror in the seclusion of her bedroom and developed the first lipreading exercises, which thereafter had always remained at the core of her teaching principles and the foundation of her belief that speech and English language were paramount for the deaf child's development, education and after-school employment. She learnt that the skill of lipreading would enable deaf children to acquire and understand the spoken English language often denied to them through lack of hearing.

Whilst in Worthing, she met Frank G. Barnes a well-known Teacher of the Deaf who in April 1928 had retired there from his Headship at Penn School for Deaf children in London. This man became one of her great friends and a supporter of her work and, having witnessed her at work, encouraged her to take up teaching a proper school class. He suggested to her that she should go to a training college and then teach ten and not one, to which she replied, "I would never teach, and boarding schools are always cold and scholars badly fed." *(Corby, p. 35)* However, he proved to be of a great influence on her teaching career; her autobiography, *Corby,* was dedicated to him.

Frank G. Barnes (1866-1932) was a prominent Teacher of the Deaf, having taught deaf children for 40 years and was heavily involved with the National College of Teachers of the Deaf (NCTD). His wife, Kathleen, and their two children also were in the same profession. He was responsible for conferences on Education for the Deaf held in Manchester (1911) and Glasgow (1913), as well as International Conferences on the same theme. Just before and after his retirement he and his wife travelled round the world, mainly the British Empire, visiting Deaf schools in Worcester in South Africa, West and East Australia and New South Wales, Vancouver and Winnipeg in Canada, and Washington in the USA during 1928-29.

He originally trained as a Pupil Teacher at St. John's School in Manchester and obtained his Elementary Teacher's Certificate after passing with honours in 1886. He was first appointed Head Teacher in Oldham, Lancashire and later Headmaster of Homerton (later moved to Rayners, Penn) School, the first residential Special School in London under the London County Council in 1900. Penn School catered for the young non-oral, delicate semi-blind and blind-deaf children who, "though unpromising at the start, were turned into reasonably capable workers and decent citizens" with the help of Mr Barnes' zeal, firmness, encouragement and creative ability. (*Teacher of the Deaf, June 1951*)

Having a blunt and cheerfully common-sense approach to all he undertook, Mr Barnes was very interested in education for deaf children and always had a moment for everyone involved in the profession. He was responsible for raising the need for a proper recognition of the Teachers of the Deaf as a specialised profession, and for a Diploma for their qualifications, the examinations for which were introduced by the NCTD in 1921. He was the Secretary for the International Conferences on the Education for the Deaf in 1907 and 1925. In recognition of his services for the 1907 Conference in Edinburgh he was awarded the honour of *Officier d'Academie* by the French Government of the day. (*Teacher of the Deaf, April 1927*) Upon retirement, he and his wife lived in Worthing, a move which was opportune, for he was later to meet and encourage Mary Corbishley.

Mary Corbishley spent the next few years learning and developing the skills of teaching deaf children under Frank Barnes' mentorship, and was soon teaching a class of deaf children as well as making private visits to other young deaf children and in addition instructing adults who had lost their hearing on how to communicate through lipreading. She found the latter more difficult as the adults needed adjustment to a different lifestyle *sans ouïe* requiring an entirely different approach to teaching.

She had always been conscious of her insufficient educational background by reason of her farm life and early termination of her grammar school years, but strove to overcome this discrepancy solely by on-going nursery teaching which she loved and by stretching her mental resources when teaching the more senior scholars. She was very much aware of the necessity of obtaining a diploma for the Teacher of the Deaf qualification which was essential in those early years of deaf education. Those who were keen to acquire qualifications of Teacher of the Deaf had two options which were the NCTD's own specially devised examinations for a Diploma in Deaf Education and the Teacher Training courses at Manchester University run by a Professor and Mrs Ewing.

She knew about or had heard of a training college for Teachers of the Deaf where she could have studied for such a diploma, but her increasing involvement with deaf children's education and other responsibilities put paid to her studying opportunities. That college might have been Ealing Training College for Teachers of the Deaf. But she was prevented from attending the College by her lack of a School Certificate. However, years later a teacher and member of the NCTD Joint Board Diploma for Teachers of the Deaf wrote in her *letter of reference (typed) dated 10th December 1937*:

"I first knew Miss M. S. Corbishley about six years ago, when she started work at the same private school for the deaf [Ed. believed to be Dene Hollow Oral School in Burgess Hill] in which I was already working as a full qualified teacher. Miss Corbishley proved herself, from the first, a born teacher and was exceptionally quick to appreciate the special difficulties of the deaf child. She showed great readiness and enthusiasm in tackling the work, and her sympathetic handling and her sense of humour easily won the confidence of her pupils.

"Miss Corbishley was ineligible, on technical grounds, to sit for the Special Diploma, but for all practical purposes I consider her a thoroughly trained and experienced teacher of the deaf, qualified in all but name. I should say her personal character, her skill as a teacher, her sound common sense, and above all, her great love of children, eminently fit her for the charge of deaf children in her own residential school." This letter was written nine months after Mary Corbishley left Dene Hollow, but merely showed that she already was well aware of the lack of a Diploma in her chosen field of teaching which would be essential for her future plans; such lack of qualifications would prove to be her Achilles' heel which threatened to recur several times later in her career.

In the 1930s which were the most critical years of her teaching career with long-lasting consequences, she was determined to improve her own general knowledge and acquisition of literature for sharing with deaf children in her charge. She had a new vision of higher education for the deaf, although it is not clear from her autobiography that she was aware of this vision already being on-going and fought for in the teaching profession where many teachers of the deaf were propounding their aims and beliefs at many conferences and meetings around the country. This vision was referred to in several issues of the *Teacher of the Deaf* in the 1920-40s.

Having no appropriate diploma or qualifications, Mary Corbishley determined to believe in God's mysterious ways governing her future, such a strong belief which she never wavered from nor did she give up right up to the end. She always felt she was guided by her faith in the Maker and sought guidance and comfort in her Bible for big decisions she was called upon to make.

In 1929 or 1930 Mary Corbishley was nominated by Frank Barnes and others for the Associate Membership of the NCTD, regardless of the fact that she had no diploma or qualifications. The Rules of the NCTD laid down that associate membership was to be offered to teachers in training as well as those without appropriate qualifications but involved in teaching deaf children at deaf schools. According to the Rules, associate members were not eligible for election to the Executive Committee. Mary Corbishley, who joined the Metropolitan and Southern Branch, most likely attended annual general meetings and branch meetings as a participating observer, although her name was mentioned a few times in the journal *Teacher of the Deaf* but she did not appear to have raised any points. Nevertheless, she was one of the most regular attendees and benefited much from meeting other teachers of the deaf, although she did not appear to recruit them for her teaching staff.

In spite of shortcomings in her professional qualifications, Mary Corbishley continued teaching speech, English and lipreading to deaf children in various places and settings on the South coast of Sussex; parents and teachers commended her work in their letters of reference (typed copies):

"Miss Corbishley has been with us for nearly two years looking after my little girl, who is now nearly eight years old. Under Miss Corbishley's care, she has been delightfully happy and has become unquestioningly obedient. Miss Corbishley is most capable. She is able to give first lessons and has also had experience and success in teaching lip-reading to the deaf. She is an excellent needlewoman and has devoted every care to the girl's clothing, appearance, manners and general deportment. I consider her unusually good at training and guiding a child's mind. She is, of course, absolutely trustworthy." *Letter (typed) dated April 1931 by a mother from Worthing.*

"Miss Corbishley has taught my little girl lip-reading for nearly a year and during the last two terms has combined this with lessons in English subjects. ... she has extraordinary patience in teaching lip-reading and a sympathetic understanding of the needs and difficulties of children who are partially deaf, and so has been able to devise helpful games and exercises to meet their particular needs and mitigate their difficulties. With regard to the teaching of English she has been very thorough." *Letter (typed) dated June 23rd, 1931 from a father in Shoreham-by-Sea.*

"I have much pleasure in testifying to Miss Mary Corbishley's ability as a successful teacher of lip-reading and speech to deaf children and adults. She has had experience in dealing with totally deaf and partially deaf children and adults, and has handled pupils suffering from defective speech with most satisfactory results. Miss Corbishley has a bright appearance and an attractive personality which readily induces response in her pupils. I am certain that she will give entire satisfaction in any work which she undertakes." *Letter (typed) dated June 1933 from a teacher and member of the NCTD.*

It is likely that it was at one of the NCTD meetings in *c.* 1930 when Mary Corbishley was first introduced by Frank Barnes to Miss Mary Hare and her sister, Ethel. Mary Hare was Principal of Dene Hollow Oral School for the Deaf in Burgess Hill, Sussex, and offered Mary Corbishley a trainee teacher post. She accepted the offer and went there in 1931 to start her serious training for the following six years and enjoyed employment there. She was encouraged to teach various classes from the preparatory up to the 5th form, thus gaining an all-round experience. *(Miss Hare's letter of reference (typed), 9th March, 1937)*

She wrote about her experiences at Dene Hollow Oral School in the defunct *Dene Hollow Association Magazine, 1936 (edited):*

SCHOOL NEWS by Mary Corbishley, L.A.M.

"In January Miss Chatterton, whose percussion Band is rapidly becoming a big noise, returned to the staff as a qualified teacher of the deaf. We hear too little about this side of Miss Hare's work. She turns out many teachers with ability to spread her oral system to others not fortunate enough to receive it personally. Some few years ago a Dene Hollow candidate won the Eichholz prize [*sic*], awarded for distinction in practice and theory, in the examination for the Teacher's Diploma.

"In the Spring term, our pupils danced with perfect rhythm on the platform and later tripped an enjoyable measure with parents and friends, who we love to see. We also love Madame Garbutt with her joyous movements and ability to bring forth the best results from each individual.

"In June, the day dawned for the Royal Drawing Society's examination. Most of us felt more like a nightmare, but determined ambition supported us as we gazed upon grotesque structures perched upon tables, and so the work began… Several weeks later we gather together in the Garden room, with the spirit which inspires us, the brain which has nourished our infantile efforts, and the hand which is proud to present concrete proof of our ability to accomplish great things. The juniors, two years under age, first step proudly out to grasp a slip of paper, which should it be *Honours* colour carry out it with joys untold. This year we had a bumper crop: 17 Honours, 23 Passes and NO Failures.

"During the summer several tennis matches were played against other schools with successful results.

"The new schoolroom is nearly finished for our very bright young people. Unfortunately, 'Birdie' [Ed. Surrendra Kumani] is going home to Patiala for three months, as her father, the Maharajah finds her so bright and intelligent. Who knows what this might lead to, in a land where women still live in purdah, cut off from all knowledge. How fitting, if our Miss Hare, one of the finest, most intelligent, and yet the most understanding women of our age, should through a child, bring about the emancipation of Indian women." (*UBL – Department for Special Collections*) This last paragraph reveals Mary Corbishley's thoughts and views on and support for women's rights and suffragette movements then, although she denied in her *Corby*: "I enjoy men's friendships. Bless them all! But no nonsense for me about equality – let them cherish us all!" (*p.17*)

[Ed: Eichholz referred to in her article *School News* was Dr Alfred Eichholz, CBE (1869-1933) from Manchester, Lancashire who was a highly-respected and much-admired Her Majesty's Inspector of Schools for the Deaf for 32 years (1898-1930) and was devoted to the care, social life and education of deaf children whom he loved. He also was a strong advocate of oralism for deaf children and adults – a belief Mary Corbishley would undoubtedly share with him. Being a modest gentleman, he upon his retirement in September 1930 wished his presentation cheque be used by the NCTD for the purpose of further educational research for deaf children. The NCTD subsequently decided upon the Eichholz Prize for the most outstanding trainee-Teacher of the Deaf of the Year while studying for the NCTD Diploma.]

She had a very useful learning curve for her teacher training, from which she benefited to a great degree. Being a lover of outdoor activities, she acquired a keen-ness for tennis, cricket and swimming as well as dancing and art which were to be incorporated in her future school curriculum.

An ex-Dene Hollow pupil, Sybil Sanders, who remembered Mary Corbishley in *c.* 1931-1932, told the author: "At Dene Hollow Mary Corbishley slept in the same room as the girls. She drew a curtain suspended on a wire across the room between her bed and our beds. We used to watch her silhouette thrown up on the curtain by a candle behind her. We were fascinated by her shadowy movements of brushing her teeth, washing her hair and dressing for bed. She had lovely curly brown hair, I remember."

Mary Corbishley met a member of the staff, Miss Jessie B. Hancock who in 1935 had returned home from the United States of America, a vital meeting leading to a potential future professional partnership for Mary Corbishley's school at Cuckfield House in Cuckfield, Sussex later in 1939.

She, Mary Corbishley, must have proved to be an enthusiastic and capable worker helping not only with teaching but also with dancing displays and games, which impressed Mary Hare who wrote:

"Miss Mary Corbishley came to me nearly 6 years ago, strongly recommended by the late Mr F. Barnes who had coached her in the teaching of speech and lip-reading to the deaf. She took further training from me and has, for the last 5 years taught the various classes in my school ….. I have always found her thorough and capable, an excellent organiser and enthusiastic worker in whatever she undertakes. In addition to the scholastic side of her duties, she has been a splendid helper to the dancing mistress, carrying on the latter's tuition in the practising classes and helping to make a great success of the annual displays. I wish her every success in whatever branch of teaching she takes up." *(Letter of reference (typed) dated 9th March 1937)*. It is to be noted that Miss Hare wrote this letter only the day before Mary Corbishley walked out of Dene Hollow after much disagreement with her.

Tennis players with Miss Mary Hare 1932
(L to R:) **Front row:** Miss Marrow, Miss Lear, Mary Corbishley, Doreen Biggs,
Margaret Greenwood
Middle row: Miss Evans, Miss Nash, Miss Chatterton, Margaret Gamlin
Back row: Laura Mona Camayer, Joan Connew, Miss Hare, Nancy Past, Miss
Cormack, Barbara Green
Miss Hare is seen holding a prize box of chocolates for the winning pupils
who beat the teachers.
©Photograph on loan by Joan Hannah

Mary Corbishley perched on a school desk
in the back garden at Dene Hollow.
©*Mill Hall OPA archives*

Sports Day at Dene Hollow c.1936
Miss Hancock is seen on the right
watching the relay race.
©*Jean Landriani's album*

Another ex-Dene Hollow pupil, Margaret Parry, e-mailed to the author from her New Zealand home: "I knew Miss Corbishley from 1931 to 1937 when she was on the [school] staff; she was my form teacher. I was fond of her and have good memories of her; she was always gentle, patient and understanding with us [the pupils]. I was quite upset when she suddenly left Dene Hollow, and I, like others, was puzzled by her disappearance for some time."

According to Mary Hare's letter of reference, Mary Corbishley was training to be an elocution teacher with the Royal Academy of Music (RAM) and had gained her Silver medal towards the Licentiate of the Academy. Old records at the RAM offices were destroyed by the bombing in London during the World War Two and no evidence of her records could be retrieved. She recorded in her book that "somewhere in the thirties it seemed a good idea to use the confident voice which then was mine … I attended elocution classes. The teacher soon tacked my interest onto the literary foundation Mother had laid. …soon medals of differing metals were won but best of all were the poems. They helped in the difficult task of overcoming self-centredness." (*pp. 37-38*)

Noami Harrison's 1934 School Report. Mary Corbishley's initials
can be seen for Nature, Arithmetic, Dancing and Games
©School Report on loan by Naomi Woodcock

During school holidays she took up jobs taking her away to Fife in Scotland on one occasion, and abroad in Europe on several occasions with deaf children. Such jobs helped with her finances which had always been problematic. Once she went home to Pershore with one of the pupils from Dene Hollow, as her niece recounted in her letter to and in conversation with the author: "…. my first memory is her bringing an Indian Princess to her home (in Pershore) for the summer holidays while I was also staying and playing with this deaf child, possibly in about 1934. When news came of her impending visit, there was great excitement and anticipation of seeing this Indian princess arrive attired in her beautiful colourful sari and bejewelled finery as befitted her status, but when she arrived in her plain green tunic school uniform we were rather disappointed!" The Indian Princess was Surrendra Kumani, also known as

"Birdie", whose father donated towards the open-air swimming pool at Dene Hollow in gratitude for her education.

In the meantime, Mary Corbishley had developed problems with her teeth which at her dentist friend's encouragement had all been extracted and re-inserted back in her gums with no further ill-effects; also, she had her tonsils taken out under local anaesthetic enabling her to watch the operation in the mirror, which she found very interesting but thought it was unnecessary.

The year 1936-37 was for Mary Corbishley the most crucial time as she was beginning to have serious thoughts and doubts about the teaching methods at Dene Hollow and was disturbed by the innermost conflicting emotions and agonised over the clash of her spiritual belief versus the more secular teaching ethos at the school. She confessed in *Corby*: "I was endeavouring to live according to the Bible as I understood it. Doctrine is not my strong point but rather truth in the inmost parts … The test came roughly after twelve years' joy in teaching the deaf … The choice was between my material job and spiritual endeavour …" *(p.38)*

One of the ex-Dene Hollow pupils, who had learned with Miss Hare, recalled that she could not remember Scripture being taught at the School, and she and other pupils were relieved when the succeeding Headmaster, Mr Mundin of Mary Hare Grammar School in 1946, brought Scripture back into the school curriculum. Another ex-pupil of Mill Hall School had the impression that Miss Hare was not as keen on religion as Mary Corbishley was; hence possible disagreements and arguments between the two women as witnessed by several pupils who in some cases saw them through the glass panel of the door at loggerheads whilst neither understanding nor hearing what they were arguing about, as recalled by ex-Dene Hollow pupils.

Another ex-Dene Hollow pupil, Jean Landriani (neé Baldry), who was to leave the school to become the first pupil of Mary Corbishley's school in Hassocks, put forward her thoughts to the author that there could be a question of differences in the ethics of discipline of deaf children, an issue which brought about Mary Corbishley's decision to leave Dene Hollow as she did not believe in caning the children which was being practised at the school. She believed in gentle non-corporeal discipline and guidance through the Bible and was a strong advocate of her God's fair judgement.

So for Mary Corbishley things had come to a head and she made the biggest decision of her life to leave Dene Hollow and so left on Wednesday 10th March 1937. That day she chose to be her Thanksgiving Day which she thereafter always shared with her pupils, teaching staff and friends, and which her school celebrated every year ever since. To her that cardinal day must have brought a great sense of release from her personal torment over what was happening at Dene Hollow where, apparently in her view, learning Scripture was not encouraged.

On that significantly historical day heavy snow had fallen the night before in Sussex, blanketing the countryside white, and children were tobogganing down the hillside of South Downs, and the new £30,000 airport was opened in Jersey in a blaze of publicity when two 14-seater aeroplanes of the Jersey Airways Fleet landed to open up a new air service from Shoreham Airport in Sussex to the island. (*Sussex Daily News, Thursday 11th March 1937*) National newspapers were full of news of preparations for the coronation of King George VI and Queen Elizabeth due two months later in May. One may imagine Mary Corbishley, fully occupied with her own problems, was hardly aware of the news.

She bravely walked out of the security of her employment at Dene Hollow into the cold and heavy snow-covered country, thinking to herself: *"That's the end of teaching the deaf as I have no qualifications."* She mentally avowed her faith in God: *"Thy Will be done … Show me thy Will, please."* For the next two days in brilliant sunshine she was all alone, walking alone, being confronted with never-ending questions of what to do with herself in the future. Looking back on this significant phase of her long career of teaching deaf children, she remarked in her autobiography:

'What seemed to be the end, was the beginning' (pp. 38-39)

CHAPTER III
1937 – 1947

Bed-sitter in Hassocks – First pupils –
Cuckfield House Oral School for the Deaf –
War Years – National Deaf Children's Society –
Recognition by the Ministry of Education –
Move to Mill Hall

In 1937 Mary Corbishley, at the age of 31, was now alone at the crossroads of her life and career, uncertain of her future. She turned her eyes to the far horizon, perhaps feeling somewhat intimidated, but her strong sense of trust in her Bible and her strong belief in "God's mysterious ways" helped to sustain her inner strength, character and fortitude which she had inherited from her parents during her early years on the family farm, and which she attributed to her rheumatic fever attacks when she was a young woman.

The next few weeks were difficult times as she found herself in the wilderness with no prospects of work or money coming in, though she was fortunate in staying with her few faithful Bible-reading friends. She was faced with countless questions about her future which appeared bleak.

One sunny day she was travelling by train to visit the doctor's family in Worthing when she passed through Hassocks and found it a very attractive place to live. Having been given an address, she stopped off at Hassocks on her way back and after a few house calls seeking accommodation she found herself a bed-sitter on the first floor of a large three-storey Victorian house *The Hayes* on 17th April 1937. The house was owned by a widow whose husband, an architect, had died the previous January and she had put it up for sale. It was opportune for both women who were in need of, respectively, accommodation and useful income.

Hassocks was part of the parish of Keymer and Clayton and was served by the Southern Railway from London to Brighton. It was a small village with a long road of private Victorian houses, a hotel and a few outlying farms, leading from the west side of Hassocks station (originally Hassock's Gate) up to the main London Road (B2026) from Burgess Hill to Brighton. It was an extension of Keymer, a village 7 miles south of Cuckfield and was supplied with water from Burgess Hill Water Company's works on the South Downs and lighted by gas from Hassocks and District Gas Company. Electricity was also available. The main crops were wheat, oats, beans, peas and turnips; the soil was loam and sand with underlying clay. The population of Hassocks and Keymer in 1931 was approximately 3190. (*Kelly's Directory for Sussex, 1938*)

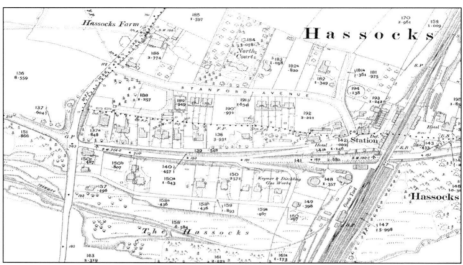

Reproduced from 1910 Ordnance Survey Map, with kind permission of the Ordnance Survey. ©*Crown copyright. All rights reserved.* (BHC)

Mary Corbishley moved into *The Hayes* and set about making her home in her bed-sitter with a kitchen at the back on the same floor. Her good Bible-group friends got together some items of furniture and china and gave them to her to furnish her one-room accommodation. She said in *Corby*: "*These believing friends, one after the other, laid the foundation of what was to become Mill Hall Oral School for the Deaf*." (p. 40)

She was soon asked to teach a deaf girl, Jean Baldry, 11 years of age, her first school pupil. Jean remembered: "My parents took me to Hassocks and found a very old-fashioned house; a very sweet lady, Mrs H., the owner, took us upstairs to the first floor where I met Corby waiting for me – one floor of sitting room, bathroom and kitchen. I came as her first day pupil and was interested in Corby and soon started to study from the English book. I had lunch and tea with her. I waited by the bay window, looking out for Mother

who came to pick me up. I asked her if I could stay on learning with Corby."
Jean stayed on at her school for the next few years and was very happy there.

Bed-sitter with bay window on first floor
where Mary Corbishley started her school
©Photographs by Ian M. Stewart 2006, with owners' kind permission

Top (second) floor where rooms
were rented for additional pupils

Her first pupils Jean Baldry and
Catherine Hutchison in the garden
©Jean Landriani's album

Mary Corbishley at the cooker in the kitchen
next to her bed-sitter *©Mill Hall OPA archives*

The following week, a 13-year-old girl, Catherine Hutchison, arrived from Cupar, Fife in Scotland and was the first boarding pupil. Mary Corbishley offered up her bed and slept on the floor. Catherine recalled vaguely in her letter to the author: " I can't remember some of the rooms at the house as it (the bed-sitter) had only very small rooms." The girls were later followed by another boarder, a 3-year-old boy, David Kimbell who told the author that his mother drove him from Chichester to Hassocks (to *quote him*): "to Miss Corbishley's flat where I was warmly welcomed with her open arms." Two more deaf children, Eleanor _____ and Hugh Mitchell, were taken in, necessitating renting further rooms on the second floor. The latter was believed to be deaf and partially sighted and did not stay long as Mary Corbishley probably found herself unable to teach him due to lack of appropriate training in the area of teaching those with additional sensory needs, even in those days.

In her autobiography *Corby*, there is reference, though in nebulous language, to the incident of being threatened with litigation from her former employer, Miss Hare of Dene Hollow: "Legal problems and threats of damage developed around my late job. A letter arrived in May." (*p. 40*) She quickly sought advice from the son of her landlady, who was studying for his finals in Law, on how to cope without defence as she did not wish to involve the pupils' parents in damages. For her defence she told this student-lawyer: "*My defence is the truth, the whole truth and nothing but the truth.*" So upon the young man's advice, she travelled to his firm of solicitors in Brighton where she presented her case based on "nothing but the truth." The firm's headed letter carried much weight … She ended the matter abruptly: "Further details are not necessary. Truth prevailed; the matter was closed." (*p. 40*)

Mary Corbishley was not alone in setting up her school; another teacher, Miss Jessie B. Hancock joined her from Dene Hollow where they had already met. Miss Hancock came from Sholden near Deal, Kent where she was born in June 1914, a daughter to George Hancock, a poultry farmer. When she was 15 she went to the United States of America as a nurse to a deaf boy in 1929. The boy was being educated at the Central Institute for the Deaf (CID) in St Louis, Missouri and Miss Hancock at the age of 16 applied for a teaching training post there and was accepted in October 1930. From then on, she attended classes of the Teacher Training College at the CID for two years and, according to Max A. Goldstein, the Principal, attended all the courses (except Physics of Speech) of the entire curriculum with excellent grades and credits. But her insufficient education and training prior to the CID proved an obstacle and prevented her from being awarded a Degree of Bachelor of Science in Special Education normally granted by the College and Washington University at St Louis under their Rules, despite the fact that she was for a year an assistant to the instructor of lipreading for adults and older pupils and spent the third and fourth years teaching first grade deaf pupils under supervision.

Max A. Goldstein, in his letter of recommendation dated March 22nd 1935 to Miss Mary Hare of Dene Hollow, had found her to be a "very intelligent and estimable young woman whose educational equipment before her arrival in the USA was very limited, mainly because of circumstances and finance." He continued (*verbatim*): "Since Miss Hancock has come to St Louis she has proven herself a very industrious, alert and intelligent young woman … In my conference with her today I find that she is seriously interested in continuing her work as a teacher of the deaf and wants an opportunity to enter your school as a pupil or apprentice teacher or whatever your regulations require in order to continue along the right course towards qualifications and recognition as a regular teacher of the deaf in England. In making the recommendation of Miss Hancock for your favorable consideration, I do so after five years of observation of her work and with the conviction that she will make an excellent teacher if given such opportunity. She is ambitious, a willing worker, a young woman of fine character and a good practical and resourceful teacher with a head full of common sense …"

The philosophy of the CID was and still is auditory-oral education for deaf children. The Institute's Oral School was originally set up with a small class in two rooms in 1914 by Max A. Goldstein who had previously travelled to Europe to study the methods of oral teaching in Vienna, which convinced him of the credibility and feasibility of the oral education that congenitally deaf children could be taught to speak intelligibly. Owing to the success of the CID, the Teacher Training College was affiliated to the University of Washington in 1931 and became the first teacher training college in the country.

When Miss Hancock had imbibed this philosophy, she proved to be an ideal young potential teacher for Mary Corbishley to invite to collaborate with her in her future school's management, aims and curriculum based mainly on speech, lipreading and English. It seems apparent that Miss Mary Hare, a qualified Teacher of the Deaf, the former employer of both women, passed onto them what she had been trained in at Ealing Training College in London in 1881-1883. The College's headmaster, Arthur A. Kinsey, believed in and encouraged by training the teacher-candidates in the German system of phonics-based education deemed suitable for deaf children. As a result, Miss Hare received her Certificate of Teacher's Qualification in the *"Diffusion of the German System in the United Kingdom."* (BDHS' *The Lady in Green – A Biography of Miss Mary Hare, 1865-1945*)

The German system of oral teaching to deaf children was first conceived by Johann Conrad Amman (1669-*c*.1730), a Swiss physician of Schaffhausen and later Amsterdam where he gained a good reputation for instructing "deaf and dumb" children to speak in their Teutonic language. He developed a system whereby he encouraged his deaf pupils to pay attention to his lip movements and his larynx, which he induced them to imitate, until they were able to speak distinctly with clearly uttered letters of the alphabet, syllables and words. He wrote a book *Surdus loquens* (1692) which was often reprinted and referred to by oral teachers of the deaf as a basis for training. [Ed: *Surdus loquens*, Latin for silent/deaf, words/language]

One of the oral teachers was Samuel Heinicke (1727-1790) who later developed the first German method of the systematic education for "deaf and dumb" children, based on Amman's *Surdus loquens*. His first successful experience of teaching a "deaf and dumb" pupil encouraged him to devote his life to this work of teaching deaf children, and after his work having been interrupted by the Seven Years' War between Prussia and the alliance of France, Russia and Sweden and subsequent imprisonment from which he escaped, he went to Hamburg and in 1789 successfully taught a "deaf and dumb" boy to speak. He then established in Leipzig what was claimed to the first "Deaf and Dumb" Institution in Germany in 1778 where he continued teaching until his death in 1790.

Alongside the sign language used in deaf schools, the German oral system appeared to have been the main and undisputed basis of oral deaf education before and after it was resolved at the International Conference on the Education of the Deaf in Milan in 1880 that this system be adopted *in lieu* of sign language as a teaching medium in deaf schools world-wide. It has been a great controversy since.

Arthur Kinsey, with his deputy head teacher from Ealing Training College, Miss Susannah Hull, attended the 1880 International Conference where he was elected one of the vice-secretaries and she, who was lately converted to oralism, presented a paper on the advocacy of the German System, which had a great impact on those present. The five-day Conference, attended by over 160 delegates, resulted in wide repercussions all round the world when the delegates passed a proposal put to the vote in three languages, Italian, French and English, that: "The Congress, considering the incontestable superiority of speech over signs – first for restoring the deaf-mutes to social life, and secondly, for giving them greater facility of language – declares that the method of articulation should have the preference over that of signs in the instruction and education of the deaf-mute." (*Report, The Times, September 13th 1880*) The proposal was passed by a huge majority with four against. It should be noted that the Americans and the English though in the minority at the Conference raised objections to the proposal, but were outvoted by well over 90% of the delegates who were mainly Italian and French oral teachers and educationalists; the proposal became a controversial resolution – and, ironically, there appeared to be only one German oral teacher present at the vote.

This resolution was one of eight passed. However, it would appear that the resolution represented the delegates' considered preference for the oral method for educating deaf children during school term and at the same time did not actually ban sign language outside the school, although another proposal was passed expressing its discouragement. The teachers of the deaf were merely encouraged to adopt the oral system of instilling speech, lipreading and language in deaf pupils *during time of instruction* [Ed.'s italics]. Consequently, this was to have a lasting effect on Mary Corbishley's oral teaching philosophy indirectly through her training in the German System at Dene Hollow.

In 1935 Miss Hancock returned home from the USA with the boy to England where they both arrived at Dene Hollow under Miss Hare's Principality. On account of her prior American training being probably unacceptable to Miss Hare who had received letters of reference and recommendation from the CID, she was appointed as a nanny to the young children, rather than as a trainee-teacher, although she might have done some elementary teaching. When Mary Corbishley walked out of Dene Hollow in March 1937, she, Miss Hancock, followed six months later to Hassocks. Miss Hancock later in retrospection wrote in her letter to Dr Richard Silverman of the CID on 5th November 1959 from Cape Town (*verbatim*): "Ever since I left CID I have worked with the deaf. At the late Miss Hare's School, I hoped to gain School Certificate but found it an impossibility with a full day's teaching plus all the out of school duties which go with an English boarding school! For a number of years I worked with Miss Corbishley. I feel sure you have heard of her school in Sussex, England. From a few rooms in a private house we expanded to a recognised boarding school." (*CID Records*)

At *The Hayes* the two women began to work in a professional partnership and taught the children speech, lipreading and English. The extra rooms on the upper (second) floor were slept in by the children and Miss Hancock.

At the same time they were conscious of inadequate understanding of deaf education by government officials. There was an article by the Editor entitled *The Bondage of Silence* in *The Times, 24th March 1938* on the Government's Board of Education's lack of provisions for dealing with problems of deaf school-leavers getting vocational training for work in industry. The Editor pointed out that out of some 35,000 "deaf and dumb" persons in the UK nearly 4,000 were children; these persons were excluded from intercourse with their peers whose communication depended on "language, song and music", thereby being prevented from full expression of their feelings.

He went on to express his regret that their status made no impact on the Government of the day and on private benefactors and so it all meant that the Blind Persons Act had no such counterpart as a Deaf Persons Act, though it had been suggested that local authorities might use the Poor Law Act, 1930 to make grants to Missions for the Deaf to provide work placements for deaf adults after leaving school. There were many regional associations for the welfare of the deaf, and they were responsible for helping deaf school leavers obtain suitable training and employment and for providing interpreters. At the same time they encouraged public awareness of the problems and treatment of deafness. The article ended: "These activities are serving, in the case of large numbers of men and women, to break effectually the bondage of silence."

In response, Miss Hancock wrote to the paper, expressing her concern over lack of interest by the Board of Education in deaf children's education for after-school employment (*verbatim*):

"Your leading article on May 24th adequately brings to the eye of the public the sympathetic understanding shown by authorities towards the deaf at school-leaving age, enabling them to become better citizens. Are they adequately educated in our deaf schools to take full advantage of these resources? Where is the board responsible for the education of England's deaf citizens? This oral school has been in existence for one year; we have deaf children here whose future is our sole responsibility. The Ministry of Health seems the only authority interested in the welfare of the deaf child, for not one member of any educational branch says yea or nay to our existence. Why not? Does this indifference apply to all schools?" (*Extract from her letter* published in *The Times, 28th May 1938*)

The Ministry of Health referred to in the letter was meant to be known as the Medical Department of the Board of Education after 1925, and a Chief Medical Inspector of the Board of Education was appointed with the task of checking on deaf and [then] handicapped children in schools. Miss Hancock was probably encouraged by Mary Corbishley to write to *The Times*; Miss Hancock could not have written without her, Mary Corbishley's, knowledge. The two women clearly disapproved of the way in which deaf children were determined by the then educationalists who believed that deaf children should be categorised with other groups of educationally defective pupils (classified as those not being imbeciles or dull or backward), namely the maladjusted, educationally sub-standard, blind, epileptic, mentally defective and those suffering from speech defects (as defined in the Education Act, 1921). The manner in which deaf children were regarded in the same class as such children had never been accepted by Mary Corbishley who fought a long hard campaign to remove this stigma as clearly expressed in a letter she wrote to the parents of a deaf pupil in the 1940s. The Medical Department was subsequently renamed Special Services Branch of the Ministry of Education on and from 1st August 1947 as announced in the *Teacher of the Deaf, October 1947*.

After two more pupils, Colin Galbraith and Simon _____, were accepted, it became clear to Mary Corbishley that the accommodation at *The Hayes* was becoming over-crowded with seven pupils, and she now had a serious need to move to more spacious accommodation. It was Mr Baldry, the father of Jean, who helped by finding a more appropriate house in Cuckfield, a few miles north of Hassocks. This house was Cuckfield House, a listed building which was later registered in the Amendment of List of Buildings of Special Architectural or Historical Interest – Urban District of Cuckfield (East Sussex) dated 23rd April 1971 under the Town and County Planning Act, 1968, Section 104 (3): "Listed Grade 2: Late 18th century or early 19th century. Two storeys and attic. Four windows. Four dormers. Painted brick. Parapet. Glazing bars intact. Porch with flat entablature and iron railings over it. Semi-circular fanlight."

Historically, in 1785 a wealthy gentleman, Francis Warden, one of the most distinguished men in Cuckfield and steward of the Manor of Cuckfield, died unmarried at the age of 85 and left his estate to, among many beneficiaries, his clerk, James Waller, whose son Samuel, an attorney and churchwarden, built the "late Georgian" Leyton House in circa 1815-1820. Upon his death in 1820,

Leyton House was then passed to his son, Samuel the Second and subsequently was renamed Cuckfield House. His surviving son, Frederick Waller, a Queen's Counsel, died unmarried in 1893 and his niece inherited the property and in turn died in 1928. It was then left to her only surviving child, Mrs Waller-Bridge, wife of the Rector. Early in the 1900s it became available for letting purposes. Their daughter, Etta Revell, used to live next door to Cuckfield House School during the war years, as the School Secretary, Mrs Treganowan, remembered in her conversation with the author.

Leyton House *c.* 1835 ©*Cuckfield Museum, with kind permission*

Cuckfield House ©*Ian M. Stewart 2006*

Cuckfield House ©*Ian M. Stewart 2006*

Kelly's Directory for Sussex, 1938 described the country town: "Cuckfield is a parish, pleasantly situated on an eminence in the centre of the county and about two miles west from Haywards Heath on the Brighton section of the Southern Railway. It gives its name to a rural district … and is now under the control of an Urban District Council, created by the Local Government Act, 1929. In 1934 the UD of Cuckfield and Haywards Heath were amalgamated to form the new urban district of Cuckfield … The town is lighted with gas and electricity from works at Haywards Heath, and supplied with water from works at Balcombe under Mid-Sussex Joint Water Board. The soil is principally loam with clay subsoil. Chief crops are oats and wheat with a large percentage of pasture. The population of Cuckfield in 1931 is 2197."

At one time a flourishing country town with weekly markets, forges and flour mills, Cuckfield was also a well-known staging post for London to Brighton stagecoach runs taking two days in the 18th and 19th centuries.

In the year of 1939 in April or May Cuckfield House was rented as temporary accommodation where Mary Corbishley set up her first private school proper for the education of deaf children, albeit a few months before the World War II broke out in September of that year. She recalled in *Corby* her response in challenging the critics who joined in a loud chorus that "the woman's mad!" "Yes, maybe, but by being mad it helps the deaf, but why be sane? There are lots of sane people about and quite a few deaf." (*p. 40*) In Clarke's *Mid-Sussex Directory for 1939*, there was the first-time entry (*verbatim*):

CUCKFIELD: Schools: Cuckfield House Oral School for the Deaf –

Principal: Miss Mary S. Corbishley   (WSRO *Local Studies*)

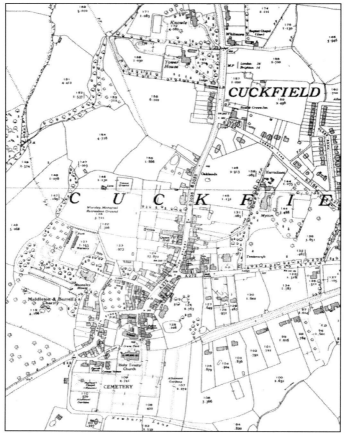

Reproduced from 1937/38 Ordnance Survey Map, with kind permission from the Ordnance Survey ©*Crown copyright. All rights reserved.* (BHC)

How could one set up a new private school with little or no finances or staff or enough pupils to start with in the 1930s? It must have been daunting in those male-dominant working days for a woman to embark on such a career with the first stepping stone of establishing a school, let alone an oral school providing primary (and to some extent secondary) education for deaf children in a quiet country village such as Cuckfield. In fact, according to Jean Ward's book *Education in Cuckfield* printed by West Sussex County Council in 1980, there were already many private hearing schools for girls and young women up and running in Cuckfield in the late 19th and early 20th centuries.

The World War II broke out with Germany in September 1939.

For her new school, Mary Corbishley would have to rely on local friends, school contacts and perhaps one or two parents, or rally a few loyal friends round to form the nucleus of the school staff for not only teaching academic subjects but also for domestic and health duties including cooking and gardening. Mr Jarvis, the gardener, tended the vegetable garden providing vital fresh produce for the school particularly during the war years when food was rationed while his wife was responsible for the domestic side with two cleaners, Misses Alexander and Sayer assisting her.

The original staff comprised, in addition to Miss Hancock, Ian N. W. Mackie BA (Oxon) who taught Geography, Roy Gornold who encouraged pupils to study Art for the Royal Drawing Society examinations, Captain Frank L. Rolt who ran physical exercise classes and Madame Vera Garbutt who arranged dancing classes and displays. A new school prospectus was produced with the details of the school's aims and objectives and a curriculum. One of the subjects being taught was Greek New Testament (as written by Erasmus in the 16th century) clearly regarded by Mary Corbishley as suitable for her deaf pupils' spiritual guidance. The author remembers her instruction: "Never believe in the Old Testament; always believe in the New Testament." To this day, he never found out the logic behind this strange instruction as he had enjoyed the O. T.

Ian Mackie, a very popular teacher with the pupils, having already taught them Geography and a few Greek words at *The Hayes* in Hassocks, designed the School's badge and logo with the Greek word εγθουσιασμος meaning *"God Inspired Zeal"*. He, who lived in Hove, held the rank of Flight Lieutenant in 22 Squadron of the Royal Air Force.. At the breakout of the WWII, he had to leave the school as he was stationed at many different airfields around the country from Caithness in the north to Cornwall in the south-west in response to the heavy and relentless demands of the aerial surveillance of the surrounding seas. He was eventually based at St Eval in north Cornwall for anti-submarine (U-boats) operations in the English Channel with the RAF Coastal Command, and was presumed shot down and killed on 27th April 1941 at the age of 27 by the Luftwaffe while flying home over the Channel from a mining operation, code-named "Gardening", in the Brest area off North-West France. The RAF records state: "Failed to return from a mining operation to the Brest area." (Ross McNeill's *RAF Coastal Command Losses 1939-1941*, BHC) He was a Flying Officer on

CUCKFIELD HOUSE ORAL SCHOOL FOR THE DEAF
PROSPECTUS, 1939 *(Original on loan by Catherine Penrice)*

Cover of prospectus showing the school logo
designed by Ian Mackie BA (Oxon)

CUCKFIELD HOUSE

ORAL SCHOOL FOR THE DEAF

Principal:
Miss MARY S. CORBISHLEY

Staff:
Miss J. B. HANCOCK
(late of Central Institute for the Deaf, St. Louis, U.S.A.)

I. N. W. MACKIE B.A. (Oxon.)

Art:
ROYAL GORNOLD

Gymnasium:
Captain FRANK L. ROLT
(Asst. Supt. A.P.T.S., Aldershot).

Dancing:
Madame GARBUTT

Introduction page of the Principal and staff

CUCKFIELD HOUSE ORAL SCHOOL FOR THE DEAF
PROSPECTUS, 1939 *(Continued)*

Rear view of Cuckfield House
The Main School Hall is on the left with tall bay windows

View of lawn and tennis court from the Main School Hall
The School Hall was used as a "gymnasium" for Capt. Rolt's PT classes

CUCKFIELD HOUSE ORAL SCHOOL FOR THE DEAF
PROSPECTUS, 1939 *(Continued)*

The Aim of Cuckfield House

is that deaf children should grow up in a healthy environment, with a variety of interests and the ability to enter into the normal activities of hearing children.

To achieve this, special attention is given to Language, Speech and Lip-reading. A wide experience of the needs of the deaf has proved the necessity for constant intercourse with hearing people. A child accustomed to read only the lips of the teachers is at a disadvantage in both social and business spheres. Cuckfield House is fortunate in that it has a large circle of hearing friends, who frequently visit the School.

The School stands in its own grounds, with playing fields adjoining, and is situated in the village of Cuckfield, one mile and a half from Haywards Heath.

Aims of the School

Syllabus

SPECIAL SUBJECTS
English Language.   Speech.   Lip-reading.
Acoustic Work (Multitone installed).

EXAMINATION SUBJECTS
Oxford Junior Local Standard.
English.   Geography.
English History.   Scripture.
Mathematics.   N.T. Greek.

EXTRA SUBJECTS
Art.   Royal Drawing Society Examination Standard.
Domestic Science.   Carpentry.

Fees

Boarders per Term, £50   Day Pupils per Term, £25
Extras (each), 2 gns.

Riding and Sailing by arrangement.   Fees (inclusive of Laundry, Text Books and School Stationery) are payable in advance.

Syllabus

Diet

Vegetables and fruit from the school garden; local Jersey milk, fresh eggs, plenty of butter, and a variety of fish and meat dishes.

MEALS: Breakfast, 8 a.m. (Saturday, 8.30); Sunday, 9 a.m.)
        Mid-morning Lunch, 11 a.m.   Dinner, 1 p.m.
        Tea, 4.30 p.m.   Supper, 7 p.m. (Seniors).

Health

A careful observation is made of each child so that their individual needs may be catered for.
Medical advice is given by Dr. D. Clement Howard and carried out by the Principal.

Games

Tennis.   Cricket.   Hockey.   Daily Physical Training.

Extras

Dancing.   Gymnasium.   Tennis (Coach : Capt. Frank L. Role).
Riding.   Sailing.

School Provisions and Extra
Curricula Activities

Nursery/classroom

Ian Mackie on the right waiting for a scramble at an airfield (unknown)
©Mill Hall OPA archives

a Beaufort Mark I plane with three other sergeants all presumed missing. Ian Mackie's name and those of who were with him on that fateful flight are commemorated on the Runneymede Memorial Panel 49. (*Commonwealth War Graves Commission*) Incidentally, his father was Captain George N. Mackie of the 54th Sikhs, who was also killed in action at Ypres in 1915.

Ian Mackie's wife, Barbara Hazel (neé Gornold, sister of Roy), upon being widowed, retired from Cuckfield to Bournemouth. She was one of Mary Corbishley's oldest friends and associates of Mill Hall and was the guest of honour for prize-giving at the Parents' Day at Mill Hall in 1961. She, Barbara Mackie, became involved in setting up a National Cycling Proficiency Scheme as a voluntary Organising Secretary and Instructor of children for cycling proficiency certificates. Howard L. Gregory, an ex-Police Special Constable attached to the then Dorset and Bournemouth Constabulary in the 1960-70s, wrote to the author:

"Having telephoned her, I made my way up to her flat … went into the lift on the ground floor in 1968 and emerged on the fifth floor somewhere in the 1920s! Quite literally, I walked through a time warp! The Great Lady rose to her full 5' 4", held out a well-manicured hand and graciously welcomed me to her 'team of friends'. She explained how she came to terms with her loss. Her husband was reported missing but as time went on she knew before it was confirmed. She said: "I knew he was dead and he was with God. Since then I've been waiting my turn so that we can be together again."

"She, her brother, Roy Gornold and one other volunteer carried on with the NCP scheme at Bournemouth Police station, building up a small but willing and experienced team of Instructors/Examiners including me. Mrs Mackie received her just desserts by being awarded the MBE at the Palace for services to road safety. In the 1980s she retired to a nursing home and died from Alzheimer's disease."

Although Roy Gornold taught art at Cuckfield House for a short period, little is known of his life in Bournemouth to where he presumably retired after leaving the Royal Navy. He is believed to have died suddenly in the 1950s.

Captain Frank L. Rolt was an Assistant Superintendent (Gymnasia) with the Army Physical Training Staff (APTS) based at the Headquarters of Army Gymnastic Staff – the Army School of Physical and Bayonet Training at Aldershot in 1917-19. He was first commissioned as 2nd Lieutenant in 1915 with the Royal Sussex Regiment, 4th Battalion (Territorial) and later promoted to Lieutenant before he was seconded for duty with the Army Gymnastic Staff.

He lived in Hove and with his father and other male relatives ran a Gymnasium in Western Road since 1914 with C. H. Moss, the proprietor. It is not clear from records what happened when the WWII broke out, so he might have been recalled by the Army Training H/Q, although he continued to live in Hove until the late 1960s. This may explain why he was at Cuckfield House for only a few months before he had to leave upon being called up for the Services.

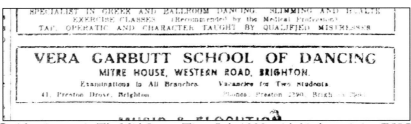

©Advertisement in The Mid-Sussex Times July 1938, with kind permission (BHC)

Madam Vera Garbutt, whom Mary Corbishley had helped with supervising her dancing classes and displays at Dene Hollow, had her own school of dancing in Western Road, Brighton. She, probably in common with other teachers, was a peripatetic dancing instructor who visited Cuckfield House in addition to other hearing schools. Mary Corbishley's enthusiasm for dancing which she claimed had helped her with her erect posture and breathing when young was borne out of her love and enjoyment of ballroom dancing when she used to be escorted by a young deaf gentleman, Dick Murphy – who was later to be the Chairman of the London Spurs Oral Deaf club (officially closed in April 2006) – to London for fashionable tea dances at a hotel before the War. They were dressed up to the nines, he in his top hat and white waistcoat and she in long evening dresses, and travelled by train from Burgess Hill.

During school-term she would invite local people of Cuckfield to her school for dances with the senior girls as part of her school's aim to promote a full social intercourse with the hearing in social and professional environments. She believed that this aim was a vital element in the build-up of character and confidence and trust at an early age in the deaf child's life while moving between two different cultures. This is truly what multi-culturism, diversity and multi-lingualism between differing peoples are all about. That was her idea and belief well before their time. During a conversation with the author who remarked to her within the context of the conversation that "no-one is perfect", she in her no-nonsense manner for which she was well-known, agreed: "*Yes, no-one is perfect.*

You are quite right.", clearly without any doubt at all about the validity of the point made, having regard to different speech styles and communicative skills of the deaf and the hearing.

Another member of the school staff who joined Mary Corbishley was Mrs Phyllis Treganowan, affectionately known as Mrs Treg by the pupils, who arrived at Cuckfield House at the outbreak of the war in September 1939 and was appointed as Secretary. She had previously taught at a Secretarial College in London and her teaching experience was invaluable in training senior girls in typing, book-keeping and other commercial office duties for after-school employment. She was the longest serving member of the staff and retired in *circa* 1968-69.

For the years of 1939 till 1942, the pupils grew from the original seven to eleven – after several of other pupils had left in the meantime – and were taught Arithmetic; Art, Dancing, Deportment (for girls), English, Geography, Handicrafts, Lipreading, Physical Exercises, Scripture, Speech(with individual speech/hearing aids) and Typing, book-keeping and other secretarial duties (for senior girls).

The demands of the war, unfortunately, meant the cutting down of the teaching staff with the loss of the male teachers. It was a serious setback for Mary Corbishley who was left with a much reduced but predominantly female staff in charge of the eleven boys and girls entrusted to her for her educational and spiritual guidance.

Despite war shortcomings, she wrote weekly letters to all the parents of her pupils, giving reports of their progress until 1944 when printed School Reports were introduced for the Spring term and continued henceforth, relieving her of the burden of writing letters by hand.

Just before the war began, the Board of Education organised the mass evacuation of children from London schools to the outlying safe havens around the country out of harm's way from the anticipated bombing. *The Mid-Sussex Times of Tuesday 5th September 1939* reported (*verbatim*): "…the population of Mid-Sussex has been nearly doubled in three days by the reception of over 10,000 evacuees – schoolchildren, mothers, teachers and others from Greater London. Trains arrived on time, the children were sorted out and despatched to the receiving towns and villages with a minimum of delay, and billeting was carried out methodically and quickly. Apart from mothers and children received by train, 36 [sic] pupils of a London school for "deaf and dumb" were brought by road to Cuckfield on Friday. They are staying at Cuckfield House." At the same time other deaf children were also evacuated from their London deaf schools and dispersed to other hastily-set-up deaf schools in such places as Brighton (school), Bognor Regis (holiday camp), St. Athenes (camp) in Glamorgan and Exeter (school). (*The Teacher of the Deaf, October 1939*)

Mary Corbishley offered to take in 34 deaf evacuees from Randall Place School for the Deaf in Greenwich, London. Staff who moved in with the pupils from Randall Place were Miss G. A. Kirby (headmistress), Mr R. Robin (teacher), Mr Oxlade (teacher), Miss Davey or Davis (in charge of the very young) and Mrs Slobrook (cook).

Mary Corbishley soon became very much troubled to find the London children using sign language and little oralism so much so that she kept the two "halves" separate by allocating her own oral-taught pupils to one set of rooms downstairs and upstairs, whereas the London "signing" children and their teachers were accommodated in the Main School Hall on the ground floor at the back, the only large area available in the building where they slept, ate and had lessons together – with the result of an "invisible wall" between them as Jean Landriani (née Baldry) told the author. Mary Corbishley forbade the mixing of the children and would reprimand any of her own pupils caught "signing" to the London pupils from outside through the windows. She probably underestimated the strength of the Londoners' signing and was perturbed lest it might ruin her pupils' carefully-taught speech and lipreading.

One ex-London evacuee, Lewis Roberts, recounted to the author that he remembered his time at Cuckfield House when the Londoners were confined to the School Hall for the whole of 18 months they were there, having to set up classes with chairs, desks and a blackboard which they folded away to one side of the room for putting up their beds for the night, and never being allowed to communicate with "Corby's own pupils". The bathroom and toilet were shared with the other pupils, though under strict supervision of the eagle eye of the nurse or matron. Nevertheless, the older London children helped with the gardening including sorting out the apples in the stable loft; one boy helped with the boiler in the basement.

Another London evacuee, Harold Dyckoff, who was born in 1927 in Rotherhithe, a parish in east London, wrote of his experience (*verbatim*): "I was on holiday on 3rd September when the war was declared, and was rushed back to London only to find the whole of my school had been evacuated! It took my parents a week to find out where my classmates were; they were evacuated to Cuckfield, Sussex and were taken in by the kindness of Miss Corbishley at her school then called "The Oral School for the Deaf". There were some 35 of us with our own teachers, cook and lady helper. I believe our cook, Mrs Slobook, took over the kitchen for both schools and was much loved by all. …we were under our own teachers and were not any way connected to "The Oral School" under Miss Corbishley. I being the head boy had the responsibility of both the older and the younger pupils, and that if there was any trouble I was blamed, hence Miss Corbishley calling me the most naughty boy of the lot! But, bless her, she knew and loved me. I was very fortunate in that I was the most oralist pupil, being the only one who spoke rather than signed…

"Miss Corbishley allowed a few of us older pupils to mix with hers and I was told to make sure that the others tried to be oralist too! We were not mixed with Miss Corbishley's school but separate as such. The whole of my school started at Cuckfield in September and left in 1941 after 18 months about February. I went to Exeter School … What a wonderful school [Cuckfield House] … All in all I must say that during my sojourn at Cuckfield House, I had the privilege to be able to learn all about country life which I fell in love with, seeing I was what is known and called a Townie. Yes, I had a great deal to be thankful for and especially Miss M. Corbishley for having taken us in September 1939." (*Harold D's letter, 1997 – Mill Hall OPA archives*)

London evacuees at Cuckfield House School
Lewis Roberts is sixth from the left; Harold Dyckoff is in the middle
at the front; Catherine Hutchison sitting at the back ©*Jean Landriani's album*

Group of London boys with their teacher, Miss Davey
Lewis Roberts is second from the left ©*Jean Landriani's album*

Harold Dyckoff, a great wartime favourite with Mary Corbishley, had remained in contact with her throughout the subsequent years, right up to her retirement and beyond. She often mentioned him to the author.

The Editor of *The Teacher of the Deaf, December 1939* wrote about the impact of evacuation on deaf children (*verbatim*): "At the moment, more than half probably of the deaf children in the evacuable areas are receiving little or no education, and of those evacuated some are working under great difficulties. These are abnormal times and everyone recognises that the difficulties are exceptional and can only be met in an exceptional way. … when lives are in jeopardy everything has to give way to secure for children comparative conditions of safety, but once that purpose has been achieved, then the conditions thereby created should be adapted for normal activities to function as far as possible.

"From the accounts given by the [deaf] schools, it is apparent that unusual conditions are being faced with good humour and patience, and both the pupils and teachers are having experiences, pleasant and not so pleasant which are at least a change from the routine of normal life. Deafness does not in itself entitle any child to special conditions as regards measures of safety, but the Board of Education have recognised, by stipulating that deaf children should be evacuated *as a school unit* [Ed.'s italics], that the needs of deaf children call for special consideration."

Mary Corbishley set aside a room or two for some of the parents of London evacuees, who also came from Greenwich. She was well up to her eyes with great responsibilities of not only looking after her own pupils, but also taking care of the London children and some of their parents all under one roof. What an indomitable woman she was! In addition to that, she offered an Open House at her school on Sundays for Bible reading sessions attended by the Pioneer soldiers who were in camp on Oaklands, an open field opposite the school, and for Cuckfield residents.

The Pioneers, originally the Royal Pioneer Corps formed in 1762, was re-formed as the Auxiliary Military Pioneer Corps within the British Army in 1939. The Pioneers – "the men who led the way" – were groups of intrepid, tough and skilled "worker-adventurers" who went ahead in advance of the Army to prepare the way. The role of the Pioneers, some of whom were conscientious objectors who opposed the war, was multi-various as their jobs were to build up stores and handle ammunition, erect camps, lay out airfields, and pull down and clear roadblocks. They also built roads, railways and bridges, loaded and unloaded stores and ammunition on and off ships, trains and planes, built aircraft pens against enemy bombing and carried out various works of fortification. One instance of their work is the first amphibious landing in North Africa with the First Army in 1942, which earned them a great reputation for their bravery and fearlessness in carrying out the advance work of preparations during the six-month campaign.

The aerial Battle of Britain with Germany raged over Sussex and Kent from August till September 1940, resulting in the defeat of Germany's Luftwaffe Air Force, thus causing the Germans to abort their planned invasion of England. This famous Battle could have been seen to a small extent from the roof of Cuckfield House, but for the summer holidays when the pupils were away from school.

As she once told the author, Mary Corbishley would climb onto the roof of Cuckfield House with a blanket, chair and torch to keep a look-out and pray to her God for the School's protection and safety from the Blitz, a German bombing raid on British cities which lasted from September 1940 till May 1941. The bombers passed over Sussex and Surrey, targeting at London, the capital. In *Corby* she described the darkened evening lit up on the horizon with a tinge of red glowing over London. Recalling such fearful experiences, she always believed that her prayers were answered as her school escaped unscathed by the ravages of the war. Even, some of the boys including myself boarding at the School would peer through a chink in the bedroom curtains to see the long beams of the searchlights sweeping across the evening sky in the distance and were awed by the sight, the author recalls.

Mary Corbishley usually spent her school holidays with her mother in Pershore, but this time she decided her place was with the "London children" and her mother would understand her decision to remain with them. (*Corby, p. 41*)

Catherine Penrice (neé Hutchison), an ex-pupil, told the author in her letter about her experience of being aware of the bombers flying over Cuckfield: "When I touched the wall of my bedroom with my hand, I could feel the noise of the German bombers over Cuckfield House. I saw the red glow of the fire in the sky over London. When the siren came on, Miss Corbishley called us downstairs to her private study and we all put on gas masks and waited until the raid was over. Thankfully, Cuckfield House was safe."

Diana Messer (neé Whitby), another ex-pupil, wrote: "Whenever air-sirens were on, senior girls took charge of juniors and looked after them."

David Kimbell remembered finding a large firebomb while walking in a field. John Perrett, his classmate, stopped him and warned him not to touch it and reported to Mary Corbishley who phoned the Army. The Army bomb disposal men defused and took the bomb away for safety.

Black-out regulations were strictly enforced where no lights should be visible through the windows at night. All windows were blacked out to ensure complete darkness in order not to reveal locations of towns and villages to attract the bombers flying in from Germany. In such a large house like Cuckfield House, Mary Corbishley as the responsible occupier had the additional worry of checking all the windows with blackouts and as a result of neglect was summoned to court on one occasion for contravening the black-out regulations. One night there was a black-out and she, feeling very much alone and exhausted after a year's coping with the evacuees at her school, received an unexpected visitor at midnight. She was a bit scared when she heard a knock on the front door and, expecting more trouble from the police, opened the door to find a desperate ambulance man asking for directions to the local hospital to which he was taking a dying man. She was mortified for having such an unfounded fear and learnt to overcome fear – or never to fear again – with God's help. (*Corby, p.41*)

She was also an Air Raid Warden whose job was to oversee the black-outs in the village and to ensure that the residents were aware of the impending air raids, the warning of which was sounded on a manually-operated air-raid siren. There were only three sirens nearest to Cuckfield (but none in the village), one at Oaklands (Cuckfield Urban District Council offices) in Haywards Heath, one at Brighton County Borough Mental Hospital in the same town and one in Lindfield, three to five miles away. As reported in *The Mid-Sussex Times, Tuesday 12th September 1939*, at a meeting of Cuckfield Urban District Council a point was raised that several Cuckfield residents had complained about not hearing the air-raid warnings, particularly at Whiteman's Green. It was felt that there should be a warning siren in Cuckfield as the wind from the south-west would blow the sounds of the Haywards Heath sirens away from the village. It was agreed that a siren should be provided and Mr Hoadley's grocer shop was chosen for the site in High Street. Mary Corbishley was now well within earshot of this siren.

Despite war difficulties, those of the senior pupils who stayed at the School at weekends attended Sunday services at the restored 13th Century stone-built Holy Trinity Church in Cuckfield, walking down the street in a crocodile file with Mary Corbishley who wrote notes of the sermons during the service to pass onto them. On one occasion some of the girls misbehaved themselves by giggling and being noisy and Mary Corbishley came round and fixed them with wide-open reprimanding eyes: "Be calm and quiet", recounted by Diana Messer. Occasionally instead of going to church, they had prayers led by Mary Corbishley in the School Hall.

The author was informed by some of the former pupils who were at Cuckfield House that they had fire drill practice with the help of local firemen who demonstrated the use of ropes and pulleys over the roof parapet for their escape from the upper rooms. One said the experience was fun but scary.

In defiance of the German threat, Mary Corbishley gave a Christmas party from 7.00 pm to 11.30 pm for members of the London Spurs Club at the School on 13th December 1941. The arrangements were dependent upon war conditions and the guests were advised to arrive at around 5.00 pm to "avoid the black-out". The charges were 2/- (10p at 2007 prices) for the party only inclusive of a buffet supper and 5/6 (27½p) for "all-in" accommodation including supper, bed and breakfast at the School. Tea would be taken at a nearby café, Kingsley's Cottage. The guests were advised that evening dress should not be worn for the occasion. (*Spurs Club Newsletter undated from Dick Murphy, the Chairman*)

It was in June 1944 when the first of the flying bombs launched from Germany fell on London. Many sinister, black, jet-fired, pilotless flying bombs, nicknamed "doodlebugs", though mainly aimed at the capital, dropped instead *en route* on the south-east counties of Sussex, Surrey and Kent. She said in her *Corby*: "Now life was almost too real and earnest as the war progressed with the first flying bomb very near us at Cuckfield House. We could see London burning ..." *(p.40)*

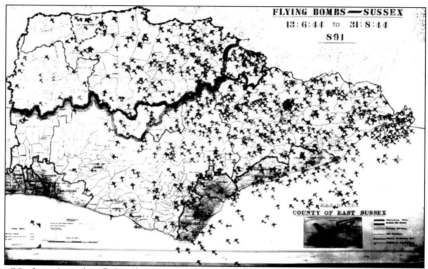

©Map 80 showing the flying bombs over and dropping in Sussex during August 1944. Cuckfield is where a few bombs dropped in the North-West of the county.
With grateful acknowledgement to West Sussex Record Office, Chichester

During the years of 1941-44, Cuckfield was a hive of military movements with the Pioneers and Canadian Infantry Brigades of 1st Canadian Infantry Division encamped locally, preparing for D-Day invasions of France on 6th June 1944. The author wrote to his parents: "We saw a lot of soldiers." *(June 1943)*; "We saw some American soldiers with a gun and a car in the field." *(May 1944)*; "The people [Army] were gone."*(June 1944)* A year later the WWII ended with the surrender of Germany on V-E Day, 8th May 1945, and Japan capitulated on V-J Day, 15th August 1945. Peace at last reigned over Great Britain and the world.

Two new teachers joined Cuckfield House; they were Miss Monica Martin and Miss Blanche Nevile. Miss Monica Martin (1903-1992), whose Australian father moved to England from Melbourne in the 1880s, was born in Caterham, Surrey where she had lived all her life. She was educated, and later became a teacher, at Eothen Public School for Girls in Caterham where she met a girl, Margaret Taylor, who was to become a qualified Teacher of the Deaf and set up her first school in Hampstead, London and later opened Hamilton Lodge School in Brighton, Sussex. It was through this Old Girl that she became a teacher of the deaf and began her career at Miss Taylor's school in the 1920s. As she needed teacher's qualifications, she moved to Doncaster School for the Deaf and trained for and obtained her Teacher of the Deaf qualifications. In 1928 she went by invitation to Johannesburg, South Africa where she was a governess to a deaf sister and brother, Ann and Michael Sutton, who benefited greatly from her tuition and who went on to become qualified architects for, respectively, landscaping and architecture.

Miss Martin once again was on the move, returning to England with her two pupils, Ann and Michael, in 1938 for them to enter the best deaf schools available at that time. After a short spell of teaching at Springhill School for Deaf Boys in Northampton, Miss Martin joined the staff at Cuckfield House in the summer of 1945 and subsequently at Mill Hall, teaching English until she retired in 1963, although she continued working part-time for a short while at a deaf school in Caterham. At Cuckfield House she also taught the author and his classmates Arithmetic.

Miss Blanche Nevile (1871-1962) was a very well-known and well-respected woman in the field of deaf education for many years and was trained at a school run by the Association for the Oral Instruction of the Deaf and Dumb in Fitzroy Square, London, where she qualified with a First Class Certificate in 1894 which empowered her to run institutions, schools or classes as Principal. She was appointed by the Local School Board of Tottenham, London to start a school for deaf children in Tottenham, which she ran for 30 years. A few years after her retirement in 1925, she moved to Cuckfield where she ended her days. It was sometime during 1944 when she visited Cuckfield House to teach junior pupils English. She was a very active member of the NCTD and strongly advocated the introduction of finger-spelling for senior pupils in schools, and gave many talks on the subject, which led to debates and arguments among the teachers of the deaf. She believed the young deaf would find finger-spelling a helpful tool for acquiring a better level of the English language and for self-expression in English, without the extra stress of trying to speak perfectly, a skill she thought was impossible or non-achievable among the young and senior deaf pupils through lack of hearing.

At a meeting of the NCTD Metropolitan and Southern Branch in July 1926, she gave a talk on language and speech teaching for deaf children. She believed that every deaf child was entitled to language training as an important part of elementary education. She, however, ruled out sign language as she considered it was not a language medium for teaching, although she would accept it outside or after school. She regarded writing as an excellent learning medium, and propounded that finger-spelling should be encouraged as a reliable skill for language development and acquisition.

She put forward her opinion that: "… in my own experience the speech of a deaf person was never understood by everyone [sic]. It was sometimes intelligible, but always queer. On the other hand, speech is good for the health, the young [hearing] child itself wants to speak, and there is something normalising about speech that is not found in other methods. …speech [is] the best medium for teaching language, but if the main aim, language, is to be attained, the speech must be definite, every word must consist of absolute sensory expressions, approximations will not do. If it is to be definite, then the speech must be simple and the same principle of analysing words must apply throughout the scheme. Personal idiosyncrasies cannot exist." (*Teacher of the Deaf, August 1926*)

She, nevertheless, supported lip-reading as an essential skill for communicating with hearing people, though she would caution against what she called "synthetic lip-reading" involving guesswork. Her talk was enthusiastically received by those present at the meeting. Had Mary Corbishley, who was not yet an Associate member of the NCTD, been present at the talk, she would undoubtedly argue against the imposition of finger-spelling on deaf pupils in schools as well as against the notion that deaf children's and adults' speech was "queer". Had the meeting been held today (2007), Blanche Nevile would have been accused of discrimination against deaf children and adults by virtue of political correctness.

Mary Corbishley never accepted finger-spelling as she was seriously concerned about its impact on speech which had been painfully taught to and acquired by her deaf pupils under her guidance and tuition. Her main task as an oral teacher/Principal of her school was naturally to steadfastly uphold the ethics of oral teaching, encouraging not only carefully acquired speech and lipreading but also the ability to understand spoken English by teachers and hearing people. She wrote to the author's father, expressing her views and perhaps doubts and fears (*verbatim*):

"With our increasing numbers it is necessary for the school to be run on slightly different lines without changing the character and standard of education.

The present plan is a trial with Miss Nevile, a retired qualified Teacher of the Deaf as Educational Advisor teaching juniors… If possible please visit and consider the methods and standards of any Deaf School you know especially private schools – Northampton for boys. We believe that Speech and Language are of equal importance to our pupils. Miss Nevile thinks Language of more importance and she believes in finger-spelling when teaching Language to older pupils. …Miss Hancock teaches speech, Miss Nevile has much language to give our juniors and so the pupils can have the best of two splendid teachers. Miss Goodwin [Ed. Teacher of the Deaf who taught English] would I am sure give you her views on finger-spelling and she would know Miss Nevile's work well."
(*Letter, 25th April 1944*)

Significantly, in the same letter she wrote: "Eventually we hope that Miss Hancock will qualify and that I shall go into partnership with a qualified teacher of the Deaf. We would like all parents of the deaf who are able to come here on 3rd June to discuss the future of this school in particular and Deaf Education in general." No records exist as to what was discussed or determined or what action decided upon, but it seems likely that the first seed was sown leading to the setting up of the Deaf Children's Society later in December of the same year and the first Committee in January, 1945.

She wrote another letter to the author's father: "I must admit that the future holds no fears for me as I know Miss Nevile's work so well, but as she is older parents may question her methods, to me it is terribly important that we remain an Oral School. There seems very little education between Manchester University costing hundreds per annum and the Council Schools. I would like to be a step between the two, just because I feel so much for these children and not because of any experience or qualification. So long as I can serve this purpose in no matter what capacity, life will be worthwhile, perhaps character training means more to me than actual teaching of facts, and if our present plan works out I shall have more and more scope out of school and energy to enjoy it all." (*Letter, 4th May 1944*)

One may observe that the teaching staff was predominantly female, and male teachers of the deaf were scarce in those days – in peace or wartime. Mary Corbishley always professed her preference for her school be for girls only; yet, she took in boys, most likely by persuasion of their parents desperate for good oral education for their sons as well as by their willingness to pay private fees which she had found to be helpful for the viability of her school's management. She wrote to the author's father (*verbatim*): "I often have fears re. boys &

wartime measures with no men on the staff, for I must admit I like boys to be boys and girls girls but he [Ed: Ian] would have your influence at home and so remove that difficulty." (*Letter, 4th May 1944*)

She clearly knew it was obvious that she was unable to impart her understanding of female emotional and sexual development to young boys on the verge of puberty leading into young manhood, and would want male advisors and mentors to guide the young developing boys towards a balanced male adulthood. She had to rely on their fathers to carry out their duty – for better or for worse …

Mary Corbishley's oral teaching laid the foundation of deaf children's speech training and acquisition by coaching them by gradual steps in breathing, voice production and projection, pitch control, pronunciation of words, articulation of the alphabet, aspirate and clear diction. Every morning she held classes and conducted breathing exercises for sibilants and aspirates by going through f, th, s, sh repeatedly to enable the deaf pupils to develop a natural breathing movement for these and other consonants.

She, having herself suffered from her many childhood health setbacks, was able to quickly establish an excellent rapport with young deaf children because she had known what it was like as a weakened child to be living in an otherwise healthy and strong world. She empathised – not sympathised – with them as she well understood how they had suffered from silence due to lack of awareness and to bewilderment of the incomprehensible world where "normal" people were fortunate to communicate with each other through hearing, speech and voice.

For lay people technically uninitiated in the connection of imperfect speech with loss of hearing, it may be explained that speech – or, technically, production through the vocal chords of sounds articulated into intelligible words – is naturally connected with the hearing of the sounds by which the speaker as a developing child or an adult is enabled to imitate other speakers' way of uttering a vocal language, with global and regional variations of accent and dialect. Thus the hearing child's brain is stimulated and becomes receptive to the new vocal language which he or she imitates. A deaf child is denied this means of hearing the language being spoken by his or her parents and teachers and thereby is delayed in developing his or her vocal chords and mental receptivity, a vital element of verbal communication in the hearing speaking world and community. For this reason which Mary Corbishley recognised early in her teaching career in Worthing and Shoreham and at Dene Hollow, she aimed to encourage her deaf pupils at a young age to open up their undeveloped vocal chords, develop the modulation of spoken words and speak as intelligibly as they could, relying on their new skill of lip-reading. She well understood the impact of deafness which stunted the natural development of the deaf child's brain – forever hungry for language, knowledge and information – leading to poor receptivity skills.

Apart from training her pupils in articulation and modulation by phonics, she would invariably begin with simple sentences: "I am a boy. I am a girl. He is a boy. She is a girl." The next lesson was with several pictures and captions saying: "This is a car. This is a boat. This is a man. This is a lady." These first two lessons were given in order to embark them on the rudiments of English grammar at an early age as she recognised that most deaf children through lack of hearing were still unschooled in such elementary sentences. Thus began the long process of developing their mental receptivity skills, the most essential basis of education. Alongside her, Miss Hancock used the modern American methods of speech coaching with the use of a speaking tube to enable deaf pupils diagnosed with useful residual hearing to learn how to recognise the spoken words and to articulate them, and to project the voice. She, undoubtedly, brought in the strong influence of the oral philosophy she had acquired at the CID in St Louis in the USA.

Lip-reading – another life-long skill – needed to be encouraged among deaf children. Watching the hearing speaker's lip movements in shaping words into sentences and questions puts a lot of strain on the young deaf child's eyes after a long conversation. To many deaf children (and adults) many words uttered by hearing speakers look the same e.g. *man, pat, mad, bad, mat, ban* and can lead to misunderstanding and uncertainty – nothing to do with mental agility or brain – and the topic of the conversation can easily be lost through no-one's fault.

Lip-reading is a useful tool required by the deaf – both child and adult – for the facilitation of communication. Every deaf child or adult is often confronted with multiple choices of lip-reading, acquired/taught speech, sign language, finger-spelling whereas his or her hearing counterpart merely uses natural hearing, speech, and voice. Acquired English language, or any other acquired language around the world, in speech, writing and reading is common in both cases of the deaf and the hearing and is prone to unfortunate misunderstanding.

HAPPY DAYS at CUCKFIELD HOUSE, 1942-1944

Smart boy David Kimbell
in school uniform c. 1942
©*David Kimbell*

Children playing on the lawn c. 1943
©*Mill Hall OPA archives*

Dancing display - Finale by pupils, June 1943
L. to R.: Brenda Tilley, Mary Hardy, Rosalind Momber (?), John Perrett, David
Kimbell, Ian Stewart, Colin Galbraith, Michael Long, Robert Riseley, Brian ….(?)
Diane Whitby, Madeleine Reid, June Hursey, Gabriel Saunders, Lorna Drillon,
Catherine Hutchison ©*Jean Landriani's album*

HAPPY DAYS at CUCKFIELD HOUSE, 1942-1944 *(Continued)*

Group of four-year-old infants in 1944
L. to R.: Susan Munt, Carol Sanderson, Patrick Chapman, Sarah Hutchinson,
John Scott, Julia Blakeway, Robert Riseley
©*Mary Hare Primary School archives, with kind permission*

Pupils outside the School in the garden, Summer 1944
L. to R.: **Front row**: Julia Blakeway, Susan Munt, Sarah Hutchinson,
Robert Riseley, Carol Sanderson, Patrick Chapman, John Scott,
Back row: Rosalind Momber, Mary Hardy?, Brenda Tilley, Ann Down,
_____?; Ian Stewart, David Kimbell, John Perrett ©*Mill Hall OPA archives*

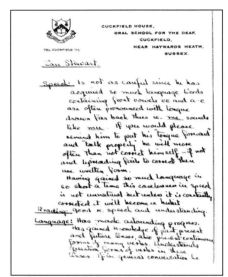

Miss Hancock's handwritten report on the author's speech training c. 1944/45
The author recalls that for the first time he saw the bottle of mauve ink which she
used to fill her fountain pen for writing the report and was fascinated by the strange
colour which he had never before seen for the ink. ©*Ian M. Stewart's collection*

It was probably during the 1940s when hearing aids were first introduced to Mary Corbishley who saw the potential of encouraging her deaf pupils who had varying degrees of residual hearing to wear them. It was, apparently, at the Deaf Education Department of Manchester University when Dr and Mrs Ewing, well-known advocates of oral education for deaf children in the 1940-50s, carried out their pioneer work in researching and developing hearing aids which were to become a permanent feature of several oral deaf schools. This led to three main types of hearing aids produced by Manchester University, Multitone Electric Company Ltd of London and Amplivox Ltd of Wembley, Middlesex, though they differed in several technical aspects and had both advantages and disadvantages in group hearing aid systems. (*Teacher of the Deaf Journals, August and October 1941*) At Cuckfield House Multitone hearing aids were used for speech training; later at Mill Hall from 1948 onwards Amplivox group hearing aids were used for speech lessons.

She believed that such mechanical stimulation of residual hearing by means of hearing aids was likely to increase the deaf child's awareness of the language – both spoken and written – and the world around him or her. Some deaf children developed a good sense of rhythm for dancing; some gained enjoyment of music, singing and spoken language in films and theatre and on television; many became better acquainted with worldly current affairs, politics, cultures and languages, art and the like, often leading to world-wide travel and adventures, all regardless of the restrictions of deafness.

Mary Corbishley early in her career became aware of the additional learning needs of deaf children and sought the best method of encouraging them to learn speech and lip-reading *at the same time* as learning to write and read. She therefore knew her foremost duty was to start her young deaf children on these skills at an early age of 2-3. She had instinctively developed what might be termed a "deaf mind" so as to fully understand the impact of deafness (or loss of useful hearing) on the young deaf child's mental development and communication skills. She thus took upon herself this vital task of preparing and equipping her deaf pupils with such skills as would enable them to fully participate in the hearing world outside her school, particularly at work. At the beginning at her School, she would tend to employ hearing teachers of like mind who were not necessarily qualified teachers of the deaf.

She did not accept, nor did she ever believe in, social exclusion (euphemism for stigma, isolation or ostracism) and institutionalisation of deaf children even during their early years. She would encourage them to go out into the hearing world, e.g. shopping in the village or going to the cinema or theatre or the local church, or join the local Girl Guides or Brownies, so that they were able to develop confidence, self-esteem and strength of character when living and working in the hearing world post-school. Her straightforwardness sustained by a "no-nonsense" attitude though tempered with Christian values of humility, kindness, succour and thoughtfulness was inherited from her mother who was described by one of her relatives as "straight as a die". She considered it was her task to instil these values in every deaf child in her charge, enabling him or her to understand and appreciate the right and the wrong.

She also inspired loyalty, love, friendship, modesty and fairness in discipline. Three former teachers from Mill Hall told the author of their praise for her fairness in disciplining her recalcitrant pupils.

For a long time she campaigned against the official opinion of the Board of Education that deaf children should be regarded "ineducable" compared with their hearing counterparts and on one occasion she expressed her fear of her deaf pupils being classified as mentally deficient or defective ("M.D.") by the Ministry of Health and Board of Education – a real sore point with her – in a letter to the mother of her pupil, Deirdre Millin (*verbatim*):

"There will be many moments when you doubt everything & everybody, there's one thing you must not do, that is doubt yourself. God knows I burn when my family [Ed: her pupils] are termed M.D. & when Mothers have to hear that, I know not what they feel. <u>But</u> remember you will not be termed M.D. I have been, for about five years. There were two years when I said, 'Well I may not be able to live for them but to give up never because I never for one moment doubted the faith that works within.' We will prove *none of the deaf children are M.D.* You will no doubt have to forgive many people much, but no bitterness must stand in our way. I have much reason to be bitter, but am I not right in saying that you admired me because I was not. "*…the more others say "M.D." the more we need to fight this battle for them.*" (*Letter 30th December 1944 – Deirdre Taylor's collection*)

In an earlier letter to the same mother, Mary Corbishley mentioned her support for and approval of the School Doctor, Dr Farr from Cuckfield, for not "treating the Deaf as M.D." With her fighting spirit and unstinting determination she undoubtedly became – consciously or not – a true champion of deaf children's – and adults' – right not to be stigmatised as "M.D." but be treated on an equal footing with their hearing peers at all levels from primary to university and beyond.

The Education Act passed in 1944 produced the most profound changes in the system of education with important repercussions for deaf children. For the first time since the first Education Act 1870, the Education Act (Blind and Deaf Children) Act 1893 and subsequent Acts of 1902 to 1937, all children – hearing, deaf and disabled – were treated equally within primary, secondary and higher education areas. Significantly, deaf children were no longer subject to certification under the Mental Deficiency Acts of the past as this form of certification was finally abolished, except where in special cases parents of deaf children applied for such certificates to enable their children to enter special schools rather than county schools if the latter were considered to be to their disadvantage.

Nationally, all children, both deaf and hearing, of 5-6 years of age were required to attend school for compulsory education, although those of a younger age group of 2-5 would be admitted if their parents so expressed their wish. At the same time schools were either under the direct control of local education authorities or managed by private Boards of Governors, and all schools were visited by His Majesty's Inspectors from the Ministry of Education. This was to later encourage Mary Corbishley to take action in applying for her school be recognised and certified by the Ministry of Education in May 1946.

Two historically significant events occurred in her life at Cuckfield House School. She had long been keen on the subject of higher education for deaf children as were other teachers of the deaf, especially the members of the NCTD who had been discussing ways and means of raising the profile of the subject. At the time there were few opportunities for young deaf pupils to receive higher education at secondary schools. This led to the founding of the Deaf Children's Society (DCS) in 1944. Fourteen parents and guardians of deaf pupils at Cuckfield House School, inspired by Mary Corbishley's far-sighted vision and belief, met at a flat in London on 15th December 1944 at which the chairman stated: "the purpose of the [inaugural] meeting is to form an association of parents of deaf children, to deal with the various problems connected with their education." (*Minutes of Meeting of Parents of Deaf Children*)

The first committee elected comprised seven members, Mr Stewart (Chairman and Treasurer), Mrs Millin (temporary Hon. Secretary), Mrs Shear (Association Hon. Secretary), Mrs Chapman, Mr Jarrett, Mr Layton and Mr Perrett. The Committee was authorised to formulate a Constitution and Rules of the Association, and to arrange for the Association to be set up. The first Committee meeting took place on 11th January 1945 at which it was unanimously agreed that: "The Association to be called the Society of St. John of Beverley; its object being to further in every way possible the provision of full modern education for all deaf children in England, as already accorded to hearing children." (*Minutes of Committee Meeting*) The Association upon legal advice was later renamed The Deaf Children's Society (DCS). It subsequently became the National Deaf Children's Society (NDCS) in July 1958, a very successful nation-wide organisation having celebrated its 60th Anniversary of its founding in 2004.

As announced in the NID's *The Silent World, June and September 1946*, Mary Corbishley organised a Garden Fête and Sale of Work at Cuckfield House which raised £200, and later in 1947 another Summer Fête, raising £140, both for the DCS funds. (*NDCS: the first 60 years 1944-2004, p.7*) She had always been a keen supporter of the DCS who expressed their grateful thanks to her and her staff for their successful efforts. (*DCS Minutes of Committee Meeting, 7th July 1947*)

Incidentally, on 2nd December in 1964 at a Reception held at the Mansion House in London to celebrate the Society's 20th Anniversary, Mary Corbishley, with the founder members, was presented to the Royal patron, Queen Elizabeth the Queen Mother. Whilst looking upon the scene Mary Corbishley turned to the author's parents and remarked with a great sense of pride: *"This is my brainchild!"* It was apparent that she believed she was the true inspiration behind the founding of the DCS, the aims of which had always been at the bottom of her heart. Her dream of higher education for deaf children was being fulfilled with the passage of time – eventually.

Royal Reception for the NDCS at the Mansion House, December 1964
Mary Corbishley can be discerned sixth from the right of the
line-up, just behind the Royal visitor
©Photograph from the NDCS' Talk No 34 - Winter 1964-65

The other historical landmark was the approval and recognition of her Cuckfield House Oral School by the Ministry of Education. Clause 9 (5) of the Education Act 1944 stipulated that schools which were especially organised for providing special educational treatment for pupils requiring such treatment and were approved by the Minister of Education would be known as special schools. According to *Corby*, she had a series of meetings at the Ministry from 1943 till 1946, at which she had great arguments with a sceptical and disbelieving Board over her oral-based teachings, administration, her own lack of teacher's qualifications and other related issues. Her main object was to secure the Ministry's agreement to grant her school eligibility for local education authorities' fees for the parents of deaf children and for boarding accommodation at her school as well as for her teachers' pension superannuation.

Finally, the Ministry arranged for HM Inspectors to visit Cuckfield House School in or before May 1946; it appears that they were satisfied that the School met with the criteria set out in the Handicapped Pupils and Medical Services Regulations, 1945 issued under the 1944 Education Act and so granted approval of Cuckfield House Oral School as a special school for Deaf children. She said in *Corby*: "Victory came on 8th May 1946 when the Ministry finally recognised the place in every respect as a proper and efficient oral school for deaf children." (*p. 46*) She also talked at length about this episode in her interview on Radio Brighton on 27th March 1980.

For her School's approval and recognition as a special school under Clause 33 (3) of the 1944 Education Act, the Minister laid down conditions and requirements which had to be complied with, regarding effective management, school attendance, categories of deaf and partially deaf pupils, provision of hearing aids, compulsory medical and dental inspections, approved scales of teachers' remuneration, register of pupils and minimum numbers and sizes of classes. Up to 1946, parents had been paying private fees to ensure their children received good proper education.

These two historic events were the proudest times of her life and career, for which she had striven for so many years from the humble beginnings at her bed-sitter in Hassocks, and upon which she often reflected with gratitude for her own steadfast and unwavering belief in her faith.

In the intervening years of 1942 – 1947, pupils who entered and left the School at different times increased from eleven to thirty seven (not including the London evacuees who had left in February 1941); they were of two-and-a-half to thirteen years of age and had lessons in Art, Arithmetic, Dancing, Geography, English, Lipreading, Physical Training, Scripture, Speech and Nature.

A new staff member, Ann May, at the young age of 15½ joined the School as nursery assistant with the task of washing the children's hair. Later she stayed on for seventeen years and trained and taught elementary English, becoming an excellent Teacher of the Deaf. (*Corby, p.45*) She was also responsible for the well-being of the children and organised games and country walks.

Although the war was on, some of the pupils were encouraged to take external examinations for art and were awarded Certificates from the Royal Drawing Society.

In 1946 two pupils, Rosalind Momber and Ian Stewart, were the first to pass the Entrance Examination for Mary Hare Grammar School (originally Dene Hollow) in Burgess Hill. Mary Corbishley had an excellent professional relationship with the Headmasters of MHGS, Mr E. L. Mundin (1946-50) and Mr R. Askew (1950-72) as she strongly supported the aims of the Grammar

School and believed in the deaf pupils' capability of taking Oxford 'O' and 'A' levels offered by the Grammar School, regardless of the fact that she had earlier walked out of Dene Hollow School under Mary Hare's Principality in 1937.

Typical Certificate from the Royal Drawing Society
©*Ian M. Stewart's collection*

Last group photograph taken at Cuckfield House in 1946
L. to R.: Front row: Julia Blakeway, Sarah Hutchinson, Jennifer Bray, Patrick Chapman, Carol Sanderson, Jean Warburg, Sarah Woodhouse
First row: Denela Platt, Paricia Johnston, Anne Bower, Susan Munt, Robert Riseley, Angela Batten
Second row: Michael Long, John Scott, Lois Raffery, Belinda Curling
Back row: Julia Crummy, Ann Down, David Kimbell, Brenda Tilley
©*Photograph on loan by Julia Crummy*

A new staff member, Mrs E. Askew, whose husband, Mr R. Askew, started teaching at the newly established Grammar School in 1946, joined Cuckfield House in circa mid-1947 for teaching Arithmetic and folk dancing.

Miss Hancock, whom the children called "Hanks", left the School in 1947, having accepted an offer from a mother of two deaf children to set up her own small private oral school for deaf children at the mother's large country house, Bepton Grange, in Midhurst, Sussex and taught there until April 1949 when she left for South Africa. For health reasons as she suffered from cold winters in England (the winter of 1947 was one of the coldest and most severe experienced) as well as for reasons of war hardships, she emigrated to Cape Town as governess to a deaf girl who was returning home from that school. In 1951 Miss Hancock (known as "Bea") with a small group of parents of deaf children set up yet again a small private school, Brook House School for the Deaf, in Claremont, a suburb of Cape Town with, initially, five and later increasing to ten pupils. The school was very successful with excellent results of preparing many deaf children for passing into hearing schools, and was recognised by the Department of Education of Cape Town.

Caption created by Dick Murphy who visited with his wife, Jeanne, in May 1970

Miss Hancock in conversation with Jeanne Murphy in Durban

©*Colour slides, Jeanne Murphy*

In 1965 she was invited by the Chairman of the Board of Fulton School – founded in January 1959 – in Gillitts near Durban, Natal (now Mozambique) to apply for the appointment of Principal. She was accepted and took up the post in 1966 which she carried out and enjoyed until 1970 when she stepped down to become Vice-Principal as she wished to devote more of her time and energy to teaching in class. She was well-liked and admired for her three "gifts" which were her "unique ability to facilitate language learning for deaf children, her astonishing success in speech correction and the manner in which she became one of any group of children with whom she worked." Such skills she had acquired at the CID, Dene Hollow and Cuckfield House. She eventually retired in 1979. It is believed that she, shortly after having visited her two sisters in England, died in Durban in the early 1980s.

An article, entitled *"Congenital Deafness following maternal Rubella during Pregnancy"* appearing in *The Teacher of the Deaf, August 1946*, mentioned an investigation being conducted at three selected schools for deaf children in the UK, one of which was Cuckfield House. Retrospectively, there had been an epidemic of German measles (also called Rubella) in the UK during the years of 1939-40 with the resultant record of babies being born with congenital risks of cataracts, deafness and heart problems. It appeared to follow a bigger epidemic found in Australia in 1939-40 where it was rampant among young Australian men in army training camps. An ophthalmologist from Sydney, Norman McAlister Gregg, discovered a link between rubella and deafness when he first observed several pregnant mothers with Rubella giving birth to deaf babies. As Mary Corbishley was approached by the investigators, she agreed to allow a Dr. Clayton-Jones of *The Lancet* staff to carry out the investigation at her school; it was found that out of eighteen children, eight had "positive history of rubella", all having born in the same year of 1940. These eight pupils and five others called themselves Rubella babies, and together with five more of the same year of birth got together to celebrate their coming of age in 1961 and their fiftieth birthdays in 1990, an ex-Mill Hall girl Jean Carter (Warburg) recalled.

In the Autumn of 1947, nearly eighteen months after the Ministry's recognition of Mary Corbishley's school, Cuckfield House was becoming over-crowded with 37 [*sic*] pupils mainly of primary age of 2 to 7 plus staff. The building, being already old due to its 1815-20 construction, was in serious need of repairs, the costs of which were too high for the school as its finances were proving inadequate for this contingency. She knew it was time to make another move to a bigger premises as of necessity; not only that but also Cuckfield House was temporary accommodation on account of war conditions, inadequate monies and an uncertain future, so obviously a more permanent school needed to be established. An incident occurred with the sudden collapse of a ceiling. She recalled in her autobiography: "The final move came when the house was found to be in dire need of attention and it was clear that something had to be done quickly – action was finally precipitated with the collapse of the main ceiling." *(p.46)*

The father of the first pupil, Mr Baldry, who from the beginning had given much support and business advice to Mary Corbishley, spotted a suitable larger property, Mill Hall, further north in Whiteman's Green, up for sale by auction in an advertisement in *Country Life, 26th September 1947*. An offer was made by Mary Corbishley in partnership with a couple, Mr and Mrs Warneford, for the property and a transaction took place on the 19th January 1948 for the conveyance to the Warnefords as the purchasers and Mary Corbishley as the sub-purchaser. (*Land Registry, Edition date: 1 November 2004*) To help finance the purchase, she received a personal loan of £5,000 and took out a 25-year mortgage with a High Street bank.

On that momentous day, she moved out of Cuckfield House to a more spacious Mill Hall, thus fulfilling her life-long dream and hope of establishing a permanent Oral school for Deaf children. In telling the author, former pupils remembered leaving Cuckfield House for the last time for Christmas holidays in 1947 and afterwards returning to a new school at Mill Hall in the New Year. Sarah Holtby (Hutchinson) and Carol Fraser-Evans (Sanderson) recalled that when they and other pupils arrived at Cuckfield House, they found themselves having to walk nearly a mile up the hilly road, carrying their small luggage, in the cold wet wintry weather to Mill Hall, with Mary Corbishley, Mrs Treganowan and Miss Martin who were waiting for them at the old school.

Mill Hall
©*Photograph from 1979 School Prospectus*

For the next 48 years Mill Hall Oral School for the Deaf was finally and permanently ensconced at the new address in Whiteman's Green, much to Mary Corbishley's great sense of achievement, pride and happiness.

'*Yes, beginning as a prayer and founded on the Bible, is what*
Mill Hall will always remain in my heart.' (*Corby, p.46*)

CHAPTER IV
1948 – 1975

Mill Hall Oral School for the Deaf, Cuckfield

[Author's Note: This Chapter covers a large span of 27 years
under Mary Corbishley's Principality when many changes
occurred in the classrooms, sleeping accommodation and
teaching staff, hence the overlapping of episodes and activities.
The two time spans relate to 1948-65 and 1965-75.]

Mill Hall Oral School for the Deaf came to symbolise what Mary Corbishley had always believed in, which was a permanent school for the education of young deaf children who needed specially-devised oral instruction whereby they were taught speech by phonics and articulation, lipreading, reading and writing English, the four most essential elements of their character, educational and spiritual development in a normal learning environment. She had argued that it was not beyond the deaf child's ability to learn to speak, lipread and understand spoken English at the same time as to read, write and comprehend written English. To quote from *Corby, pub.1980 (edited)*:

"These [special and skilled methods, normality and happiness] were built up from the very beginning upon the early experience (or, as I call it, training) in an isolation hospital. Certainly, it was perfect training for this adventure. I understood what mothers and silent, small children register, their need of security, with a home atmosphere; trying to live what one cannot fully explain to a totally deaf child, that Mother is not leaving him or her for ever. The requested bed-covering, brought from home, was so essential at bed-time to give security.

"The actual teaching was based on games in most homes with all children. I had great fun working it out. One game was blowing coloured wool to encourage watching. That was lip-reading. They would be familiar with the wool through Mother's knitting. This activity would help deep breaths; good speech is dependent upon deep breathing, not upon microphones. The fun of blowing wool and bubbles advanced. The bubbles were not burst; this would have been too explosive and clumsy for deep breath building.

"Later the wool was blown on to the back of little hands so that they could feel the breath when starting off with 'wh', 'f', and 'th'. These are never vocalised. Tiddlywinks were used for explosive consonants such as 'P', 'T' and 'K' (again no vocalisation). Over fifty years ago [1927] it was all too often thought and said that "the deaf will never read." May I emphasise that I am talking about the child born totally deaf, not the partially deaf. The game of Tiddlywinks was most useful for voice placement. Consonants should be as explosive as pistol shots and this game, combined with explosive breath on the counter and felt on the hand, gave much fun, encouragement and progress.

"I spent considerable time and contemplation upon voice placement in the nursery, often working back from employment and normal speech requirements." (*pp. 48-49*)

Thus was developed and maintained, throughout her career, her "*unorthodox*" philosophy of teaching her deaf children speech and lipreading from an early age as such was already practised at Cuckfield House.

Undoubtedly upon moving into much larger premises, Mill Hall, in cold and wet January 1948, she wasted no time in rising up to the daunting challenge of organising rooms for the class, dormitory and common hall. Mill Hall, a typical large rambling Victorian house built in *circa* 1845, originally comprised four reception rooms, billiards room, five principal bedrooms, three secondary and four servant rooms, and was surrounded with 53 acres of rich pasture and arable land, ample outbuildings, small farmery and three cottages. (*Country Life advertisement, September 26th 1947*).

Photograph of original painting of Mill Hall c. 1850
©*Mary Hare Primary School; photograph by Ian M. Stewart 2007, with kind permission*

Photographs of Mill Hall taken in c. 1910-11
©Cuckfield Museum, with kind permission

The 53 acres were composed of 6.2 acres pertaining to Mill Hall itself and 46.8 acres forming part of the adjoining farm and riding stables as well as the open land across the road on the South side. The last-named area was later sold and converted to playing fields and a rugby club. A well-known Victorian address in the 1850s and clearly indicated as a landmark on Ordnance Surveys of Cuckfield since that time, it was constructed with brickwalls hung externally with ornamental red tiles to most elevations, with tall bay windows and sash windows and topped with decorative brick chimneys over pitched tiled roofs. An extension with a single large reception room (later named the Garden Room) was added onto the back in the 1920s with some classic Art Deco features.

A large paved terrace at the rear of the house, enclosed on two sides with a low ornamental brick wall and a wrought iron gate, overlooked a wide Northern panorama of green lawn, a summer house and acres of fields beyond a steel field fence towards the Southern London to Brighton railway line running in the North-East. On the South side was a gravel drive leading up to the twin-columned portico over the panelled front door which faced acres of open fields across the road. To the North-East were the riding stables owned by the Warnefords who gave supervised riding lessons to the pupils for the first few years of the school's extra-curriculum activities.

On the West side were orchards of apple and pear trees, and rhododendron shrubs, and on the East side were a long greenhouse and a Victorian brick-walled vegetable garden tended by a long serving gardener, Mr Jarvis who had moved from Cuckfield House. After his retirement, Mr Leslie Charles Taylor took over the job, with his assistant, Mr Mitchell. Mr Taylor, an ex-Army man, tended the large vegetable garden with neat rows of vegetables of most kinds and also cultivated a peach tree on the garden wall and would give

Mary Corbishley a basket of peaches whenever there was a good crop. He normally did not like taking orders from women, but she was an exception for whom he was happy to carry out orders, as recalled by an ex-pupil, Funda Saleh (née Gürel). He also used to go into the basement by a wall ladder under the dining room to stoke up the coal-fired boiler.

According to Mary Corbishley's autobiography, she had thirty seven boys and girls being taught in the preceding Autumn of 1947, all of whom moved to Mill Hall on that cold and wet day in January. [Ed: One of the former teachers, however, mentioned to the author that 25 pupils were present at Cuckfield House at that time.] One of the former pupils, Sarah Redshaw (née Allan), while recalling her first days at Mill Hall described the ground floor accommodation: "As we entered through the white portico-ed main entrance door, we saw a huge hall with its blue linoleum covered floor and a series of wall shelves filled with books to which the pupils helped themselves for leisure reading and Mill Hall's scrapbooks which the pupils loved browsing through for memories of their times. Mary Corbishley's private sitting room on the left was decorated in her favourite colour of purple, and no-one was allowed in that room unless for a good reason.

"At the end of the hall was a red-carpeted main staircase aptly named Corby's Staircase which was out of bounds to the pupils except when they were recovering from their illness and had the privilege of walking down and up the Staircase in bedroom slippers to boost their morale. The room opposite her private sitting room was the "Study" with its wooden floor – a classroom for senior pupils who sat in a semi-circular arrangement of desks facing the teacher, Mrs Morris, in front of a blackboard with wall shelves and cupboards on each side.

"The dining room was magnificent, a lovely big room with blue floor linoleum and blue flowered velvet embossed wall paper above a painted timber dado. It had six tables, a large highly-polished one for senior pupils sitting with Corby, three medium-sized tables for other children and two corner ones for day pupils for lunch only. Corby normally served from a sideboard on one side to queues of pupils waiting to be served. All pupils had their own napkins and rings from home.

"The School Hall was where the pupils could relax by playing games or watching television only at restricted times. The girls loved leapfrogging over four high square stools or walking and balancing on or swinging round a long pole clipped on between the stools; the most popular plaything was the "famous

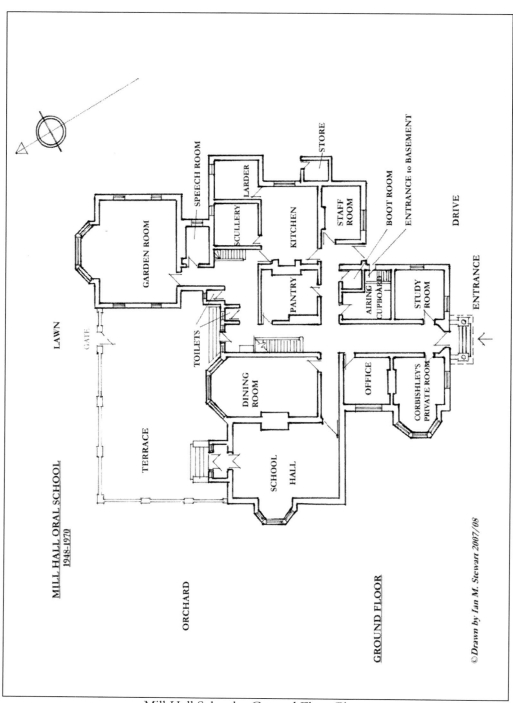

Mill Hall School – Ground Floor Plan
©*Ian M. Stewart*

and popular" red seesaw on which they tried to go up as high as they could towards the lofty ceiling. The small external lobby was used for the storage of gym equipment. Speech classes also took place in the School Hall for which the Hall was heavily lined with acoustic panels on the walls and ceiling to deaden the echoing noises during speech lessons.

"The Kitchen was big with a huge table in the middle, an Aga oven, a small electric cooker and several cupboards, and had a scullery and larder leading off it. The Pantry with its glazed roof lantern light was where the pupils were allowed to keep their own food from home in the cupboards as well as their dishes brought in from their cookery lessons at Cuckfield Secondary Modern School. Opposite the Pantry across a short lobby was the Boot Room with its strong smell of shoe polish, where the pupils polished their shoes, especially for the Brownies and Girl Guides.

"Down the hall and leading off on the right was the Garden Room, a large square oak-panelled room with bay windows overlooking the garden, with a raised floor with blue-cushioned seats below the windows. The room was used for, mainly, morning assembly and prayers, indoor games, sewing lessons, drama lessons and stage performances. Next to the Garden Room was the Speech Room with group hearing aids for speech lessons with Corby (shortly before its transfer to the first floor "Westrex" Room)." An ex-pupil, Sarah Holtby (née Hutchinson) told the author: "My parents kindly donated the first black and white television set to Mill Hall; we [the pupils] were allowed to watch television for two hours every Friday and Saturday, sitting on a plank supported by vaulting horses."

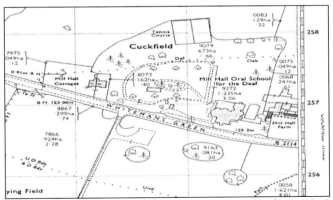

Reproduced from 1971 Ordnance Survey Map with kind permission of the Ordnance Survey. Licence No. 100048368 ©*Crown copyright. All rights reserved.* (WSRO)

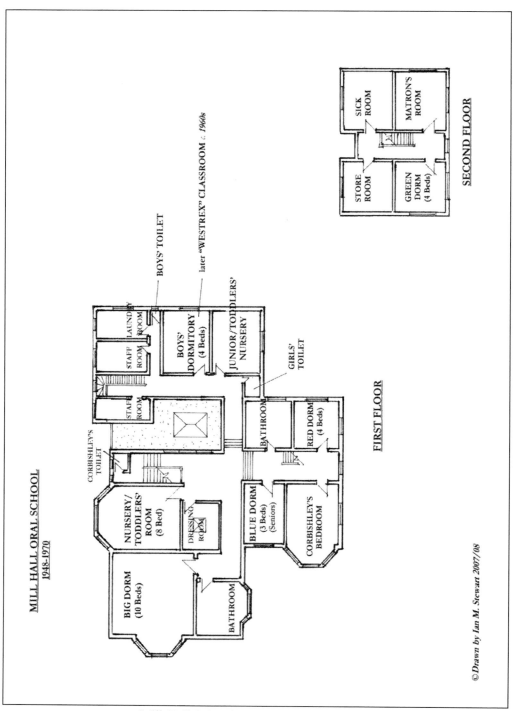

Mill Hall School – First and Second Floor Plans
©*Ian M. Stewart*

Mary Corbishley organised the allocation of the pupils according to age to various dormitories, some of which were aptly named after the colours of the floor linoleum; they progressed onto the next dormitory at each age stage of seniority.

As at Cuckfield House, young deaf children continued to be admitted to Mill Hall mainly on the recommendation of several Teachers of the Deaf, Professor A. W. G. and Mrs Irene Ewing of Manchester University Training College and other teachers at times when parents sought their advice, and, even, the Headmaster of Mary Hare Grammar School, Mr R. Askew, whom some of the parents met at conferences of the National College of Teachers of the Deaf. Mary Corbishley had already built up a reputation for running an efficient school on the lines of her philosophy of Christian-based oral education for deaf children in a happy family-orientated environment.

Mary Corbishley having sorted out the accommodation and classes, Mill Hall soon settled down to a permanent regime of daily activities as expected of a normal boarding school as observed by former pupils. She was at her happiest, knowing at last after eleven years of struggling for and seeking a more stabilised career and school she could now feel more contented with the unstinting help of her loyal staff, parents and friends. She stood ready to take on more challenges without fear or doubt, sustained by her unfailing faith in God, her guiding hand in all matters, temporal or spiritual.

It appears that the only original teaching staff, who moved in with Mary Corbishley from Cuckfield House, were Miss M. Martin, Mrs P. Treganowan, Miss Anne May and Mrs Askew; they were joined in the early years of Mill Hall by new teachers, Miss E. M. Hartley (*circa* 1949), Miss R. Milton (1951) and Mrs M. Morris (1954).

Mrs Morris applied for her teaching post in response to an advertisement in the *Times Educational Supplement* which sought a qualified teacher for teaching deaf children up to GCE standards.

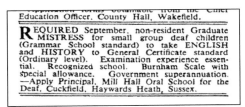

Education Officer. County Hall, Wakefield.

REQUIRED September, non-resident Graduate MISTRESS for small group deaf children (Grammar School standard) to take ENGLISH and HISTORY to General Certificate standard (Ordinary level). Examination experience essential. Recognized school. Burnham Scale with special allowance. Government superannuation. —Apply Principal, Mill Hall Oral School for the Deaf, Cuckfield, Haywards Heath, Sussex.

©Times Educational Supplement, 9th April 1954,
with kind permission of Mr Tony Shaw, Principal of MHGS (BHC)

HAPPY DAYS at MILL HALL 1948-1960s

Group of first Mill Hall pupils 1948-49.
L to R: Jean Warbug, Wendy Mears, Patrick Chapman, Michael Long,
Margaret Murray, Ann May (teacher), Jennifer Bray, Sarah Hutchinson,
Susan Munt, Sally Woodhouse, Angela Batten, Carol Sanderson, John Scott
©Photograph on loan by Jennifer Greenfield

Corby in the garden with Cherry
MacKenzie, Susan Hayward,
Terry Prickett (1949)

Corby in the garden with Terry Prickett,
Sally Crouch, Diana Butler, Elizabeth
Mortimer, Julia Crummy, Cherry
MacKenzie, Susan Hayward (1949)

©Photographs on loan by Terry Sutton

HAPPY DAYS at MILL HALL 1948-1960s *(Continued)*

Corby on terrace with Angela
Bodenham c. late 1950s
©*Jean Landriani's album*

Relaxed Corby outside the entrance
porch c.1951
©*Mill Hall OPA archives*

Three-legged race with (left to right) pair of
hearing (?) girls, Eleanor Chapman and
Angela Bodenham, Helen MacKenzie and
Diane Purcell (1953/54)
©*Angela Charles-Edwards*

Character Prize annually awarded
for good behaviour, 1951-1968
(believed to be St. Nicholas, patron
saint of children and scholars
©*Ian M. Stewart 2007*

HAPPY DAYS at MILL HALL 1948-1960s (*Continued*)

Group in 1952

L. to R.:

Front row: Paula Norton, Sarah Allan, Veronica Armstrong, Helen Cunningham
1st row: Diane Rowe, Lynda Fox, Helen MacKenzie, Rosemary Gilbey,
Angela Bodenham, Margaret Murray, Eleanor Chapman
2nd row: Angela Batten, Elizabeth Mortimer, Wendie Mears, Terry Prickett,
Sally Crouch, Angela Rosen
3rd row: Jean Warburg, Diana Butler, Anne Bower, Wendy Holloway, John
Scott, Sarah Hutchinson, Cherry MacKenzie, Susan Munt
Back row: Sally Woodhouse, Carol Sanderson
©*Photograph on loan by Terry Sutton*

HAPPY DAYS at MILL HALL 1948-1960s *(Continued)*

Warnefords' Riding stables next door to
Mill Hall
©Photograph on loan by Ann Allen

Ann Down and Rosalind
Momber with "Gimlet"
©Ann Allen

She, Mrs Morris, was promptly invited to the interview by Mary Corbishley at the English Speaking Union in London and was impressed by her direct, frank and down-to-earth approach. In her brief unpublished typed account in 1968, Mrs Morris recounted: "Two things that she said stand out: "I've no qualifications and I do everything on a spiritual basis." She asked me why I wanted to teach the deaf, something very different from what I had been doing. I told her that if I had to lose any of my senses, hearing would be my great loss so I felt sympathy for deaf people. I also admitted I'd no experience of the deaf at all. "Fine", she said, "just what I require. I want them to go on to higher education under normal conditions; it's an oral school; we don't use sign language. We lipread." Mary Corbishley interestingly used the pronoun "we" to include herself.

Mary Corbishley must have appeared to the interviewee to be very much an authoritarian and practical person in control of the situation. Mrs Morris visited Mill Hall one day in May and was shown around the school, visiting classrooms where she met some of the girls who impressed her with their clear speech. Mrs Morris was duly appointed and started in the following September. She was immediately thrown in the deep end but loved her job of teaching

English literature, history, current affairs and drama in which she excelled. She concluded:

"As time passed, I was to discover many things about Mill Hall. Not only was there discipline in the classroom. There was an orderly running of the school, completely devoid of rigidity. After prayers at Assembly, which the staff were not required to attend, an explanation rather than orders were [*sic*] given; a stress put on doing unto others what one would like done to oneself; morality without hypocrisy, Christianity as opposed to 'religion'. It was a happy community, one which balanced work and play, the spiritual and the practical – so well embodied in Corby herself. When problems arose they were dealt with promptly and with the minimum of fuss."

The author, having himself experienced such learning times with Mary Corbishley at Cuckfield House in 1942-46, can vouch for that. Mrs Morris summed up: "The school badge bore the Greek word "εγθονσιασμος" – *God inspired zeal*. There was indeed, zealousness and enthusiasm in the atmosphere of Mill Hall. There was also dedication, joy and much fun. "Try it here for a term", said Corby when she engaged me. "And see how you like it." I did, and stayed for fourteen years. They were among the happiest of my life."

Mrs Marjorie Morris, born in Hackney, London, went to King's College, London at the age of 18 to study English and French. An accomplished pianist and singer with an excellent ear for languages, she, after teaching training, was employed as an English teacher at a girls' school in Cairo, Egypt in 1935 for six years. She became fluent in Arabic and French and, in addition to her post in the Egyptian Ministry of Education, she became an English tutor to the Egyptian royal family. She returned to England in 1947 and obtained a journalist's job at the cultural section of the Egyptian embassy in London.

In 1952 when diplomatic relations with Egypt became difficult leading to the Suez Canal crisis, she left the Embassy and found herself a teaching job at Oxted Grammar School in Surrey where she taught until April 1954 when she eventually went to Mill Hall. After having taught at Mill Hall until 1968, she left England for Malta as her husband needed a warmer climate for recovery from his serious illness. In 1974, after her husband's death, she returned to England.

Mrs Morris was one of Mary Corbishley's great friends who believed in her and the latter often spoke highly of her to the author. During retirement they continued meeting for social pleasure upon her return from Malta. She died in hospital on 7th October 1999 at the age of 90.

Another great friend of Mary Corbishley was Anne May who started her career at Cuckfield House and moved to Mill Hall. She was very popular with the children and soon got married in 1951 to Glyn Bright, a dog breeder; they lived next door to Mill Hall. In *circa* 1964 they moved to Ontario, Canada to live. She remained in contact with Mary Corbishley, making regular visits to see her at the Orchard Cottage.

Miss Martin continued with her excellent teaching of general knowledge by keeping the pupils up to date with everyday news. She was a keen botanist, teaching them how to breed silkworms in the Garden Room by feeding them with the leaves from a mulberry tree in the garden. She also demonstrated the life cycle of tadpoles and frogs in the garden pond, and identified stick insects. She started handwriting competitions for good handwriting styles and encouraged the pupils to keep holiday diaries for homework and handwriting skills. She, being a strong believer in sports, encouraged the pupils to play cricket, netball and rounders, and at the same time as a keen gardener taught gardening skills and allocated plots to encourage self-learning experiences for self-sufficiency.

As part of character training, the pupils went through their daily rotas for laying and clearing tables in the dining room, washing up in the kitchen and other chores as well as sweeping their bedrooms and cleaning classrooms weekly. Daily they made up their beds in hospital style with turned corners under the strict eye of the Matron or nurse. They went through an annual ritual of shaking their blankets on the terrace early one morning at springtime as one ex-pupil, Ebrahim Saleh, recalled. A typical timetable was adhered to: 7.00 am – Getting up; 8.00 am – Breakfast; 8.30 am – physical exercises; 8.45 am – Assembly; 9.00 am – Lessons; 11.00 am – 15-minute-break for milk; 1.00 pm – Lunch; 1.30 pm – Playground; 2.00 – 4.00 pm – Lessons; 4.30 pm – Tea followed by evening prep work; 6.30 – 8.30 pm – Bedtimes."

Every morning shortly before breakfast, the pupils assembled on the main landing by Corby's Staircase and waited as they watched the bell to summon them to the dining room; just before eight o'clock the cook (Jill Conquest, née Jenner) in the kitchen below pulled the rope to toll the bell: "it's breakfast time", recalled a former pupil, Sarah Redshaw. After breakfast the pupils were led outside by Miss Rose Waller onto the terrace or in the playground for short physical exercises before trooping back indoors for Assembly in the Garden Room. For lunch they enjoyed fresh produce from the kitchen garden, along with fresh meat and fish from local village shops, and fruit from the orchard, black/red currants from the garden patch which was later uprooted to make way for Mary Corbishley's cottage in 1961.

The deaf cook, Jill Conquest, narrated how she got the job at Mill Hall: "After having been taught at a private primary school for deaf children in Durrington, Sussex, where one day Corby came to see me in class, I entered Mill Hall in 1953 at the late age of 12 and stayed there until 1955. It was during the summer holidays when I was offered two posts, one with a bakery in Worthing and the other one at Mill Hall. I chose to accept the latter and started my job in September in 1955 which I enjoyed until I left to get married in 1973." She learnt the skills of cooking from her mother as well as teaching herself and attending cookery classes with senior girls at Cuckfield Secondary Modern School.

Fully mindful of the School's finances, Mary Corbishley kept a very strict regime in the kitchen, deciding on the daily menus for the week and keeping the pantry cupboards locked, handing out food supplies whenever it was necessary. She ordered meat from the village butchers and grocery from the local grocers, apart from home-grown vegetables. The cook prepared breakfast, lunch (with the help of her assistant, Nancy) and tea for the pupils, and cooked evening meals for the staff who ate in the kitchen and for Mary Corbishley who ate alone in her private room. Additionally, Jill Conquest recalled a chicken run tended by Mr Taylor who collected eggs. For two or three years, the children had a special Christmas treat with chicken from the run.

Jill Conquest at her wedding, March 1973
with Mary Corbishley (bridegroom not shown by request)
©Photograph on loan by Jill Conquest

In the dining room Mary Corbishley sat with the children for breakfast and at lunchtime was always present, supervising the children's table manners and behaviour. While the pupils waited in a queue at the sideboard, she sharpened the carving knife with a flourish and carved a large joint and served out the meat and vegetables, or dished out the fish. Being a typical country farming woman at heart, she encouraged or obliged them to eat up fresh garden produce without wasting it or leaving it uneaten on the plate. However, the children were allowed to have second helpings of the sweet if they so wished as Mary Corbishley ensured that they were well-fed. She would reprimand "naughty" children by sending them out of the room to the hall or the pantry or by sending senior children down from the top table to the bottom table to sit with young infants. Before bedtime the pupils had biscuits and milk.

Occasionally, on exceptionally hot days in the summer, the pupils had their picnic lunch or tea *al fresco* on the lawn, a treat which they were always delighted to indulge in as much as Mary Corbishley who loved the joy of watching this happy brood enjoying themselves, which was a pleasure continued from her Cuckfield House days. One ex-pupil, Ebrahim Saleh, recalled that picnic lunches were one of the highlights when the pupils brought out their raincoats and plates of food onto the lawn.

In the winter Mill Hall, being a large 105-year-old Victorian house, was often cold with inadequate central heating from a few antiquated ribbed radiators in some of the rooms. The pupils used to huddle around the fireplace in the Garden Room for warmth until one day Mary Corbishley marked out a line in white chalk around it, forbidding them from moving near to the fireplace so that the heat would fill the room. They had to don several layers of clothing to keep warm and they even sat on the radiators for the little heat they could enjoy. On one occasion the condensation froze on the inside of the windows in the Garden room; they had the fun of scratching the ice to form patterns which they used to call Jack Frost. They were instructed to shut the door of every room they entered or left at all times to conserve as much of the little warmth as they could. It was believed that such cold wintry experiences would fortify the young pupils' character development.

Whenever an Open Day, Parents' Day or some other important outdoor occasion occurred, Mary Corbishley often served tea, inviting the guests to help themselves to the fare of sandwiches and home-made cakes displayed on a large table on the lawn or terrace. She supervised the whole of the queuing of guests and pupils in such a manner that one guest remarked to the author that: "*She was dictatorial!*' The author reminded the guest that it was typical of her to organise or marshal people into orderly queues in an efficient manner. That was the result of her experience of working as housekeeper and office co-ordinator for a London lady employer in Hampstead in the 1920s.

In maintaining her strict control of all movements at Mill Hall, Mary Corbishley took upon the task of handing out letters to the pupils after breakfast every morning in the week and on Fridays acted as "banker" paying out their pocket money – often 2/6d (13p at 2007 prices) – for shopping at a popular sweet shop, Marshalls, in Whitemans Green. She also had on the table beside a pile of letters a daily newspaper which she held up to show to the children, quoting some news item of interest. On one occasion in February in 1952, she solemnly announced the death of the King, George VI and the accession of the Queen, Elizabeth II and held up the newspaper with pictures of the two monarchs. She made sure that her pupils were continually aware of the current events happening outside the school as part of their education, recalled a former pupil, Angela Barker (Batten).

Lessons taught to classes of varying age groups of 2-16/18 by the teachers covered a wide range of subjects, and most teachers taught a medley of subjects (1948-*c.*1960): Arithmetic, Art, Arts & Crafts, Biblical stories, Biology, Book-keeping, Current Affairs, Dancing, Drama, English, English Literature, General Knowledge, Geography, History (British Empire), Lipreading, Nature, Needlework, Scripture, Speech, Physical Training, Typing and commerce secretarial work (senior girls).

One of the teachers, Mrs M. Hogwood, was probably invited by Mary Corbishley when they met in the 1960s at Cuckfield Baptist Chapel, where the former and her husband were very much involved in the renovation work for the re-opening and re-establishment of the Chapel in April 1957. Mrs Hogwood, who started teaching at Mill Hall in 1962, was Headmistress of High School for Girls in Lewes, Sussex until her retirement in *circa* 1973.

Some teachers were brought in from other hearing schools for part-time teaching or short periods: Mrs Breeds (from the Sacred Heart Convent in Brighton) for Dressmaking and Needlework, Mr Gooch (from a local Preparatory School for Boys) for Maths, Miss Higgs for dancing and piano teaching. One of the girls obtained her Pass for pianoforte playing at the Trinity College of Music in London in 1951.

Some senior girls attended the Domestic Science College in Cuckfield Park (in the early 1950s), and others later went to Cuckfield Secondary Modern

School (opened in 1956) in Warden Park for cookery lessons with Mrs Barrowman and for typing and technical drawing lessons.

The pupils were divided into Forms according to their age and ability and moved upwards to the next Form at every appropriate stage: Form C; Form Junior B; Form B; Form B Garden Room/Study B; Form Study A; Form A1/Form Study A1. In the early 1960s they were renamed Nursery, Junior Classroom, School Hall, Westrex I and II Rooms, Orchard Classroom and Study.

Those with promising prowess in art continued to be encouraged and taught to develop their potential and took Art examinations with the Royal Drawing Society and were awarded with Honours and Certificates of Merit for various categories of subjects and also for picture-making. One pupil, Wendy Mears, won a Certificate of Merit for "Excellence of Work" displayed at the Deaf Children's Art & Crafts Exhibition in 1954.

Elizabeth Seneff's Certificate, 1953
©*Elizabeth Seneff*

Wendie Mear's Certificate, 1954
©*Wendie E. Mears*

Rosemary Hackforth (née Gilbey) recalled: "Assembly took place at 8.45 every morning from Monday to Friday, at which the Psalm, The Lord's Prayer or the hymn *All Things Bright and Beautiful* were sung in rhythm." Angela Barker (née Batten) remembered: "As part of lipreading practice, we had to read the *Illustrated London News* weekly on Fridays and Miss Martin would fire out questions to us orally! Also, we read books in our dressing gowns before going to bed." Lesley Hunter (née Walker) wrote: "Before bedtime we were given an extra half an hour for reading in the Summer – with curtains or blinds undrawn."

According to former pupils who told the author about how they learned to read Shakespeare and other classics in the 1950-60s, Mrs Morris either spoke in clear English or wrote on the blackboard short versions of Shakespeare's plays such as *The Merchant of Venice, A Midsummer's Night Dream, Romeo and Juliet* and *Much Ado About Nothing* as well as Charles Dickens' *Christmas Carol* and Charlotte Brontë's *Jane Eyre* and Jane Austen's *Pride and Prejudice*. She also wrote lines on the blackboard for the pupils to write down for learning and speaking as characters in role play in the classroom. They did not give performances of these plays outside class. However, she introduced a shortened version of Oscar Wilde's *The Importance of Being Earnest* to the senior class who had the fun of performing the play to the School in the Garden Room in 1962.

Senior girls on terrace with Mrs Morris 1962
L. to R.: Lynda Fox, Terry Prickett, Susan Cox, Angela Bodenham,
Mrs Morris, Rosemary Gilbey, Diana Rowe, Diane Purcell
©*Rosemary Hackforth*

Mary Corbishley led weekly sessions for Scripture on Monday mornings and Bible readings every Tuesday evening in the Study or the Garden Room where the pupils sat in a semi-circle facing her as she told Biblical stories. They would enact some of the stories so that they understood their morals. She often quoted from her Bible her favourite Psalm 23: "The Lord is my Shepherd; I shall not want ..." In the early days at Mill Hall on Sundays she and her pupils, who were full boarders, walked in a crocodile file for nearly a mile down through the village to the Holy Trinity (C.o.E) Church; however, it was sometime in the late 1950s when, after an altercation with the vicar, she withdrew her pupils from the church and took them instead to the Baptist Chapel. In his eulogy at her Thanksgiving service in December 1995, one of her close friends, Barry Laflin, spoke of how she used to take her pupils to the Holy Trinity Church and thereafter the Baptist Chapel in Cuckfield:

"The story of how she came to Fellowship in this Baptist Church was to do with practical faith. She was brought up in the C. of E. and when she first set up her Cuckfield School she took her pupils to the C. of E. Parish Church here in Cuckfield. Naturally, as she was a great believer in lipreading for the Deaf, she seated herself and her pupils in the front row of the pews. Hearing aids (then) were cumbersome and noisy... lots of crackles and whistles.

"[One Sunday] at the end of the service the priest stood at the church door to bid farewell to his congregation. Corby told me that on this occasion the priest took the opportunity to request that in future she kept her children at the back of the church as the hearing aids interfered with the service. Knowing Corby as we do, can you even begin to imagine her retort? From now on it was the Baptist Chapel for her and her pupils. No reflections on the C. of E. in general but for her a practical pastor was preferable to a pompous priest! Her deeds always matched her words."

According to a former pupil who indeed was told many times by her of this incident, the story of her retort to the vicar goes that the vicar said to her: "Your children's hearing aids are very disturbing." Corby, rising to the occasion and bristling with justifiable disgust, replied in a clear voice: "Oh, you heard the whistling. You get on your knees and thank God you can hear!" So she stood up against what would undoubtedly have been in her eyes and mind the bigotry of the vicar – newly appointed to the church in 1957 - and so removed her pupils from his church and never went back again.

Mrs Hogwood's *The History of Cuckfield Baptist Chapel, 1772-1984* contains information on Miss Corbishley's attendance with her Mill Hall pupils: "One great encouragement during those early days was the interest shown by Mill Hall School for the Deaf. Its principal, Miss Corbishley, was among the first attenders at the service held in the re-opened chapel but after the appointment of Mr Hulse as pastor she, accompanied by a number of her pupils, was a regular worshipper at our morning services. It was always a delight to see the first three pews on the right hand side of the chapel filled with girls, all neatly dressed in their red coats or blazers and gazing attentively at the preacher as they lipread the message. When the chapel was later being extended the loan of Mill Hall School for Sunday School use and teas was of the utmost benefit in maintaining a witness." *(p.13)*

Cuckfield Baptist Chapel   Mill Hall girls with Mary Corbishley
©Sketches from Marion Hogwood's *The History of Cuckfield Baptist Chapel 1772-1984, with kind permission*

At the same time Mary Corbishley started giving Sunday School from 10.00 to 11.00 am in the Garden Room on most Sundays, alongside visits to the Baptist Chapel on other Sundays where they sat through two-hour services from 10.00 am to 12 noon. Jill Conquest, the cook, recalled that she and two pupils used to travel in Mary Corbishley's car to the Chapel and, after the service, had to dash back to the School to cook lunch for 1.00 pm. However, on some Sundays in the 1960-70s, they attended services at the Chapel in the morning and later had Sunday School in the afternoon with one or two of the elders from the Chapel for Bible readings.

An ex-teacher from the 1960s made her observation to the author that Mary Corbishley, being an unconventional woman in her ways and beliefs, was not keen on traditional customs of worship and disliked church buildings (symbolic of materialism) and preferred praying with the children at the School to nurture their spiritual well-being.

It appears from *Corby* that earlier on at Cuckfield House she had doubts about accepting pupils of different races and faiths. She had already accepted Jewish pupils at Cuckfield House School who were prepared for the old Junior Oxford examinations in the Old Testament and passed. In the case of children from abroad, she felt that care was needed. They could be black or ethnic and she wondered what the Bible had to say about that. She was especially concerned lest some parents might query the wisdom of mixing children of different races and denominations. She asserted that she never had this problem, but if confronted by the objecting white parents, she would rather remove the white child than fail to observe the Bible on which her School was based for equal rights regardless of race or denomination.

So she wrote to five Bible colleges asking for advice on the race problem, seeking hope that the Lord would have an answer to the problem which was not of her own making. The Bible colleges in responding convinced her that the differences at human level were only "male and female as God created them" and, spiritually, the only difference was between believers and non-believers." (*p. 44*) Thus she was guided by the Bible colleges to accept children whose religions were not compatible with hers. When the first Muslim pupils arrived at Mill Hall in 1959-63, they were at first obliged to attend the Baptist Chapel but were unable to participate in the services; after a time they asked Mary Corbishley to exempt them from future Chapel services, which she reluctantly granted.

Senior Roman Catholic pupils received weekly visits from a Roman Catholic priest from his church, St Paul's in Haywards Heath, who gave religious instruction; they attended Mass at the church with one of the teachers, Mrs Maureen Wood.

Mary Corbishley was lucid, honest, unambiguous and straightforward about the School's curriculum based on Christianity and the Bible. When confronted by parents of potential non-Christian pupils (from different faiths), she pointed out to them this significant philosophy and asked the parents to either accept it or otherwise. In most cases they agreed to accept, bearing in mind the foremost aims and benefits of oral education for their children.

For speech lessons Mary Corbishley introduced to her new young pupils of 2-5 years of age speech and breathing sessions with visual aids such as a yellow wall chart with all the different sounds like ar, or, oo, ee / f, th, s, sh / p, t, k, / m, n, ng, involving exercising vocal chords and aspirating 'h' with controlled breathing and pitch of the voice, as she had already done earlier at Cuckfield House. By this time she had developed her own – what one would call – *unorthodox* system of encouraging or persuading her young learners to open up their undeveloped vocal chords and start articulating sounds into intelligible words at an early stage of their educational development. Also, she induced them into repeating the sounds by placing their hands on the piano while she played out the rhythm. Rosemary Hackforth reminisced: "I can remember us all the girls standing round the piano, feeling the different sounds while she played the piano; it was during my early part of my school life."

In a school magazine *Mill Hall News, Summer 1960* a parent of one of senior girls wrote about a performance by senior pupils during Dramatic Hour on March 11th to celebrate Thanksgiving Day: "On Friday afternoon many parents gathered in the Garden Room to watch 'Dramatic Hour'. Miss Corbishley told us that the plays were being presented exactly as though it were an ordinary English lesson. There were historical playlets about King Alfred's burnt cakes, King Canute's control of the sea and St Augustine's conversion of King Ethelred to Christianity. They were easy to follow because the speech as well as the acting was so good. Each word was pronounced carefully and clearly. The star play about a submarine adventure in a bathyscope was specially written by Mrs Morris and was performed with zest and enjoyment. Miss Corbishley's words *"The deaf are born actors"* are enough to show the high standard of acting, but the confidence with which the girls spoke their lines – without any prompting – was so encouraging that we were all certain that these pupils at least face the world when they leave Mill Hall, well equipped for whatever is in store for them."

Parents continued to receive reports of their children's progress and, also, school bills for extra-curriculum activities and additional needs.

School Report signed by Mary Corbishley ©*Rosemary Hackforth*

Mary Corbishley had been interested for several years in the benefits of group hearing aids for her pupils with residual hearing and in *circa* 1961 decided to introduce Amplivox and Westrex group hearing aids for speech training. The general idea was to construct a purpose-made central desk fitted with the teacher's microphone connected to the pupils' headphones with their individual L & R volume controls to suit their varying degrees of deafness. The teacher would speak into the microphone while the pupils learnt to repeat after him or her. Later the Amplivox aids were replaced by Westrex, a new product by Westrex Co. Ltd of London in the 1950s but it was no longer in production later in the 1960s.

 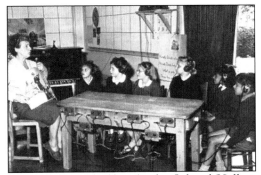

Corby's Speech Class in the Nursery with (*L to R*) …?, Fiona Damm, Joan Margeson, Kevin Cave

Corby's Speech Class in the School Hall with (*L to R*) Janette Alexander, Julia Matthew, Alison Saunders-Davies, Susan Stubbs, Haridrani de Silva, Ebrahim Saleh

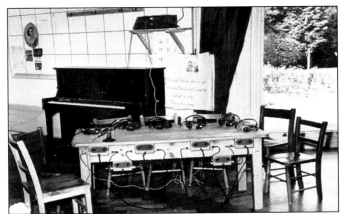

View of group hearing aid set-up with individual headphones
©*All three photographs - Mill Hall OPA archives*

Additionally, those pupils diagnosed with sufficient hearing were fitted with individual hearing aids which were either privately bought or free-issue Medresco under the NHS in the 1950s; the aids were worn in a harness fitted to the body which proved to be rather cumbersome and restrictive for their movements. Mary Corbishley, however, did not believe that totally deaf children should wear hearing aids which would not benefit them.

School bills - signed by Mary Corbishley on left and by Mr Baldry on right upon his appointment as Trustee in *c.* 1958 ©*Rosemary Hackforth*

Her Oral School at Cuckfield House having been approved and granted status as a proper and efficient school by the Ministry of Education in 1946 merely two years before its move to Mill Hall, it behoved upon Mary Corbishley to continue with fulfilling many duties of responsibility in compliance with the Education Act 1944 and its subsequent Acts and Special School Regulations, if Mill Hall Oral School were to retain its status as a recognised special school. One of the demands of the Act was Medical Health inspections carried out by nurses, doctors and HM Inspectors.

Mary Corbishley was very much aware of her girls' need for guidance for coping with puberty. She would explain to them at the start of puberty that it was a natural process of physical and emotional development into young womanhood. Angela Barker (Batten) wrote: "Obviously, Corby cared a lot about our rapid transformation into young women in spite of the fact that we never had proper sex lessons that today's [2006] young people take for granted. Corby taught young girls during puberty to be socially aware of the hearing world around them and be well mannered! I recall how we learned to stand tall and proud, and walk round the room with a book or two balancing on our heads."

For the school uniform, senior girls wore dark red tunics, pullovers or cardigans and ties with white blouses and red winter overcoats with maroon velvet collars (in the summer they wore blue or red checked dresses), whereas toddlers and junior pupils wore their own clothes, mainly sweaters and slacks. Boys had red blazers over grey shorts or trousers, red ties and white shirts with grey pullovers together with red caps sporting the school badge.

Mill Hall girls, Angela Bodenham and Rosemary Gilbey
in school uniform ©*Angela Charles-Edwards*

As Mill Hall was predominantly a girls' school, there were for a short period of time in the 1960s a few boys taking lessons and meals with the girls during the week. One ex-boy pupil, Ebrahim Saleh, recalled being a full-time boarder at a privately-run boys' school, Sharrow School in Staplefield, a few miles north-west of Cuckfield and commuting by Southdown country bus daily to Mill Hall School. Sharrow School was founded by its Headmaster for boys of 7 to 17 ('A' levels) but closed down upon his passing in the late 1960s. He remembered his first day at Sharrow when the Headmaster, already primed by Mary Corbishley, introduced him to the boys: "We have a deaf boy. Please make sure you turn your face to him and speak clearly. He lipreads." The Sharrow's boys were asked to put their arms round his shoulder to talk to him in clear spoken English. He felt heartened by the warm welcome extended by the understanding Headmaster. He wore Sharrow's blue and brown school uniform. He also joined the Scouts there.

Another ex-boy pupil, Ian Depledge, told the author of his daily commuting by taxi as a day pupil from his home in Lindfield near Haywards Heath. The two boys played cricket and football at Sharrow's and became long-term friends as a result. Once a week he, Ian Depledge, stayed late at Mill Hall to go to the meetings with 1st Cuckfield Wolf Cubs at the Scouts' Hut in Whitemans Green. Mary Corbishley ensured the best arrangements for the boys' natural development, unencumbered by the dominating presence of girls at Mill Hall.

Extra-curriculum activities included dancing lessons, horse-riding sessions at weekends for senior girls and boys at the Warnefords' stables next door, swimming lessons, weekly country walks and sports (netball, rounders and tennis). Horse-riding lessons were discontinued in the mid-1950s, possibly due to some disagreement between Mary Corbishley and her neighbours, the circumstances of which still remain unexplained to this day.

In sports the girls played netball in the winter and spring, and tennis or rounders in the summer. If it was raining in the winter or spring, instead of netball they had to run round the orchard "four times" as one pupil recalled. Two tennis courts were laid out in the school grounds by the summer house. For tennis coaching, they had Mr Basil F. Bourne-Newton, a professional coach from Hove, for six summers of 1957-62. He died suddenly in October 1962 as Mary Corbishley sadly announced to the pupils. He was 46. No further tennis coaching seemed to continue afterwards.

In 1954 Mr Baldry, the father of the first pupil, Jean, kindly donated the Baldry Tennis Cup for tennis tournaments which were played on Parents' Days and won by the following champions whose names are inscribed on the Cup: 1954-56: *S. Woodhouse*; 1957-58: *D. Platt*; 1959: (*not played*); 1960-62: *A. Bodenham;* 1963-64: *D. Rowe;* 1965: *V. Armstrong & A. Turner;* 1966: *V. Armstrong;* 1967: *C. Carter;* 1968: *Helen Parr & Carole Carter.* Runner-up and double finalist winners received the Capelin Spoons donated by Mr F. W. Capelin, the Headmaster of Cuckfield County Secondary School. (*Mid-Sussex Times, June 1964*). It is believed that as a natural progression the tennis tournaments were discontinued after 1968 as the last of senior pupils were leaving school for higher education and employment, thus reducing the number of senior pupils of secondary age.

School Badge
©*Veronica Savory*

Ian Depledge in his school uniform
©*Ian Depledge*

Keen tennis players c.1962
L. to R.: **Front row:** Diane Purcell, Rosemary Gilbey, Helen MacKenzie,
Terry Prickett
Back row: Angela Bodenham, Diana Rowe, Helen Cunningham, Lynda Fox
©*Rosemary Hackforth*

MILL HALL TENNIS TROPHIES

Baldry Tennis Cup
©*Ian M. Stewart*

Capelin Spoons
©*Ian M. Stewart*

Junior Tennis cups
©*Angela Charles-Edwards*

One of the former girl pupils, Lesley Hunter (Walker) was disappointed that: "There were more girls than boys, so there was no football!"

Dancing lessons were supervised by a Miss Higgs in the School Hall in the 1950s; once weekly senior girls went to Haywards Heath for ballroom dancing lessons.

At weekends the full-time boarders who remained at the school enjoyed country walks with Mrs Treganowan and Miss Hartley through fields and indulged in blackberry picking in the autumn and visited shops in the village with Anne Bright. Some of the boarders went home for occasional weekends. Additionally, those whose families lived or worked abroad spent weekends at the school, being cared for by Mary Corbishley and some of her staff. Some helped in the kitchen with shelling freshly picked peas and broad beans, topping and tailing gooseberries and stripping red/black currants. For the last weekend of the Summer term, former pupils were invited to the School where they enjoyed a reunion and were looked after by senior pupils.

For swimming lessons in the summer Mary Corbishley and Mrs Anne Bright escorted the pupils by bus to the Birch Hotel in Haywards Heath where they learned and practised in an open-air swimming pool under instruction of Mrs Partridge. However, swimming was shortlived as further sessions were discontinued after only one or two summer terms in the mid-1950s, much to the great disappointment of the pupils. Consequently, there were neither swimming certificates being awarded nor racing competitions held with other schools.

For leisure they had traditional parties to celebrate annual festivals such as the Hallowe'en and Christmas. On one occasion in 1953 they celebrated the Queen's coronation with a special lunch of roast lamb, roast potatoes and Brussels sprouts and jam tart with custard for the pudding, and the pupils each received a mug decorated with pictures of the new Queen, recalled by Elizabeth Seneff, a former pupil.

Upon earlier encouragement by Mary Corbishley at Cuckfield House in 1946-47, senior girls enrolled with the 1st Cuckfield Girl Guide Company who held weekly meetings at the Queen's Hall in the village, where they participated in various activities with their hearing counterparts. In 1957 they re-formed into a new company, the 2nd Cuckfield Girl Guide Company, under their Captain, Mrs D. Canning from the village and her Lieutenant, Miss K. E. Mitchell who later became their Captain with a new Lieutenant, Miss Hill ('Lefty'), as recalled by a former pupil and Girl Guide, Terry Sutton (Prickett). They held weekly meetings in the Garden Room. They also went camping occasionally and hiking.

In 1957 the first Brownies at Mill Hall formed the 2nd Cuckfield Brownie Pack who met on Tuesday afternoons/ evenings in the School Hall.

On one occasion in 1960 the Guides attended the Golden Jubilee celebrations at Withdean Sports Arena, Brighton where one of them, Angela Barker (Batten), was chosen to represent the Guides and presented the Birthday Cake to the Princess Royal to mark the 50th anniversary of the Sussex County Girl Guides' founding. A few partially-deaf senior girls joined the 1st Cuckfield Girl Guide Company and enjoyed the experience of taking part in various activities with hearing Guides including camping.

2nd Cuckfield Girl Guides 1957
© Carol Fraser-Evans' album

After receiving new colours at the service
at Holy Trinity Church, Cuckfield
©Mill Hall OPA archives

Their Captain, Miss Mitchell, wrote in the *Mill Hall News, Summer 1960* that she found them very keen and enthusiastic and working hard for their second and first class badges. Proficiency badges were won by several Guides for child nursing, hostess and cooking. One Guide, Elizabeth Mortimer, went further and gained the Queen's Badge, the highest award "believed to be the first attained by a totally deaf girl, a very considerable achievement", the *Mill Hall News* reported.

Another Guide, Terry Sutton (Prickett), joined the newly formed Forest District Land Rangers Company in Sussex in 1960 and participated in many practical activities with other hearing Rangers such as training for Quartermaster camping, rope bridge-building across an actual stream, hiking with the spastic children, interior house decorations and fire fighting. She said: "It is part of our Ranger Service Star. I think Rangers is an absorbing activity." (*Mill Hall News, Spring 1962*)

Girl Guides in the Garden Room c. 1962
L. *to* R: ***Front row:*** Sarah Allan, Veronica Armstrong, Dawn Moffatt, Paula Norton
Middle row: Joan Margeson, Diane Merritt (in American green uniform), Gillian
Richards, Barbara Logan
Back row: Helen Cunningham, Helen Mackenzie, Lynda Fox, Miss K. Mitchell
(Captain), Rosemary Gilbey, Miss "Lefty" Hill (Lieutenant)
©*Angela Charles-Edwards*

On 10th March every year Mary Corbishley continued with her traditional Thanksgiving Day celebrations by granting her pupils the day off and arranging a coach trip – after a short service in the Garden Room – to Rottingdean in Sussex for a special treat. Upon arriving there, they trooped into a double bow-windowed restaurant, *The Creamery*, near the seafront and had an ice-cream. Then, regardless of the weather – rain, snow, wind or sun – they went for a bracing walk along the under-cliff promenade eastwards to Saltdean, or westwards *en route* to the marina in Brighton, stopping off at Saltdean or Ovingdean where they rejoined the coach for the return journey to the school. Several ex-pupils told the author tales of their day trips.

Ann Allen (Down): "One such journey was by train to Hassocks and we walked on the South Downs."; Jean Carter (née Warburg): "I remember we passed Roedean [Public] School for Girls on the way to Rottingdean." Carol Fraser-Evans (née Sanderson): "We stopped off at the Black Rock marina in Brighton and walked for 5 miles to Rottingdean; senior girls were in charge of the juniors. In Rottingdean we had ice-cream at a café. It was always great fun." Angela Charles-Edwards (née Bodenham): "If it was too wet, we just had the day off lessons and did what we liked e.g. hobbies or games." Funda Saleh : "We visited a farm in Plumpton to see lambs *en route* to Rottingdean." Lesley Hunter: "I think we once went out by coach on a visit to Arundel Castle and its grounds where there was a splendid swan lake."

Day outing to Rottingdean, 1958
©Jill Conquest

In the school magazine *Mill Hall News, Spring 1961* was a heart-warming article about one unusual Thanksgiving Day outing to Rottingdean which had taken place eight years previously in March 1953.

"UNDERSTANDING"

"The children were eating ice-cream in a restaurant when they were noticed by a stranger, who commented on their good behaviour and asked that they should be given ice-cream – the fact that they already had some was unbeknown to him who was blind. The children enjoyed their extra treat and returned to the school, and that might have been the end of a pleasant incident. Corby, however, was determined to know who this man was, and finally discovered through St Dunstan's [Ed: a well-known rehabilitation centre for the blind ex-service men and women near Brighton in Sussex] that his name was Leonard Curnow, and he kept a sweet-shop. She wrote and thanked him for his kindness, and at Easter-time came a whole load of Easter Eggs for the children. One of the children's parents then wrote to thank Leonard Curnow, writing to him in Braille, and telling him something about Mill Hall.

Not very long after, he arrived at the front door of the school and announced himself, saying, "I have been told things about your children which I wish to witness for myself." "By all means", Corby replied, "Come in and meet them". So, eight years ago, was born a relationship between a blind man and deaf children which developed into a lasting relationship, and which today is as firm as ever. Leonard Curnow still gives sweets to the children, still calls at Mill Hall, and never forgets a name. He observes with his ears, while the children listen with their eyes, and the result is one of the most precious requirements in human relationship today – understanding."

There are hardly any recollections or information available for the author, regarding the short-lived Parents' Association which might have been set up with its constitution at Mill Hall in the late 1950s (according to their news magazine, *Mill Hall News*). After a comparatively short period of less than ten years the Association was suddenly either disbanded or simply discontinued for unknown reasons. At the same time, Mary Corbishley did not permit, nor did she encourage, parents to ask her teachers questions about their pupils' progress or about the school's curriculum as she seemed determined to keep a strict and tight control of the school's teaching ethos to maintain its reputation as an oral deaf school. By this, she ensured or commanded all questions be raised directly with her and not with any of the school staff in her absence.

The Parents' Association edited and issued *Mill Hall News* in 1959-1962, a short newsletter containing school photos of pupils in groups, mostly outdoors, and speech lessons in class, letters from pupils and parents and occasional articles and drawings by pupils. In the first issue of *Mill Hall News*, *Christmas 1959*, the Editor introduced the idea:

"Here is a way in which we can all keep in touch with the activities of our children at Mill Hall, and of those children who have left. Here, too, is an opportunity to express our views on everything connected with the education of our children, to sing praise where praise is due and to air our grievances when just. For this Newsletter to be a success and of real value the most important need is for ideas and original thinking. We have of course talked to Miss Corbishley about all this. She thinks it is a good idea and says she is going to make use of whatever space is made available to her to record all the things she would like all parents to know but never has the chance of putting across at the right moment. Knowing Miss Corbishley, it is probable that some original thinking will find its way into print."

Further on in the same issue, the Editor wrote an article reminding the parents of deaf children of the benefit of a normal and happy family atmosphere at Mill Hall: "Like other oral schools for deaf children, Mill Hall performs a special and skilled function, fulfilling a vital need which is perhaps fully understood only by those closely associated with the problems facing the deaf child. Besides fulfilling this need, however, Mill Hall offers something else – an atmosphere of normality and happiness which it is impossible to describe adequately but which nevertheless is very evident to us and all those who have cause to associate themselves with the school."

The Editor well understood the parents' concern about their deaf children. He wrote that such parents would experience the sequence of events starting with that first suspicion of their child's lack of response to being called by name and leading to the final diagnosis: "*Your child is deaf*". To them such a truth was harsh and difficult to accept at first, although as he assured them there was no reason for despair. Their children at Mill Hall were being helped in many ways and there was great hope for the future. That was not the case thirty years previously. It was when practical help was hard to find that hope was so often destroyed by indifference, the Editor said in his editorial.

The Editor praised Mill Hall Oral School as a shining example of successful endeavour and reminded the reader that the success of Mill Hall would not have been achieved without considerable sacrifice, and the spirit of happiness which found its way into every corner of the school was blended from the purest ingredients of love and selflessness.

The Editor continued: "To parents of younger children, it is a place with future assured, where the minds of enquiry are freed to communicate with the intelligent hearing world outside the barriers of silence, and where the children's characters are developed to fit them for their proper places in life. To future parents of deaf children, as for us, it will be known and respected as Mill Hall

Oral School for the Deaf, but to those who helped to build it, surely it will always be remembered as "… a funny little school in Sussex."

How the school came to be thus called is due to the true story of a London hearing specialist who offered advice to the mother of a deaf child, who was undergoing a hearing test, by informing her that: "*There is a funny little school in Sussex where they are doing some quite good work – do you know anything about it?*" That must have occurred during the war years and Mary Corbishley with her subtle humour took great pride in telling everyone this story. She loved referring to her school being called "a funny little school in Sussex" and always invited others to laugh with her about it.

How far the reputation of Mary Corbishley and her Mill Hall Oral School had spread worldwide [mainly, the British Empire then] is illustrated by one incident in the mid-1950s when parents of a potential boy pupil born in Uganda, Africa, were told of this School and moved to England accordingly so that he was sent there.

According to the Editorial in the next issue of *Mill Hall News, Summer 1960*, the Parents' Association offered to extend its membership to friends who were keen to maintain their interest in Mill Hall and education of deaf children. The Editor wrote: "The appeal to join Mill Hall Association met with nearly 100% response, and interest in the new Association spread beyond Mill Hall parents to friends who are anxious to associate with the affairs of deaf children. It will have been noticed from the constitution of the Association that membership is not confined only to parents of Mill Hall children … Ideas which are stillborn are often so because there has been no way of promulgating them or no link with others having a common need." It was emphasized that the Mill Hall Association, though newly set up, was strong and should remain supportive of both parents and Mill Hall School. The Editor appealed to the parents and pupils that *Mill Hall News* was a forum for pupils' work progress and achievements, and ideas, articles and views of particular interest in connection with Mill Hall School.

In the third Issue, *Mill Hall News, Spring 1961*, the Editorial contained an encouraging comment: "Lady Inman [the guest of honour on Open Day in1960] who gave the prizes talked to us of the spirit of happiness she found prevailing throughout Mill Hall – an indefinable permanent quality which is vital to the deaf child's well-being – Corby's word for it, as we well know, is *Normality*. [Author's italics] Without this feeling of normality a deaf child cannot accept the challenge thrown by the hearing world. A happy, normal deaf child should be offered, and should welcome competition, both from the hearing world and from companions at school. Success in competition promotes keenness to succeed further and progress will result provided, of course, competition is not so severe as to discourage the child."

A typical page from *Mill Hall News, Christmas 1959*
©Ian M. Stewart's collection

In what is believed to be the last and fourth Issue, *Mill Hall News, Spring 1962*, the Editor in his Editorial congratulated Miss Corbishley upon the 25th Anniversary of her school's founding. No further issues of *Mill Hall News* appeared to have been produced, which might be due to the pressure on the Editor to continuously edit and complete further issues, a task which he had found difficult to carry out voluntarily, so hence the cessation of this invaluable magazine.

CHRISTMAS
1959

SUMMER
1960

SPRING
1961

SPRING
1962

Mill Hall News 1959-62
©*Ian M. Stewart's collection*

In the first issue of Mill Hall News we attempted to describe something of the growth of Mill Hall Oral School for the Deaf - 'the funny little school in Sussex'. This year is the 25th year of the little school, a quarter of a century of effort devoted to the education and fitting for life of deaf children.

The beginnings and subsequent development of the school would not strike the casual observer as anything very out of the ordinary - many schools have started and struggled the same way, with one or two pupils, growing over the years to an established and fully integrated unit.

The difference between the beginnings of most such schools and that of Mill Hall, however, lies in the reason for the beginning. The coming into being of Mill Hall was more than just 'starting the school'. It was the acceptance of a challenge to devote the whole of a life to the teaching and care of deaf children - without qualification of terms and with no conventional way clear to reach such an objective. Difficulties were strewn all along the way and even now they still appear. Each difficulty was tackled with the same confidence that the school was a right thing and must survive. Each time, there was help at hand in one form or another. The fact that Mill Hall has not only survived, but today is established as one of the best oral schools for the deaf in the country, is no accident. It was meant to be, and will continue for a long time yet. The school itself exists in the tangible form of bricks and mortar, making a beautiful building in which deaf children can learn how to overcome their handicap and take their place in the world with confidence. From the school, the lovely view of the Sussex Downs forms part of its attraction. However, the Spirit of Mill Hall is its real secret of success. It has touched the hearts of all the many people, children and adults, who have had the privilege of entering the door, spreading happiness and peace of mind to those who most need guidance and comfort.

We say Thank You to Miss Corbishley and Mill Hall for the past, wishing her and the school a Happy 25th Year with God's blessing for the future.

©Editorial from *Mill Hall News, Spring 1962*
©*Ian M. Stewart's collection*

It was in the early 1960s when Mary Corbishley became aware of the new idea of pen-pals which started among her young children at Mill Hall and issued a note of advice and caution to their parents in an attempt to encourage them, the girls, to practise their English language with hearing pen-pals; at the same time she was clearly concerned about the risks of their contacting unknown or unseen correspondents whose character and integrity might be questionable or doubtful, especially where she felt responsible for the girls' welfare, vulnerability and personal security.

```
        PEN  FRIENDS
        -------------


        I encouraged pen friends
    to stimulate language and general
    knowledge - it is now slightly
    out of hand!


        In future girls over
    16 years of age use their own
    discretion re number and sex
    but do not write letters during
    school or prep. times.


        Girls under 16 years of
    age may only have two pen pals
    and these are to be female.


            -----
```

Mary Corbishley's typed Note to parents
©Rosemary Hackforth

Though a strict disciplinarian but with a caring maternal nature, Mary Corbishley dealt with pupils who misbehaved themselves or whose behaviour did not meet with her approval. She sent them out of the dining room whenever they were being "naughty" at times or had shown unacceptable table manners. At night if caught playing about or making too much noise in the bedroom, they would line up on the landing and, one by one, go into her bedroom where she in her nightgown used her slipper to slap on their buttocks a few times. In class the recalcitrant pupils were given lines to write or sent out of the room for 10 minutes or thereabouts or given a reprimand. Some had to stand in the corner of the classroom or be sent down to the lower class to spend time and have lessons with the younger pupils or, even, babies. These appear to be the only punishments meted out by her and her teaching staff to the pupils.

Difficult or emotionally disturbed pupils were cared for by her separately from, but not in front of, other children, although she would not tolerate some of the tantrums thrown by them, and sought to calm them down with firm words of discipline. One of the former pupils pointed out to the author that physical punishment was rarely used on the pupils, apart from occasional slipper-slapping on their posterior in the privacy of her bedroom.

Many of the pupils obtained jobs soon after completing their time at Mill Hall. In the early years of Mill Hall (1948-60), a small number had their education interrupted and had to leave early to go overseas with their families to New Zealand, Malaya, Southern Rhodesia (now Zimbabwe) and the USA. They, however, were able to complete their education at local British schools in their respective countries.

At the same time when the pupils reached their school-leaving age of eleven, some went to other Deaf schools, e.g. Nutfield Priory in Redhill in Surrey, Burwood Park School in Walton-on-Thames, Surrey, Hamilton Lodge School in Brighton or Ovingdean Hall School east of Brighton in Sussex. Some pupils went onto Mary Hare Grammar School (MHGS) in Newbury after having passed the School Entrance Examination and were later successful in passing GCE 'O' and 'A' levels. Senior pupils at a later age went to hearing Secondary Modern Schools and colleges – technical, academic, arts & crafts – and to Colleges of Art, Dentistry and Floristry where they obtained Certificates or qualifications for their chosen skills or careers.

Many in the first and second generations (1948-60) at Mill Hall stayed on up to the age of 16-18 when they left, although, upon reaching the secondary age of 11, they should have been eligible for the MHGS Entrance Examination which they never had the chance of taking, due to some parents' wish to continue entrusting them to Mary Corbishley's maternal care and spiritual guidance at Mill Hall or her decision to retain them to the best of her judgement.

However, some of the pupils who studied at local hearing secondary modern schools in Cuckfield (Warden Park) and Haywards Heath and, in one case, Lewes High School for Girls passed GCE 'O' levels in a few subjects such as English, Art, Needlework and Scripture. One pupil took 5 'O' levels at a hearing school but obtained one pass in Art; another passed three 'O' levels which he took in London after leaving school. Some did not have the opportunity to sit GCE 'O' levels for various reasons. However, according to an article in *The Mid-Sussex Times, July 1964*, two girls successfully passed their GCE

'O' levels in English whilst at hearing colleges. Mary Corbishley was reported to have said: "[As] I'm preparing deaf pupils for the hearing world, regular contact with hearing people is essential. A number of our pupils have attended Trevelyan School for Girls in Haywards Heath. Seven of our junior girls attend St Clair School in Haywards Heath. We are always grateful when the hearing world is able to co-operate." Incidentally, one of the teachers from St Clair's, Miss Grant, taught Geography for two afternoons a week at Mill Hall.

Mill Hall could be regarded as a feeder school for Mary Hare Grammar School which was what Mary Corbishley originally planned as part of her life-long strong desire to see deaf children receive higher education since the Grammar School was first launched in 1946. Her continuing professional interest in the Grammar School was evident in her shrewd acumen of maintaining an excellent partnership with the Headmasters of the Grammar School, Mr E. Mundin and Mr R. Askew, for the future higher education of her pupils. This might appear to be ironic following her departure from the very same school after her disagreement with Miss Hare in 1937, but she never allowed her personal feelings to interfere with her main objective of securing her pupils' higher education.

Senior girls were annually appointed by Mary Corbishley as Head Girl or Monitor with responsibilities of carrying out duties expected of them, in which they acquitted themselves well to her delight. Furthermore, at MHGS the following ex-Mill Hall girls had the honour of being elected Head Girl (HG) or Deputy Head Girl (DHG): Rosemary (Cherry) Mackenzie (HG 1960), Eleanor Chapman (HG 1965), Lesley Walker (DHG 1978), Caroline Sanders (DHG 1981) and Annabelle Bolingbroke-Kent (HG 1983).

Over the years from *circa* 1960 to 1975 there was a high turnover of teachers and staff; new or additional teachers who joined Mill Hall were Miss Chaloner (1959), Miss Hooper (1959), Mrs Rose Hoadley (née Waller, 1959), Mr Clark (*c.*1960), Mrs Mary Bevans (1961), Mrs Johnston (…), Mrs Connie Mager (1962), Mrs Maureen Wood (1962), Miss Grant (…) and Mrs Gibbs (…). Many of them were part-time or short-term teachers.

Mary Bevans, after leaving school at the age of about 15, joined Mill Hall as a Nurse in 1961 and was trained by Mary Corbishley, becoming a qualified Teacher of the Deaf and had stayed there for her most enjoyable and happy 30 years until her early retirement through ill health. Her mother, Mrs Quinn, used to help out with the kitchen duties.

Mary Bevans with one of the boys in nursery class
©*School Prospectus, 1989*

During Mary Corbishley's retirement Mary Bevans daily took lunch from the school kitchen to the Orchard Cottage. She, Mary Bevans, took charge of the young generation upon arrival at the school in her nursery and was a much-loved teacher and friend to many of the infants who benefited from her maternal love and care as they learned new skills with her encouragement. She and her husband frequently had the children at their home at weekends. Several ex-pupils spoke and wrote about her with fond memories and affection. As Mrs Avril Hardman the music teacher told the author, Mill Hall was her life.

Mrs Mager who incidentally knew, and taught under the headships of, Mary Corbishley and her two succeeding Heads, Mrs Webster and Mr Bown until 1988, was in 1960 teaching at Cuckfield Church Primary School. She was working as a librarian in Norbury, London when she was advised by the Chief Librarian to take up teaching. She trained as a Nursery/Infant teacher at Furzedown Teacher Training College in London. She started her teaching career as a supply teacher at primary schools in Caterham in Surrey and Haywards Heath in Sussex. Her first full time teaching job was at Cuckfield Church of England Primary School where she taught 1st year classes. In her class group were a number of young Brownie Guides. Their Brownie Leader made contact with Mary Corbishley at Mill Hall to invite some of the young girls to join this Brownie group. She also sought advice on how to help deaf Brownies, so as a result Mary Corbishley visited Cuckfield Church Primary School and met Mrs Mager for the first time and was impressed with her teaching style.

Mrs Mager was already contemplating a change of employment, so she asked Mary Corbishley for advice on training for teaching deaf children. Mary

Corbishley offered to train her for the job at Mill Hall as she felt she, Mrs Mager, would be a great asset to her school. Mary Corbishley believed that it was beneficial to employ experienced mainstream teachers who would prepare and encourage deaf pupils to integrate into the hearing world because they had higher expectations. She already had Mrs Morris who was teaching the 14+ group. Mrs Mager began her job in September 1962 at Mill Hall, sleeping in a tiny bedroom on the first floor at the school; after 24 years' teaching full time she continued teaching four days a week from Monday to Thursday.

Group outside the Garden Room c.1962/63
L. to R. **Front row:** Hazel Stevens, Haridrani de Silva, Julia Matthew, Alison Saunders-Davies, Carole Carter
Middle row: Diane Purcell, Paula Norton, Helen Parr, Janet Easley, Veronica Armstrong, Judith Renshaw, Ebrahim Saleh, Susan Nash
Back row: Rosemary Gilbey, Lynda Fox, Sarah Allan, Angel Bodenham, Diane Rowe, Helen MacKenzie, Barbara Logan, Joan Margeson, Annette Turner, Carolyn Maile, Susan Cox, Susan Marshall, Ratan Vatel, Helen Cunningham
©Rosemary Hackforth

Mrs Mager set up a new club, Tufty Club, which aimed at teaching Road Safety and the Green Cross Code with bicycle riding lessons in conjunction with the local council who provided all the equipment including miniature road signs, kerb stones and traffic lights for the Proficiency Cycling Tests devised by the Royal Society for the Prevention of Accidents. A representative from the RSPA tested the children and awarded certificates to those who successfully passed the test.

She was later appointed a Governor in March 1981 and was the Secretary to the Board of Governors in the early 1990s. She was also Deputy Principal to Mrs Webster, the successor of Mary Corbishley. She, Mrs Mager, resigned from the Board in June 1992.

Trio of Mill Hall staff: (L. to R.) Mrs Treganowan (secretary), Mary Corbishley, Mrs Mager (teacher) at a former pupil's wedding reception *c.* mid-1960
©*Ian M. Stewart's collection*

Mrs Maureen Wood, who hailed from a small village near Loch Lomond in Scotland, first met a Mill Hall girl, Sally Woodhouse, whose parents were living in East Sussex, and they became friends. Maureen Wood had wanted to be a teacher from an early age and became interested in teaching deaf children. At the age of eleven she was invited by Mary Corbishley to visit Mill Hall on a number of occasions, and in 1955 started a year of teaching as a student teacher mainly with the infants, helping them with Arithmetic, English Language and speech. She also spent Friday afternoons story-telling to senior pupils of 12-14 such as Jules Verne's *Around the World in Eighty Days*, Captain Frederick Marryat's *The Children of the New Forest* and other classics. She looked after the children after school and at weekends, taking them out for shopping, country walks and various rural activities.

She later tried out teaching at a hearing school for three years before deciding to become a teacher of the deaf which was what she had wanted. With Mary Corbishley's recommendation, she enrolled at Manchester University for her teacher training course in 1961 and completed the course with a Teacher of the Deaf Certificate in 1962. She then returned to Mill Hall and taught full-time until her marriage in 1964 and left to raise her family. In 1974 she went back to Mill Hall and taught part-time until her early retirement in 1986. Like Mrs Mager, she knew and taught under three Heads from 1955 to 1986.

A four-year-old girl, Rachel Peacock, who entered Mill Hall in May 1970 made keen observations of Mill Hall as she found it: "At the time when I started at Mill Hall, there was only the main building housing all the classrooms, dormitories and staff bedrooms; there were no outbuildings in the grounds, apart from two summer houses both used as storage for games and sports equipment. Further away in the orchard was situated Corby's house, Orchard Cottage; in the orchard we used to play hide-and-seek, and the orchard was an ever changing place.

"Mill Hall was small with, at the time, no more than thirty boys and girls of ages ranging from 2 to 18, the majority of whom were under 12. Some of the older ones who stayed at weekends were cared for by Corby who acted as their guardian. With the exception of a few children, they were all weekly boarders who went home on Fridays, returning on the following Monday.

"The Nursery on the first floor was a square room with a single sash window letting in plenty of daylight. In one corner was a white cupboard with drawers which held all the exercise books for writing and drawing and 'bits and bobs'. On the opposite wall was a blackboard with two chairs in front of it for Mrs Bevans, the nursery teacher, whom the little ones called Nurse and for Corby. The mantelpiece over the small long-since-disused fireplace was used for displays of our creative work. Photographs of our families and examples of our written and art work were pinned or hung on the walls. For arithmetic lessons we had cubes for counting and doing simple sums.

"The dim and ill-lit corridor outside led up a flight of steps onto a square landing with a grey floor and white walls, and with access to dormitories and bathrooms. The babies' dormitory had six to eight beds, all painted pink and fitted with thin, narrow and lumpy mattresses and blankets which were almost threadbare in places but still serviceable. The window looked out onto the back terrace and green lawns beyond. The walls of the nursery needed redecorations like in other rooms. The older girls of ages 6 or 7 upwards had a large, rectangular and lofty dormitory with two rows of six longer beds painted in black and again fitted with lumpy mattresses. Next to this bedroom was the Green Bathroom (which later in the mid-1970s was converted into the Green Dormitory for senior girls) with a green floor and cream walls and bay sash windows overlooking the orchard. In the middle were two old-fashioned raised baths with claw feet, and a washbasin in between. A second washbasin was in the corner and all round the room were wall shelves and rails for towels. A wooden table nestled in the bay window, and in one corner stood a small cupboard containing basic first aid.

"The boys' dormitories and bathroom were reached from the square landing by going down a short flight of steps – down half a floor as all rooms were on different levels - to the south side of the building. One dormitory was small and square shaped for small boys of 5-8 and opposite was a boys' bathroom with old-fashioned raised baths like the girls', and a small single window letting in daylight. Next to the dormitory was the "purple" dormitory for senior boys in the south-west corner of the building, with its bay sash windows. [Ed: It used to be Mary Corbishley's bedroom in her favourite shades of purple until she moved into Orchard Cottage.] Opposite this room was a store-room for suitcases. On the second floor resident staff had their two bedrooms alongside two senior girls' bedrooms. [Ed: The attic in the north-east of Mill Hall was converted into a flat with sitting room, bedroom and bathroom, in which resided a male teacher in his mid-fifties, Mr Clark, who joined the School in 1969, but after two or three years he reportedly left unexpectedly. This flat was later occupied by Mrs Webster who succeeded Mary Corbishley in 1974.]

"On the ground floor the dining room, which again was in need of redecorations, had a lofty ceiling which had cracks appearing in places and was in a dirty old shade of yellow; the wooden panels to the lower half of the walls were painted blue and the faded old-fashioned wallpaper above the dado was 'long past its sell-by-date!' There were one small rectangular table for the babies, one long rectangular table for the juniors, one oval-shaped table for older children and one wide oblong table for senior pupils with a senior teacher sitting at the top end.

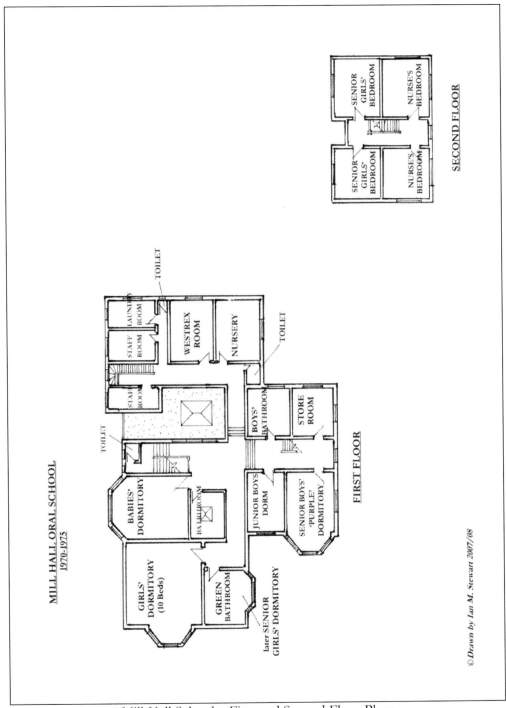

SECOND FLOOR

SENIOR GIRLS' BEDROOM

NURSE'S BEDROOM

SENIOR GIRLS' BEDROOM

NURSE'S BEDROOM

MILL HALL ORAL SCHOOL
1970-1975

TOILET

LAUNDRY ROOM

STAFF ROOM

WESTREX ROOM

NURSERY

TOILET

STAFF ROOM

BOYS' BATHROOM

STORE ROOM

TOILET

BABIES' DORMITORY

BATHROOM

JUNIOR BOYS' DORM

SENIOR BOYS' 'PURPLE' DORMITORY

FIRST FLOOR

GIRLS' DORMITORY (10 Beds)

GREEN BATHROOM

later SENIOR GIRLS' DORMITORY

© *Drawn by Ian M. Stewart 2007/08*

Mill Hall School – First and Second Floor Plans
©*Ian M. Stewart*

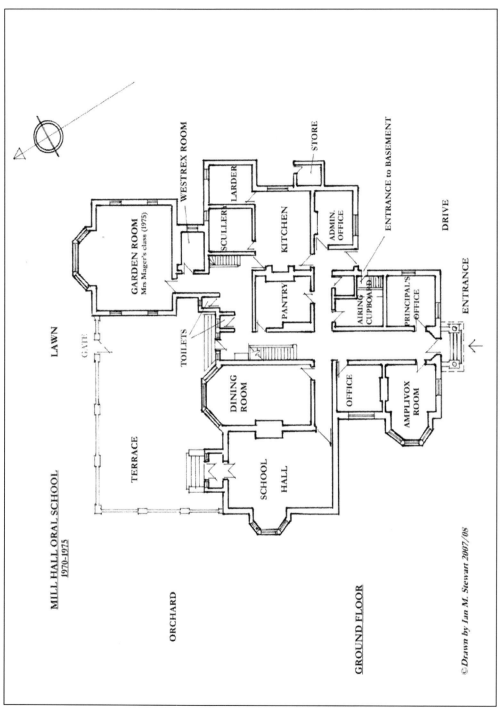

Mill Hall School – Ground Floor Plan
©*Ian M. Stewart*

"Daily after breakfast, the post was brought in and put on the senior girls' table and either one of the teachers or Corby handed out the letters and postcards to the pupils as they left the room. There was one sitting for lunch at one o'clock and Corby always served out the main course and the pudding was dished out by one of the staff. The food was brought in on a large trolley from the kitchen; there was no heater for the food in the dining room and so the food must have been almost cold by the time the older children were served. The lunch menu was a set one for each day of the week.

"On Tuesday mornings the whole of the school (pupils and staff) assembled in the School Hall for prayers before lessons began at nine. Corby still presided over the morning prayers; once weekly the senior pupils were awarded for their politeness and helpfulness with badges to pin on their school ties. The badges were shaped like the school logo with an image of the Bible on a dark red background and edged with a gold band. However, upon Corby's retirement, the badges were discontinued. Corby would preach or explain the importance of differentiating between, and recognising, good virtues and bad vices by demonstrating the two opposites under the headings of *Jesus* (virtues) and *Herod* (vices) on a large board which she brought into the room.

"Corby, though she was in her 60s, liked to drop in from time to time to participate in the lessons and activities – a 'best' chair was always reserved for her in each of the classrooms. We had to be on reasonably good behaviour for her visits. Corby had short, almost white hair that seemed to be permed and she always wore a large brooch at the front of her neck, adorning a high collar, an old-fashioned habit. She wore skirts that came down to below her knees, and always walked and sat upright in a regal manner.

"In Corby's time, all nurses wore, over their clothes, white knee-length overalls with long sleeves and pockets and buttoned up on the front, which were discontinued when Corby retired and were replaced with navy blue uniforms which were shorter and of a more modern style.

"When I was six, I moved up from the nursery to the next class in the School Hall where a different teacher taught. I recall the teacher, Mr Clark, in his blue pullover, with greying hair and metal-rimmed spectacles. There was also another teacher, Mrs Rose Hoadley (née Waller), who was a very good teacher but was fairly strict and at the same time indulgent towards us when we were good.

"In the School Hall, the desks were stashed and piled up by the wall at night and brought out to positions for morning classes. For lessons we had a free-standing blackboard. At other times outside class the Hall was used for after-school activities, one of which was the Tufty Club run by Mrs Mager for road safety awareness once weekly. Other activities were physical exercises supervised by a PE instructor and weekly dancing with Rose Waller.

"On Tuesday afternoons the 2nd Cuckfield Brownie Pack met in the School Hall for various activities and games under supervision. The Brownies were divided into two patrols, the Elves and the Pixies. While the girls had Brownies, the boys played cricket.

"At the age of seven, I moved up to the next classroom, the Westrex, named after the group hearing aids. The Westrex hearing aids were incorporated in a specially designed system with a central purpose-made table fitted with six or eight units of hearing aids individually tuned to suit the pupils' levels of residual hearing after having been tested by an auditory specialist at the auditory unit. This system was used for speech training, English and lipreading lessons. The class teacher was Rose Waller who used a wall chart with the vowels listed on one side and the consonants on the other which she instructed her pupils to learn to pronounce phonetically in order that they were enabled to form and articulate into intelligible words.

"My next move upon reaching the age of eight was the Amplivox classroom on the ground floor, named after another group hearing aid used in similar specially designed group units, where we, the pupils, remained until we were eleven, whereupon we left for other schools or, if considered academically competent, moved up to the Orchard classroom for preparation for entry to Mary Hare Grammar School, for which we had to take Entrance Examinations."

At this point Rachel Heron pointed out that all the pupils either moved up to the next class or remained in the same class, depending on their age, ability and aptitude as well as their learning abilities. Thus each class had a broad age range, some classes having pupils of 2-6, 6-9 and 9-12 years of age. The first-named started in the Nursery.

In 1975 when Mary Corbishley retired, Mrs Webster took up the Headship and introduced a large ambitious programme of redecorations, renovations, improvements and new equipment, and a change of speech and English teaching by encouraging natural conversational practice with self-expression. Naturally, Mary Corbishley, though not longer teaching, found these changes not to her liking and was clearly displeased by the conversion of what Mill Hall had always meant to her to something completely different which was not acceptable to her.

One needs to appreciate that when in 1937 Mary Corbishley herself was at loggerheads with her former employer, Miss Mary Hare, at Dene Hollow Oral School over teaching methods and children's discipline, she was 32 and a young woman with her own beliefs and ideas, and Miss Hare was 72 and an elderly woman with her set ways. Mary Corbishley would have new unconventional ideas which clashed with Miss Hare's old or long-established beliefs, which could be one of the reasons why Mary Corbishley felt unable to continue at Dene Hollow. It can be seen that history often repeats itself where a new philosophy is being introduced to replace the old in all areas of work including education, irrespective of its success or failure. Thus arose Mary Corbishley's understandably uncompromising attitude towards Mrs Webster – just as in the same way as Miss Hare must have felt towards her, Mary Corbishley, in the 1930s.

Despite this rather unfortunate turn of events brought about by a clash of ideas and personalities, Mary Corbishley now started to enjoy her retirement in her beloved Orchard Cottage, knowing that her Oral School – still within sight from her bedroom window – continued from strength to strength on the other side of the open wire-mesh fence as long as she lived and remained contented with her life's past achievements and successes in overcoming obstacles with the help of her unfailing faith in her God. She continued enjoying lunches brought in daily in the week by Mrs Bevans from the school kitchen which also provided her with Sunday roast. She must have found it hard at times to realise upon reflection how she had stoically struggled through and overcome ignorance, bias, officialdom, trials and judgements with endless doubts, trepidations, triumphs and justifications in her steadfast stand for the inalienable right of all deaf children to higher education which had always been in her heart since she first taught a deaf child to speak and lipread in Worthing in 1929. She summed up in *Corby (1980)*:

> *'Teaching the deaf, founded upon the Bible, was a time of opening minds, eyes and hearts .... Higher education now is possible ... May this educational endeavour continue and bless all concerned.'* (p. 59)

CHAPTER V
1948 – 1995

Mary Corbishley's Chronicles at Mill Hall School
1948-1975 – Limited Company – post-1975
Retirement Years – Nursing Home – Death

1948 – 1975

As she undoubtedly looked back in time over the past 27 years of Mill Hall School, 1948-1975, Mary Corbishley would recall or talk about important events which had significant influences on her life, philosophy, school, education, health and faith in her God. Also, she always maintained her deep and real interest in the progress of her former pupils' after-school lives, careers, achievements and families and delighted in hearing the news from them.

In 1948 after the Spring term ended, she opened up her new School for a social visit by the London Spurs Club on April 8th. She had been an honorary

Visit by London Spurs Club members, April 1948
L to R: Sitting on bench: Lorna Drillon, Mr Baldry, Mary Corbishley,
Jean Baldry, Rosalind Momber
Standing behind are members of the Spurs Club (defunct)
©*Spurs Club archives, with kind permission*

member of the club since the 1940s and attended, by invitation, several social functions such as dinner and dances.

In the summer of the same year, she was unable to organise another Garden Fête to raise funds for the Deaf Children's Society, due to the move from Cuckfield House to Mill Hall in the preceding January as reported in the *DCS Minutes of Committee Meeting, 10th May, 1948.*

On June 11th 1949, Mary Corbishley was one of many guests attending the second Sports Day at Mary Hare Grammar School in Burgess Hill, at which a new flag of the Grammar School was unfurled for the first time, followed by a Service for the unveiling of a memorial portrait of the School's founder, Mary Hare, during the interregnum of the sports activities. (*MHGS' The Bluebird, July 1949, pp. 10-11*) As the guests and pupils slowly filed past the portrait, how Mary Corbishley must have felt as she was once again confronted by Miss Hare's cold steely gaze twelve years after leaving Dene Hollow in 1937 is pure speculation. Mary Corbishley did not attend either of Miss Hare's funeral or memorial services in 1945, as it appears from the local newspaper reports. So the moment had come and gone away in the confrontation between the living and the dead, with their unspoken private thoughts.

Garden Fête on the lawn, 1949
©*Susan Armour's album*

On 25th June 1949 Mary Corbishley raised more funds for the Deaf Children's Society by organising once again a Garden Fête at Mill Hall, which resulted in the biggest sum on record being raised of £270 which was received with much appreciation by the Society. A report appeared in the NID's *The Silent World, August* 1949, describing the event: "The kindest of summer weather blessed the summer fête at Mill Hall Oral School, organised by Miss M. Corbishley the

Principal, in aid of the Deaf Children's Society. This is now taking its place among the major annual events of the south and weather or no weather is always very well supported. The fête was opened by Lady Bonham, who generously gave the proceeds of another fête she had already held, to the Society. Members of the Haywards Heath Soroptimists Club helped Miss Corbishley and her staff on the many stalls and side shows, and Mr A.L. Baldry brought the afternoon to a happy and profitable end with a brisk mock-auction." During the afternoon the pupils gave a dancing display under the watchful eye of Mrs Askew. Some parents and pupils also watched on television Wimbledon tennis matches and the second Test match between England and New Zealand being played at Lords. Capt. Warneford of the School of Equitation next door loaned ponies for children's rides. (*Mid-Sussex Times, June/July 1949*)

It seems that after this event, Mary Corbishley found her increasing responsibilities of running the School too onerous for her to continue with this annual fund-raising activity and felt unable to repeat it for 1950. No further Summer Fêtes took place since.

Sometime during 1949-50 Professor A.W.G. and Dr Irene Ewing, respectively, Director and Head of the Department of the Education of the Deaf at Manchester University visited Mill Hall to carry out tests on the pupils' speech and lipreading abilities with successful results. It could have been at one of the NCTD meetings when Mary Corbishley had earlier met the Ewings and found them very supportive of and encouraging for her oral methods of teaching deaf children. Her own views and aims of oral education were a perfect match for the Ewings' teacher training methods, and consequently she regarded them among her great friends who believed in her, and even dedicated her autobiography *Corby* to them.

In 1950 on 15th April a Memorial service took place for the Headmaster of MHGS, Mr E. L. Mundin at St. Nicholas Church in Newbury, which Mary Corbishley did not appear to have been able to attend, although she had known him since they met at meetings of the NCTD, and she admired his forward-thinking belief in oral education and knew that what he was doing for higher education for deaf children exactly reflected her own strong support for the same rights of deaf children.

However, later in the same year she attended with parents a Confirmation Service conducted by the Bishop of Reading at Chieveley Church near Newbury on 13th May to witness one of her former pupils being confirmed in the Christian faith.

Mary Corbishley with her Bible in her private study, *c.* 1960
©Mill Hall OPA archives

In May 1950 she hosted a Summer meeting of the Metropolitan and Southern branch of the NCTD at Mill Hall, as reported in the *Journal of the T.o.D, August 1950 and April 1951* (*verbatim*): "At the kind invitation of Miss M. Corbishley, the Summer Meeting was held at Mill Hall, Cuckfield, Sussex, on Saturday, 20th May at 2.30 pm., with Mr G. E. Whiteway in the chair. Over 70 members were present. Members stood in silent tribute to the memory of Mr E. L. Mundin, whose loss we mourn.

"(After the usual meeting business was over) Miss Corbishley introduced her children to the meeting and demonstrated the speech and language ability of a group of infant children of 5-7 years of age. She stressed the need to have the children enter school at 3 years of age, to work them together in a group of not more than six and to base the grouping on ability rather than age. In the school, we saw oralism as a success, with speech used happily and naturally from the earliest years. Miss Corbishley attributes this success to the children's ability to read. Reading is introduced at three years of age, the printed word helping towards the accuracy of speech and language which deaf children find so difficult.

"Miss Corbishley feels that co-operation with the parents is a first essential and explained her method of achieving it. The parents of nursery children spend one day per month in the school, watching teaching methods and receiving help. The parents of children 5-7 attend twice a term and the parents of older children the November Exhibition of work and the Summer Open Day. All the children take their work home for the parents to follow their progress. The end of term breaking up covers three days to enable parents of the different age groups to attend at school and receive what help they need. The school nurses, attendants and domestic staff are all regarded as important cogs in the machinery of the school, receiving training from Miss Corbishley and making for continuity throughout the child's day.

"Miss Martin gave a delightful demonstration of reading with a group of nine-year-old children. The afternoon was profitably spent. The obvious success of oralism was very heartening and the thanks of the members were expressed by a member of the NCTD. These demonstrations proved to be most instructive. Afterwards, Miss Corbishley and her staff entertained members to tea." Miss Corbishley had a big sigh of relief at the end of the memorable day as she wrote about the experience in *Corby*: "In the early 1950s a new college chairman was elected. He expressed his wish at the AGM to inspire new, young teachers to higher speech and language standards. I normally attend these meetings, but was absent on this occasion. The Chairman suggested a visit to Mill Hall for this purpose. I gather there was one voice that queried it. However, the suggestion was carried. I was asked to give a demonstration of speech and language teaching, rather like taking all examinations in one session with eighty-one examiners, including providing tea and being sociable. All was well, and Mill Hall was not publicly disgraced by the Associate Member of the College!" (*pp.49-50*) In this context, it is to be noted that, by coincidence, the newly elected Chairman, Mr G.E. Whiteway, was appointed in 1949 as Headmaster of Randall Place School, Greenwich, London, which arranged for the evacuation of thirty four of its pupils to Cuckfield House school during the war years.

Professor and Mrs Irene Ewing were invited as guests of honour for prize-giving at the annual Parents' Day at Mill Hall on 28th June 1951. As reported in *The Mid-Sussex Times, July*: "In the course of her remarks Dr Ewing expressed the hope that eventually all deaf children would have the advantages of an education such as the children received at the Mill Hall School, with its small classes and individual attention, and with children of about the same age and ability working together.

"Dr Ewing gave her audience a detailed account of the examinations which she and her husband had conducted at the Mill Hall School, with most gratifying results, in a number of cases their accomplishments nearly equalling the achievements of non-handicapped children … It was most important that deaf children particularly should have these opportunities for travel both here and abroad, such experiences which were a real training and education for them. She looked forward to the day when the training of deaf children in voice production could begin at the age of two and three, so that the real natural voice could be produced."

The fact that Mary Corbishley still opposed the use of sign language and finger-spelling as a medium for teaching deaf children since the beginning of her Oral school was manifest in her – and Miss Martin's – absence from or refusal to attend a meeting of the Metropolitan and Southern branch of the NCTD on 25th September 1954 at which an address on the subject entitled *"The New Sign Language"* was given by Sir Richard Paget. He was "inspired to develop his new sign language of 3000 words which he had evolved from his study of hand gesture languages of primitive peoples … 900 words of which he considers suitable as vocabulary for very young deaf children, thus giving parent, teacher and child a common language … But experiment is needed to prove or disprove whether the young deaf child will absorb and use these signs with as little effort as the hearing child absorbs spoken words. The New Sign Language is intended to facilitate oral teaching at a later stage when it will be possible to convert these signs into lipreading and speech." *(Journal of the T.o.D, December 1954)* Apparently, this Sign Language was not taken up successfully and was quietly dropped.

In the mid-1950s several local parents in Sussex got together to set up a new social club in Haywards Heath for young deaf school-leavers and Mary Corbishley supported the idea by attending some of the social evenings where she met her ex-pupils as well as local deaf people with whom she conversed. The Club was Medresco Club, named after the Government-issue hearing aids just made available for deaf children and adults. One evening at the club she was attempting to talk to a local deaf man who had great difficulty in lipreading her. The author who was present at the conversation assisted him by using finger-spelling and a few signs, risking her displeasure. But later she told a Parents' meeting at Mill Hall she did not object to finger-spelling and sign language *outside* her school in social circles, if the deaf adults would benefit from them, and she expressed delight with and pride in the author's help with the conversation. This alone demonstrated her flexibility towards and tolerance of the deaf people's preference for sign language or oralism.

In 1957 at the Annual Parents' Day at Mill Hall on Saturday June 27th, Mary Corbishley declared to the audience of pupils, parents, staff and other guests: "This is a most happy occasion. Grants, Ministry and mortgages were disposed of last year, and Mill Hall again stands firmly on the original foundation of character, speech and English. Pupils are taking the usual school subjects, and at about 16 years they are specializing according to ability, interest and career. If parents wish it, the Mary Hare Grammar School entrance examinations can be taken at 12." *(Mid-Sussex Times, 3 July 1957)*

Occasionally, she was invited to give talks on the education of deaf children to various interested audiences such as the Women's Institutes, Rotary Clubs, Round Tables, Young Wives, Church Fellowships, Inner Wheels and others. *(Corby, p. 60)* One particular meeting was at the District Nursing Association sometime in 1959 or 1960, at which one of the audience members said when she was testing Mill Hall girl guides for their Child Nurse badge, she found them self-reliant and courteous. *(Mill Hall News, Summer 1960)*

In 1959, true to Mill Hall's tradition, a Thanksgiving Day service for parents, pupils, teachers and friends was held at the School on Friday 6th March, to which many vicars, ministers and rectors were also invited from local churches over a wide area as far as Cuckfield, Haywards Heath, Staplefield, Lindfield, Ardingly and Warninglid. The vicar from Cuckfield Holy Trinity Church conducting the service reminded the congregation of the School's humble beginnings: "After 11 years, however, it became clear that another move would have to be made because the house [Ed: Cuckfield House] had become structurally unsound and was causing anxiety. At that time Mill Hall was on the market, but he asked, "Who could contemplate coming to a place like this with no visible resources?" Several thousand pounds were needed before the school could move to Mill Hall, but because God had willed it, and because of the faith of those who worked for the School, the problem was solved. Firmly established at Mill Hall, the works for the deaf had gone on … Unfortunately, the Headmistress was unwell but she was not going to miss the service. As she welcomed visitors from all over the country at the front door, her thoughts no doubt went winging back over the years to the School's humble beginnings and the long way it had travelled on the straight road of faith." (*Mid-Sussex Times, 11 March 1959*)

At this point Mary Corbishley was seriously ill with worries over the School's management and finances and was advised to go away on a long two- or three-week cruise to Madeira. Having thoroughly enjoyed the break, she came back much recovered with a renewed determination to take things easy. While she was recounting this experience to the author at the time, she appeared to him a much changed woman with a less severe countenance; to this day he still

Mary Corbishley with Ian Stewart and Jean Warburg
at ex-pupil Angela and Charles Barker's wedding, June 1963
© *Photograph from Ian Stewart's collection*

remembers this particular conversation about her life-changing experience during which – as it became apparent to him – she had undergone a complete transformation from a school headmistress in sombre dresses to a more matronly figure in pastel colours as seen in the photograph.

In *circa* 1961, a new small house with its attached classroom was built in the orchard on the west side of Mill Hall. The house, Orchard Cottage, was lived in by Mary Corbishley until her retirement and beyond up to 1993 when she eventually had to leave to move into a nursing home. At the beginning the classroom, Orchard Classroom, was used for the continuation of speech and lipreading lessons taught by her to young pupils. It was also used later for preparing the senior pupils for the MHGS entrance examinations, Oxford GCE examinations or higher education elsewhere. Also, a metal chicken-wire mesh fence with a timber five-bar gate was erected to mark out the boundary between the School and her cottage as required for registration in the property deeds.

Front view of Orchard Cottage
©*Mill Hall OPA archives*

Rear view with Orchard Classroom
©*Angela Charles-Edwards*

Orchard Cottage, a two-storey timber-boarded and brick-built structure, was simply designed with its front door opening into a small fitted kitchen through which visitors walked into a small lobby leading off on the left to a lounge overlooking Mill Hall on the east side, and was surrounded by the orchard to the south. A simple right-angled staircase gave access to the first floor with Mary Corbishley's large bedroom and one visitor's bedroom and a separate bathroom. Pupils entered the Orchard classroom through a side door. She comfortably settled down in the new cottage and continued with teaching small children.

As she always strongly believed in the integration of deaf and hearing children from an early age, she had the opportunity of, on one occasion in 1961, observing such integration at a meeting. She described the evening in *Mill Hall News, Spring 1962*: "On October 28th I was asked to give a talk to the "Young Fishers" at St. Wilfred's Church in Haywards Heath. I had never heard of them, their ages were 11–15 years, so I decided to start with the "wool game" as played with the smallest deaf children. It was a wonderful experience for me to have these youngsters keen, yes, keen not avoiding the issue – to join in and find out how to help the deaf.

"At first I am sure the boys thought they would be expected to knit garments and were relieved to find it was blowing pieces of wool to build speech. My talk was followed by games and the Mill Hall children were invited to join in and all had a lovely time. During my talk I had said that most of the girls I had brought with me came from long distances and were unable to get home for weekends. The next thing was invitations for long distance children to spend weekends in their homes in Haywards Heath.

"November 25th – another invitation came from the 'Young Fishers' to an Open Evening of Games, Dancing, etc. Today is November 26th – I had not spent yesterday evening at the Club because you all know how I seek opportunities to prove the pupils' normality in a hearing world. They returned delighted to tell me about 'rock and roll', fun and one ball game played deaf versus hearing and the deaf won three times. I rejoiced with them. Later I paused, reflected and blessed the adults in this Club, who were responsible for so much joy in our midst. Ordinary people but exceptional in their way of life. Surely this is Christmas in spirit and in truth."

She had a tradition of welcoming and participating in the celebrations of the School's anniversaries organised by her former pupils, apart from her annual Thanksgiving Day Services and holidays which she shared with her pupils, parents, staff and friends. The year 1962 was the 25th Anniversary of Mary Corbishley's Thanksgiving Day and her first School in Hassocks. The ex-pupils

Mary Corbishley receiving a scroll of congratulations and a Pye record player
©*Photograph of colour slide from Ian Stewart's collection*

set up an ad-hoc committee (with the author as its chairman) to plan a special party which took place at Mill Hall; they presented her with a surprise gift of a Pye record player in its handsome mahogany casing for her enjoyment of music which she loved listening to in the evenings. She was pleasantly delighted to see so many of her former pupils with their betrothed, husbands and wives, alongside their equally delighted teachers.

Later in the same year another incident occurred which was to have a lasting impact on her faith, leading to a more serious study of the Bible with a pastor from Cuckfield Strict Baptist Chapel. The Strict Baptists regard the Bible as the inspired and infallible word of God, the only final authority for all matters of Christian faith and practice. After having broken off relations with the Holy Trinity Church in Cuckfield, she started attending the Baptist Chapel with her children from Mill Hall, and so once more resorted to further Bible-reading sessions, by which she discovered the inner truth of what the Bible meant to her. What she called this truth is described in *Corby*: "… may all believers enjoy, benefit. And be blessed by their place of worship as much as I have been since attending Cuckfield Chapel, which opened over twelve years ago. After the first few years a pastor was called and he has fed me with 'meat', not 'milk' from the Bible …" (*p. 44*) This marked the turning point of her spiritual life, after which time she became more devoted to Bible readings.

It was around this time when her niece from Exeter in Devon started visiting her and staying at the cottage from time to time with her husband. It was a natural consequence that Mary Corbishley once again got in touch with her family in Worcestershire and Herefordshire – after a long interval. Previously, as the niece mentioned in her letter to the author, she and her Aunt Mary had started corresponding by letter since the 1930s; then they proceeded to telephone calls – to quote her – "*which was even better.*

Invitation from the NDCS
©*Mill Hall OPA archives*

In 1964 Mary Corbishley received an invitation from The National Deaf Children's Society to a Reception at the Mansion House in the City of London on 2nd December to celebrate the 20th Anniversary of the founding of the Society and was presented to the Society's patron, Queen Elizabeth the Queen Mother. They had already met once at a Bible Reading Fellowship at Central Hall, Westminster Centre, London during the Blitz in the 1940s. After the reception when the Queen Mother had left, the guests moved to the Egyptian Hall to enjoy a fund-raising dinner of trout, pheasant and peaches.

In the autumn of 1965 she threw Mill Hall open for a large party which was attended by former pupils and members of the Spurs Club. She had continuously been a strong supporter of the oral deaf club and had the happy pleasure of joining the gathering for the occasion.

Mill Hall/Spurs Club Party in the Garden room with Mary Corbishley (second from right) sitting on the floor ©*Malcolm Reid*

For Mary Corbishley's faith in her God, 1965 was another momentous year which represented for her the end of her "40 years of wandering". As she had effectively converted herself from the Anglican High Church to the Baptist Church, she would quote Deuteronomy, Chapter 8 from the Bible to mark that year; this Chapter reminds the reader or Bible-user of God's commandments which should not be forgotten as were observed by the Israelites during their 40 years of wandering in the wilderness after their exodus from the "house of bondage" in Egypt before finding the Promised Land. These 40 years of wandering "in the wilderness" could relate to the period starting with 1925 when she left home in Pershore to seek better fortunes in another world and had to endure trials, fears, doubts and self-questioning while venturing forth into the unknown and untried world for the next 40 years. The moment she entered Mill Hall for the first time, though in 1948, she must perhaps have told herself: "This is it – my *Promised Land."*

In March 1967 to celebrate the 30th Anniversary of her Thanksgiving Day, Mary Corbishley presented the children with a large square cake surmounted with a model of a new A-frame styled Baptist Chapel, recalled by a former pupil, Ian Depledge. Plans were being made to construct the Chapel in the orchard as announced by Mary Corbishley at the presentation as well as in the village magazine, The Cuckfield Society's *This is Cuckfield* (1967). Such plans never took off and the existing Chapel had an extension built onto it instead. The annual visit to Rottingdean for the Thanksgiving Day did not take place.

On August 17th - 20th 1970 Mary Corbishley, with one of her former Cuckfield House School teachers, Miss Hancock from South Africa, attended the International Congress on Education of the Deaf in Stockholm organised by the Swedish Association of Teachers of the Deaf and the Swedish Union of Teachers. The author met them by chance outside Drottninghölm Palace with its 18th Century private theatre before a performance one afternoon. The small theatre which was built for private Royal Court performances is the oldest theatre in the world with its original stage and machinery for shifting scenery in the slots in the boards from the wings. Mary Corbishley particularly enjoyed the performance of music and opera while the author was especially interested in the historical aspects of the workings of the stage machinery and lighting.

In September 1970 she attended her other elder sister Bessie's Golden Wedding celebrations in Hereford. Her niece from Exeter wrote to the author: "I was simply delighted, she came by taxi; mainly mixed with my mother-in-law and sat at the table with my husband and me and our two children."

For the last five years of her career at Mill Hall up to her official retirement in 1975, Mary Corbishley was to enjoy some of the most unforgettable events of her life which reflected her achievements.

In 1971 she was invited to a Garden Party at Buckingham Palace in London on Wednesday, July 21st. She sent out a letter to all pupils, parents and friends who had supported her throughout her career, dedicating the honour to "all her pupils who have attended Mill Hall School, also the Staff who have helped them." In the letter she suggested the reading of three significant

Chapters and Verses of the Bible in which she had found solace, guidance and spiritual strength which enabled her to face up to life's challenges in the three years of her life: 1920 when she was seriously ill with rheumatic fever in Pershore, 1937 when she for the last time walked out of the front door of Dene Hollow Oral School in Burgess Hill on 10th March which she called her Thanksgiving Day, and 1965 when she celebrated the end of her 40 years' spiritual wanderings since leaving home in 1925.

MILL HALL,
SCHOOL FOR THE DEAF,
CUCKFIELD,
NEAR HAYWARDS HEATH,
SUSSEX.

HAYWARDS HEATH 4000

I have been invited to the Garden Party

at

BUCKINGHAM PALACE

Wednesday, July 21st

This will honour all the pupils who have attended

MILL HILL SCHOOL

also the Staff who have helped them

In acccepting this honour on your behalf may I never forget that Mill Hall School was and is founded on Faith and the results of our work are

'the Fruits of the Spirit'

BIBLE READING

1920   I Peter Ch. I v. 3-7
1937   St. Matthew Ch. 10 v. 16-20
1965   Deuteronomy Ch. 8

Letter sent out by Mary Corbishley
©*Ian M. Stewart's collection*

She recalled the happy occasion in *Corby* (recorded *verbatim* and edited): "The great day arrived. It happened to be the time when a bomb had been thrown in Scotland on a royal occasion, so there was little of the usual fraternising with the Royal Family. The gardens are spacious and a perfect setting for the uniform and grand costumes of eastern rulers. One only needs a companion fully to enjoy all the sights. At that time, some of the young girls wore long thin dresses with hem frills and through these one glimpsed long, leather boots. Fashionable, no doubt but it struck me that they had been called rather late that morning and only had time to jump into boots, so the diaphanous nightie remained! … The Deaf left me in no doubt that acceptance was on their behalf, and as such, the party was much enjoyed." (*pp. 60-61*)

Later in November of the same year a letter arrived from the Prime Minister's Office in Downing Street, informing her "in strict confidence" that her name would be submitted to the Queen with a recommendation that she, Mary Corbishley, be appointed a Member of the Order of the British Empire (MBE) on the occasion of the forthcoming New Year's Honours. She expressed her delight in *Corby*: "I received notification that Her Majesty *might* be pleased to confer an honour on me for education of the Deaf. I was asked to indicate my willingness to accept or otherwise on the enclosed form. I returned the form stating my acceptance and remained in suspense until the 1st January 1972 when the New Year's Honours list would be published. My second-hand family of two of my children, who by this time were in their teens, were from abroad and on holiday with me. We were much too close to keep things from each other for long; one of them sensed my anticipation and cover-up and, when asked to put a note for the milkman, wrote "Five pints, please". He remarked: "Now I know something's up tomorrow!" Refusing to reveal the situation, I decided to retire early for the night. Once again, in front of the mirror, I had a good laugh wondering who the joke would be on if no name appeared in the paper on the morrow. 1st January 1972. MBE. Our celebrations went on until 3 a.m. on the 2nd January with friends blowing in, much joy and, of course, Bible reading." (*p.61*)

In 1972 three big occasions occurred with her receiving the MBE medal in February, her being Guest of Honour at the Annual Speech Day at Mary Hare Grammar School in Newbury in September and her School being incorporated as a Company Limited by Guarantee in November.

On 15th February she attended an Investiture at Buckingham Palace and was awarded her MBE. She travelled to London, accompanied by her two teenage children, Ebrahim Saleh and Funda Gürel, from her second-hand family, Mr Baldry, the father of her first pupil and a "friend who believed with me in prayers in the 1920s." She well remembered the occasion (recorded *verbatim* and edited from *Corby*):

"The day of educational honour was fixed for 15th February. The two teenagers and I arrived at the Palace at 10 a.m. as instructed. They went one way and I followed those to be honoured into a vast gallery hung with rare pictures and furnished with antiques. At 11 a.m. names were called; a mix indeed; the distinguished, sportsmen, medical personnel, boxers and the brave. I enjoyed

Mary Corbishley's MBE medal February 15th, 1972
©Ebrahim Saleh

Mary Corbishley with her MBE medal. Funda Gürel on left in her
Mill Hall outfit and Ebrahim Saleh on right in his MHGS uniform.
©Photograph on loan by Jill Conquest

Miss Mary S. Corbishley, M.B.E.

IN LOVE TO:

Mother,

Cook, my Headmaster for four terms

The late Frank Barnes, and the late Lady Irene Ewing
Two Heads of London schools for the Deaf

The parents of pupils and others prior to recognition
by the then Ministry of Education in May 1946

My dear Bob and Jean and others who encouraged the
first recordings in 1977

Pastor and Mrs. Pastor for MEAT supplied
through the Bible

These encouraged the early vision
or sustained it and were without 'partiality'.
'They never got me wrong'

"*Corby*", her autobiography, pub. 1980
©*Lawrence Littleton Evans, designer of "Corby", with kind permission.*
Ian Stewart's collection

every minute of it. As one slowly advanced, soft music from the band, the colour and beauty of the surroundings, the Throne Room and not least the hidden efficiency. The Queen Mother in her ever-charming way remembered our meeting at the Mansion House in 1964, asked after the School and its important work for the deaf children … I relaxed and thought to myself: "Certainly, she had done her homework!" We three were driven back to the hotel and enjoyed a happy and delicious lunch, very much aware of that 'funny little school in Sussex' in 1937 and not least the previous years, beginning in Worthing."*(p.63)*

On Friday 22nd September, she was the guest speaker at the Annual Speech Day at MHGS in Newbury and was introduced by the Headmaster, Mr R. Askew, as "perhaps the best teacher of the deaf who ever lived." In his last Annual Speech before his retirement, he raised a contentious point to the audience of pupils, teachers, parents and officials: "Why is it that some of the biggest best-equipped schools have not produced a single candidate for our entrance examinations for ten years, and some schools none at all in 26 years?" He reiterated the theme of his previous year's report in which he criticised insidious and ominous trends away from oral methods of teaching the deaf.

He pointed out that: "Only 13 out of 45 schools for the deaf now claim to be oral, and no one in authority appeared able or willing to halt this drift back into the 18th Century." He answered the critics of oral education: "Any attempt to forecast the future, especially in educational matters, is a risky thing to do as never within living memory has there been produced such a spate of nonsense and crazy ideas as there is at the present times." (*Newbury Weekly News, September 28th, 1972*) Mary Corbishley whilst listening to this speech must have found perfect accord with his sentiments and well understood his frustrations just as she herself had experienced in her early days of Cuckfield House and Mill Hall as amply described in *Corby (verbatim)*:

"In 1949 [Ed: corrected 1946] the deaf had their first grammar school. The opportunity to study and sit outside examinations, the same as hearing boys and girls. This would lead ultimately to fewer dead-end jobs, and less frustration and bitterness, due to unfulfilled potential ability. Mill Hall pupils had taken outside examinations and about this time some were preparing for 'O' and 'A' levels in English and a few other subjects. From the grammar school's commencement I was in favour and adapted our aims towards this goal. Mill Hall's success was publicly stated by the Headmaster of the grammar school at the Speech Day. It was to be the Head's last Speech Day after over twenty years which had seen a revolution in higher education for the deaf. His report covered a number of successes. He also spoke about large, well-equipped schools up and down the country and then remarked: "But there is one quite small school that sends us the highest percentage of totally deaf pupils. It's Mill Hall in Sussex."

"I had been asked to present the prizes and certificates to the successful pupils ... I congratulated them and then wished to say a word to the failed or, shall we say, less successful. I had no 'O' or 'A's so my advice to them was "keep a vision of what their future could be". I had had a vision of higher education for the deaf with numberless people; that was not exactly unsuccessful, as seen by today's results.

"Then in a rather quiet voice and in a secret way, I said: 'Now, I'll tell you my attitude towards your Head. He's been one of my pin-up boys for years and I hope he and his wife, having cast their bread upon the waters, will find it coming back to them as buttered toast in retirement." (*pp. 52-53*)

True to her character, she displayed her not too mischievous sense of humour, such humour few people would credit her with throughout her life. She proceeded to present the prizes and certificates. After the ceremony, Mr Askew wrote to her, expressing his thanks on 24th September:

"Dear Corby,

The tumult has died somewhat and at last I have time to record my thanks and appreciation for all you did for us on Friday. It was the easiest and happiest speech day we ever had and everyone agrees that your words to the pupils really did get across to them. Not all of them took your remark about me as a joke; some certainly think you have a large photograph in your bedroom and one or two of the boys look upon me with more awe and respect than ever before. No demand yet from the girls for large autographed copies but you never know!

I was very proud of your pupils, they were so happy and so much at ease that everyone was impressed. The only letter to reach me so far from the father of one of my prefects reveals how jealous he is of my status as your pin-up. Now we are on the last lap – with interviews for my successor on Wednesday and then all the preparations for handing over. One more Entrance exam and one set of GCE entries to be dealt with; we are already busy with the preparations. The only quotation that comes to mind this time is Tennyson – "Then slowly answered Arthur from the barge – etc."

I'm glad I'll still have some active links with you and also with Manchester University, and I hope to see you often. May I say once again how grateful I am to you.

All my best wishes,

Jack Askew"

(©Handwritten letter 24/09/1972 from Mill Hall OPA archives)

[Ed: Alfred Lord Tennyson's *The Passing of Arthur*:

"And slowly answer'd Arthur from the barge:
'The old order changeth, yielding place to new,
And God fulfils himself in many ways,
Lest one good custom should corrupt the world.
Comfort thyself: what comfort is in me?
I have lived my life …"]

Upon his retirement from the MHGS in 1972, Mr R. Askew accepted an invitation to join the Council of Management of Mill Hall School as a Director in 1973, after its incorporation as a limited company.

Towards the end of 1972, the time had come for Mary Corbishley to consider her retirement which had now become imminent as she was approaching the age when she felt the School's management and teaching a bit onerous for her to cope with. It was likely that at the same time her responsibilities as Principal might prove risky for her and so she was advised to consider converting her School by registering it as a company limited by guarantee (and not having a share capital) with the Companies House. She instructed her Solicitors to institute the formal proceedings of applying for the registration of a Company on 23rd October 1972. The Memorandum of Association was drawn up, some of which provisos were:

1. The name of the company is Mill Hall Oral School for the Deaf Limited.

3. The objects for which the School is established are:

(A) to advance education by the provision and maintenance at Mill Hall, Cuckfield in the County of Sussex …. of a School (which shall be conducted in such a manner as to be eligible for approval as a Special School within the meaning of the Education Act 1944) for the education of children of both sexes up to the age of twelve years (or such other age as the Council of Management shall in writing agree with the Secretary of State for Education and Science) who are in need of special educational treatment by reason of their being profoundly deaf or partially deaf ....

(C) To do all such other things as are necessary to be the attainment of the above objects or any of them. Provided that:-

(iv) The School shall be conducted on purely oral lines on the Hearing – Speech – Lipreading – Language method and this method shall be adopted in preference to all other methods of instructing deaf children and shall not be changed except in pursuance of a unanimous resolution of the Council of Management of the School and with the written consent of the Secretary of State for Education and Science.

Additionally, the Articles of Association were written, in which it was laid down that, *inter alia,*:

27. The Council shall:-

(d) cause the tenets of the Bible to be taught and practised in the conduct of the School. Provided nevertheless that if the parent or guardian of any child attending the School so claims by notice in writing addressed to the Council such child shall be exempted from attending the religious instruction and worship there taught and observed....

34. There shall be a Principal of the School. The first Principal shall be Mary Stephens Corbishley, who shall have only teaching and minimal administrative responsibilities. Each future Principal shall be appointed by the Council, shall in the opinion of the Council be a believer in the Bible, and shall have such responsibilities as the Council shall direct.

The first Council of Management of the Company comprised five Directors including Mary Corbishley MBE who was also appointed Secretary of the Company and Mr George B. Mansell OBE, a company director, all of whom signed the documents on 23rd October 1972. Consequently, the new Mill Hall Oral School for the Deaf Limited by Guarantee (and not having a share capital) was finally registered with the Companies House on 9th November 1972. Mr Mansell, a London businessman, was also one of the MHGS Governors from its beginnings in 1946, and brought his considerable experience and business acumen to Mill Hall, and his experience of deaf children's education and strong belief in higher education for deaf children and oral teaching for deaf children were shared with Mary Corbishley who found him an invaluable ally, friend and Governor.

The Company was also registered with the Charity Commissioners on 22nd December 1972.

On 28th December of the same year, a conveyance took place of the property, Mill Hall School from its owner, Mary Corbishley the vendor – for a token charity payment of £1.00 – to Mill Hall Oral School for the Deaf Ltd the purchaser, thereby completing the transaction of the property. (*Land Registry Property Register Ed. 1 November 2004*). The conveyance was facilitated by two mortgages, as indicated on the Mortgage Register with Mary Corbishley and the National Westminster Bank Ltd as the mortgagees. The mortgage to Mary Corbishley was redeemed in full on 17th May 1976.

In the following year of 1973 the Council was enlarged by two new Directors, one of whom was Mr R. Askew OBE, the retired Headmaster of the MHGS.

Up to 1974 Mill Hall School had been receiving fees from the East Sussex County Council, after which time under the Local Government Act, 1972 becoming operative on 1st April 1974 the urban district of Cuckfield was passed to the West Sussex County Council which took over and continued with the payment of fees to Mill Hall School.

An advertisement was placed in the *The Times Educational Supplement, 1st March 1974* and *The Journal of the Teacher of the Deaf, March 1974* for the post of Deputy Head at Mill Hall. As a result of interviews, Mrs Helga Webster was appointed Deputy Head to work with Mary Corbishley for a few months of introduction to the School's management under the retiring Principal's guidance until the latter retired at Easter 1975. In the *Journal of the Teacher of the Deaf, May 1975*

SUSSEX
MILL HALL ORAL SCHOOL FOR
THE DEAF
Cuckfield, near Haywards Heath
Applications are invited from suitably
qualified and experienced TEACHERS
for the appointment to the post of
DEPUTY HEAD at the above-named pri
mary school for the deaf. Keen oralist
essential. Salary Burnham Special Schools
3S.
Application forms and further details
from Deputy Director. Phillips Research
Unit. University of Sussex, Brighton, to
whom completed forms should be re
turned

©Times Educational Supplement, 1st March 1974,
with kind permission of Mr Tony Shaw, Principal of MHGS

Mr Askew wrote a brief appreciation of her work:

"When Miss Mary Corbishley retired at Easter it brought to an end half a century of teaching deaf children but by no means the end of her active interest in their education and welfare. Corby, as she is known to all her pupils and friends, left Dene Hollow School at Burgess Hill in 1937 to open her own school at Cuckfield. At first in the centre of the village it moved ten years later to Mill Hall on the outskirts where bigger premises within spacious gardens made possible an increase in the number of pupils, although the number was never more than forty to preserve the family atmosphere.

"Under its new name Mill Hall Oral School for the Deaf established a reputation which attracted pupils from all parts of the British Isles as well as many from overseas. Apart from a long list of academic successes former Mill Hall pupils appear to have two common characteristics, affection for Corby shown at their annual reunions and the ability to return happily and unobtrusively into normal hearing society.

"In 1972 appreciation of Corby's work for the deaf was shown in the award of the MBE. Also in 1972 Mill Hall ceased to be a small private school and gained new status as a charitable trust, the Trustees forming the nucleus of its new Board of Governors."

A brief advertisement was inserted in the *Journal of the Teacher of the Deaf, January 1975*, in which the Principal was seeking "an enthusiastic teacher":

MILL HALL ORAL SCHOOL, CUCKFIELD, SUSSEX

Due to increasing numbers and expansion — enthusiastic teacher required for juniors. Pupils are range — nursery, infants and juniors. Application forms from the Principal.

Mill Hall was evidently set for a huge programme of changes, improvements and renovations in anticipation of the enlargement of the pupil intake under the imminent Headship of Mrs Webster.

Mary Corbishley resigned as Director and Secretary from the Council of Management on 5th November 1975 and two new members were appointed in her place. One new Director was Mr M. Peacock, a local farmer, whose daughter was at Mill Hall. He was an outstanding Director who was involved in many projects for raising funds for the School and for a new classroom block which was built in the late 1970s.

After a lifetime of teaching deaf children since the 1920s, she began to settle down to a well-deserved retirement at her beloved Orchard Cottage which she called her sanctuary for her spiritual meditation. She continued to receive visits from many Cuckfield, Baptist and other friends, and former pupils, many with their families whom she always looked upon with innate joy and love. She would still offer spiritual succour, understanding and encouragement to those who were experiencing life's problems as she herself had known from her early days. She consistently quoted suitable passages from her devoted Bible for solace to her troubled friends.

Picture of Mary Corbishley believed to be taken on a cruise in early 1970s
©Photograph on loan by Ebrahim Saleh

Post - 1975

In 1975-1976 she was taken seriously ill and weakened again by another attack of rheumatic fever, this time not expecting to live. She slowly recovered with the much-appreciated help of her loyal Chapel friends, doctors and specialists. Such experience enforced her to seek spiritual explanation in the Bible with the support of the Pastor and his wife. He, the Pastor, asked her: "*As your first ministry to the deaf is ended, what are you seeking as the next one?*" This question prompted her to contemplate: "I began to seek biblically for a better reason for the faith that was in me. If one is to share one's belief, then it is a good thing to have a biblical reason and argument for the faith one has. Maybe, once again the end of one thing was the beginning of another …" (*Corby p. 56*) Having fully recovered with renewed faith, she was encouraged to start her autobiography, *Corby*, which she first dictated to a tape recorder in 1977 whereupon it was typed and printed in book form in 1980.

In January 1979 the long-serving gardener, Mr Leslie C. Taylor, retired after 30 years' service at Mill Hall, but sadly died, aged 66, a month later. Mary Corbishley, his life-long friend, attended his funeral at Cuckfield Parish Church alongside many friends and neighbours and Mrs Webster.

On 27th March 1980 she was interviewed on Radio Brighton (later changed to BBC Radio Sussex in 1983). Below is an abridged transcript of the interview with Radio Brighton (*with kind permission of BBC Radio Sussex*):

Interviewer: Mary Corbishley MBE is an amazing lady who is just about to publish her autobiography. For over fifty years she has pioneered and developed work amongst deaf children at Mill Hall in Cuckfield. For the first twenty years of her life she only had one year of formal education but let her tell her own story – I asked her first of all what was the reason she had for publishing her book.

Corby: "To endeavour to help others to overcome problems and difficulties."

Interviewer: You told me that your original thoughts were titled with 'Four Fevers'. Can you explain that?

Corby: "Yes, because my life was changed when I was four and a half by having very serious Scarlet Fever – the real old-fashioned kind – followed by five Rheumatic Fevers, Diphtheria, in fact illnesses until I was twenty and during that time I was only able to go to school for four terms. Then I was born again of the Spirit and the Lord helped me to overcome this and eventually led me into service for the deaf. I always wanted to be a surgeon … But, nevertheless, that is what I became and started teaching a child who I thought was deaf in Worthing and this built up and later in 1937 I was in a bed-sitting room with one child in Hassocks and that was the beginning of Mill Hall.

"From the bed-sitting room we moved to Cuckfield House just before the war in 1939 … I think I was going up to the Ministry [of Education] for three years from '43 to '46 and the last time I went up there were great arguments. The thing I remember best of all I think was one of the interviewers came out and said to me, "You know, you are very obstinate." And still the only thing I'm rather proud of is that I kept my cool and I looked her in the face and said "You know my friends call it tenacity!"

"And out of that interview a date was fixed for inspection, May 8th, 1946 and I can still remember the joy with which I came out of that Ministry. The inspection took place and we were passed on results in spite of me for grants for the children's parents and superannuation for teachers but it was all in spite of me because I am *still* unqualified."

Interviewer: But nevertheless this work was recognised because you got the MBE for it, didn't you?

Corby: "As a servant of the Lord, yes. False humility does not glorify the Lord at all. At one time I wondered when the school was building up and becoming successful I had to face this problem of what attitude I took and it became clear that the answer was, "Of course it is a success because it is based on the Bible.""

Interviewer: Then let us go back all those years, after all those illnesses, the fact that you were still alive again was probably very fortunate. Do you look back and see that it was God's hand at work?

Corby: "Yes, I look back and the reason the Lord did not wish me to be educated was so that I could get into the mind of a deaf child fifty five years ago and experience the awfulness of ignorance."

Interviewer: What particular things were the most difficult in teaching deaf children as compared with teaching children with normal hearing?

Corby: "I think the thing that very few people fully appreciate is that everyone realise that they have to learn speech in lipreading but fail to appreciate that they don't have language. Because they don't *hear* words they don't register them and they have to learn every word and the terminology of every subject. But it *can* be done and they are taking 'O' and 'A' levels and going to University. But fifty five years ago this was not happening."

In response to a further question, she explained that though she had no qualifications she believed that the only qualification she had was as the Lord's servant in her work with deaf children.

Interviewer: So your training came from God and through your own experience over the years?

Corby: "Yes. Diligence I think is a very important word. I often say to the young, "The Lord does not subsidise laziness.""

Interviewer: What do you hope you can achieve by this book?

Corby: "I hope it is going to encourage, strengthen and eventually inspire people who, through reading it, will turn to their Bibles and will realise that with

God nothing is impossible."

Interviewer: Thank you very much, Corby. Thank you.

(©Transcript from Mill Hall OPA archives)

During the next few years several of her former teachers, staff and governors who had worked with and supported her at Cuckfield House and Mill Hall passed away: Miss Hancock (South Africa) *circa* early 1980s; Mr Baldry 1984; Mr Mansell OBE 1987; Mr Askew OBE 1991; Miss Martin 1992. If Mary Corbishley had been informed, she would undoubtedly feel saddened by the thought that they and Mr Taylor, her gardener, figured in her life as both professionals and friends whose indefatigable work had sustained her for many years, and who had now gone.

As she later became less mobile, she had a stair lift installed in her Orchard Cottage in the 1980s. She continued receiving many friends and Baptist people, a privilege which she always enjoyed to the end. She loved her "second-hand" family of her former school children and kept a keen interest in the latest news of their activities and happenings. Despite the gradual onslaught of her immobility, she was still involved with the voluntary work of a local organisation providing victim support by telephone to people suffering from emotional setbacks. Far from being idle, she still persevered in giving spiritual and emotional support and encouragement to others.

In 1988 came another milestone with the belated celebrations of the 50th anniversary of her school for which a dinner was held at the Birch Hotel in

Mary Corbishley with Malcolm Bown
©Ian Depledge

Rose Hoardley (Waller) with Mrs Treg
©Photograph of original by Ian M. Stewart

Haywards Heath on October 8th, organised by the Old Pupils' Association. It was attended by over 100 former pupils, teachers and staff with their husbands, wives and partners, guests and friends and Mr Bown, the School Head and his wife. Mary Corbishley was the guest of honour for the happy occasion and expressed her delight and joy of seeing all those present, in her letter to the Secretary of Mill Hall OPA (typed to the best of her ability).

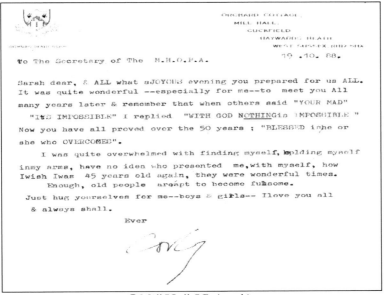

©Mill Hall OPA archives

In 1990 she sustained a broken hip but soon recovered after an operation in hospital. She was well looked after and cared for by her many Cuckfield friends.

In the early 1990s she was bedridden and her loyal local friends continued visiting her and providing her with meals daily. Former pupils dropped in to see her occasionally. In mid-1993 she first went into St Peter and St James Hospice in Wivelsfield, Sussex, but was later transferred to Compton House Christian Nursing Home in Lindfield, a few miles away on 6th December 1993 where she remained until her passing at the age of 90 at 4.15 in the afternoon of 17th November 1995. Her friend, Barry Laflin, who had known her and became her close friend for nearly 20 years was present at her final departure from the world: "…I knew Corby from 1979 until her death, I was actually holding her hand as she died …" (Letter 08/05/06 to the author)

Her funeral service took place at 1.00 pm at Cuckfield Baptist Chapel on 28th November, which was followed by her interment at the Holy Trinity

(C.o.E) Church in Cuckfield in accordance with her wish as she had said she wanted to be buried in view of her beloved South Downs of Sussex. David J. Ellis, one of the Baptist Chapel elders, gave his eulogy, some extracts of which are quoted *verbatim* therefrom:

"I'd like to welcome you all most warmly to this service this morning. You will have noticed already that it is unusual for a funeral service in that there is no coffin in the Chapel, and you must understand that what we are doing this morning is by strict instruction from Corby. So we seek to carry out her wishes in celebrating together thanksgiving and praise to our God for all his goodness. At the conclusion of this service there will be a brief service of interment at the churchyard down in Cuckfield …

"In many ways, this service ought to have been held at the graveside, but this is the month of November and there is something ironic in that November was one of Corby's most detested months and as she would have said herself, '*all God's jokes are good jokes.*' God was uppermost in her thoughts. She saw God's hand in everything, down to the minutest details of timing or provision. She had a determination second to none. That can be seen in her pioneering spirit. How often did we hear the words from her lips: 'I'm not an evangelist. I'm a pioneer.'

"And she was that in the work she did among the deaf, in the building up of Mill Hall School. She taught, she encouraged, she persevered with the slow and the difficult. She discerned potential. In ill health, which she knew quite a measure of in her youth and also in later life, she would never succumb to self-pity. She fought back …"

A Thanksgiving service for the life of Mary Corbishley was held at 2.00 pm at Cuckfield Baptist Chapel on 9th December and was well attended by former pupils, staff and friends. Her friend, Barry Laflin, gave his eulogy on her life: "Much has been said and will be said about Corby, the believer, the evangelist, the teacher of the Deaf … that character who lived in Orchard Cottage, who even when she could no longer get around, went around giving support to others in need. Some of you will remember the little yellow Escort buzzing around Cuckfield, Lindfield and Haywards Heath, carrying Corby on missions of comfort and encouragement. Even, when she could no longer drive, she carried on her work joining the 'Victim Support' organisation and being there for people on the end of the line. She called it her lifeline …

He went on to describe her strong, formidable and highly-principled character: "She was tough and gritty … she had to be. How else in the thirties could a single woman with fragile financial resources and no recognised qualification and away from immediate family have set up a school for deaf children? All God's jokes are good, she used to say and I think the one she enjoyed the most was the fact that here she was, she with but a few terms of school education she had as a child, ending up as founder and 'Principal'(I think she relished that term) of Mill Hall!

"She disliked hypocrisy and pomposity. She would not respect authority and position for its own sake; people had to earn Corby's respect. Whilst Corby did not have any truck with smut or any sort of impropriety, she was very feminine, and she made no secret of the fact that she loved the company of men, and of course us men loved her company because she had that way of talking to us, straight, direct, challenging sometimes, but with no guile, no hints, no sighs. She said what she meant and she meant what she said ... the way companionable men relate to each other. She had, as a lady, the rare capacity to be one of the lads whilst retaining her femininity and our respect, and we loved her for it! The last two years of Corby's life were difficult ones both for her and for those who knew, loved and liked her. As a Christian she had to love everyone, but if she said she liked you as well you had indeed arrived in Corby's inner sanctum of friendship." Few people would disagree with his perceptive sum-up of her character. He concluded with a description of the last months of her life, illustrating her determination to remain a true Christian helping and encouraging other people:

"She thought that her "usefulness" had run out; though it must be said that until the last few months she was still being useful and practical, and she spent some time using her skills and declining energy in teaching a fellow patient at the nursing home who had lost the power of speech through a stroke and subsequent depression how to speak again. Of course she encouraged those at the nursing home who shared her belief; I heard the phrase "partners in prayer" mentioned more than once. It had to be her dread month of November when she left us – with the words of John 3: 16 ringing in her ears: "For God so loved the World that He gave His one and only Son that whoever believes in Him shall not perish but have everlasting life." His eulogy ended: "All the way your Saviour led you."

Mary Corbishley died from bronchial pneumonia and cardiac arrest. Her last thoughts would undoubtedly be as quoted in the epitaph on many of her ancestors' gravestones at Bricklehampton and Little Comberton churches, and she quoted to the author twice or three times towards her end:

Thy Will be done.'

Pupils mourn pioneer deaf teacher

PAST and present pupils are mourning the death of a pioneering teacher of deaf children.

Mary Corbishley enabled thousands of youngsters to break the sound barrier and learn to talk.

The dedicated campaigner for the deaf founded Mill Hall School for Deaf Children in Cuckfield, near Haywards Heath, in 1937 and was principal for more than 40 years.

She died at a Lindfield nursing home, aged 90.

Miss Corbishley, known affectionately as "Corby", was a great believer in encouraging deaf children to speak, rather than use sign language.

During a royal visit four years ago, Miss Corbishley told the Princess Royal how she started the school after meeting a young girl with hearing problems.

She said: "No one wanted to know about deafness then. They said 'don't get involved' and it still happens today. I feel very humble about what we have achieved."

She forged close bonds with her pupils, remaining in contact with many of them after they left the school, and until recently lived in a cottage in the grounds of Mill Hall.

Today, the boarding school has 30 pupils, aged five to 12, from all over the country.

The school's vice-principal, Clive Rees, said: "Mary was very religious and she devoted her life to helping deaf children.

"She was a real character, a very determined lady who was much loved by everybody."

A memorial service for Miss Corbishley will be held at Cuckfield Baptist Chapel on Saturday, December 9.

News item from unientified local paper
©Mill Hall OPA archives

Mary S. Corbishley MBE
©Photograph by Ian M. Stewart 2006 (from unidentified local paper)

Mary Corbishley's grave at Holy Trinity Church, Cuckfield
©Ian M. Stewart 2006

Holy Trinity Church, Cuckfield

Cemetery and view of South Downs

©Photographs by Ian M. Stewart 2006

©Veronica Savory

CHAPTER VI
1975 – 1996

Mill Hall Oral School post-1975 – Mrs Webster – Peacocks
Classroom Block – Malcolm Bown – Royal Visit – Paul Simpson –
School's Closure – Purchase by Mary Hare Grammar School –
Relocation to Greenham Common, Newbury

The last quarter of the century saw big changes to Mill Hall Oral School, commencing with the appointment of a new Principal in 1974 and culminating, after two succeeding Heads, in the School's closure in Cuckfield in 1996 and its subsequent move to new premises in Newbury under the management of Mary Hare Grammar School for the Deaf.

Mrs Helga Webster, BSc Hons (Psych.), a young 34-year-old dark-haired vivacious woman with a warm smile, took over the reins from Mary Corbishley at Easter 1975 after the six-month induction period with the retiring Principal, and soon embarked upon an ambitious programme of renovating and modernising the School. The programme involved refurbishing throughout the building, replacing old school furniture and antiquated audio and hearing aid equipment with new alongside changes to old classrooms, bedrooms and bathrooms including improved central heating. According to the Governors' annual Statements of Accounts for 1975-78, expenditure on furniture renewals, property repairs and improvements, and hearing aid repairs and renewals amounted to approximately £65,000. Their Reports stated that: "substantial deficits for the years have been due to the improvements considered essential by the Governors, of the standards of the facilities available for the children." Undoubtedly, the Governors approved and greatly supported the renovations programme.

In her letter to the author in June 2007, Mrs Webster described the work: "I made it a condition of accepting the role of Principal, that in addition to purchasing group hearing aids and other classroom equipment there should be: roof repairs (it leaked and some rooms were mouldy); central heating should be installed in the dormitories, bathrooms and nurses' rooms; upgrading of the kitchen including purchase of a dishwater, mixer, mechanical potato peeler and bringing in additional help; general improvements including new lino flooring where necessary, new bedding … At that time a little old lady pensioner was the only cook working in the kitchen who provided three meals a day, plus Corby's Sunday roast, unaided; she used to do all the washing-up by hand; she used to get up at 5.00 am to start peeling the potatoes. The Governors were only *too* happy to accede to these requests."

External fire escape staircases were erected, doors fire-proofed and audio/visual alarm and emergency lighting systems installed as part of fire precautions work carried out in consultation with the local Fire Prevention Officer who awarded a fire certificate.

Although the loft in the north-east wing of the main building was already converted into a private flat for one of the teachers in the late 1960s and the new Principal was now residing there, it was, eventually, decided by the Board of Governors that a Principal's House be built for future Principals. The three-bedroom House, adjoining the east side of Mill Hall's grounds, was completed in 1980.

Mrs Helga Webster was born in Graz, Austria and later, when her mother got married again to a soldier from Yorkshire, was sent to Malet Lambert Grammar School in Hull of the same county. She then attended the University of Hull where she obtained her Honours degree in Psychology. She became interested in deafness when her son, Eric born in 1966, was diagnosed as profoundly deaf at the Nufield Centre in London. She continued in her letter: "Having seen what was available in the name of deaf education, I decided I had to equip myself to help him and applied to Manchester [University Teacher Training Department]. Fortunately, I was accepted almost immediately for training." She met and married William Webster while studying at Manchester University. In 1971 they both qualified as Teachers of the Deaf and were soon teaching at Woodford School for the Deaf (later renamed Sir Winston Churchill in 1975) in Woodford Green, Essex. In 1973 she moved to Blanche Nevile School in Haringey in North London as Head of Language Development.

The Websters decided to move out into the country for a quieter life, and she answered the advertisement for Deputy Principal at Mill Hall, the post of which she was immediately offered at her second interview with the Governors. She wrote: "I went home in a state of shock. Bill and Eric were shocked as it meant a major upheaval for all of us." They all moved south to Cuckfield in time for the Winter Term in 1974. Her husband, Bill Webster, went on to teach at Hamilton Lodge School for Deaf children in Brighton, Sussex and later at Nutfield Priory School in Redhill, Surrey.

However, her first days at Mill Hall were difficult as she found Mary Corbishley very determined that nothing should change at *her* School. It became apparent to her that Mary Corbishley did not encourage any input on anything as well as interaction between the staff. The retiring Principal made it clear to her that: "We are like the spokes of a wheel, and I am the hub." Mrs Webster thought it was her [Mary Corbishley's] belief that as long as the spokes did not come in contact with each other, everything would be fine. On one occasion Mary Corbishley summoned her, Mrs Webster, to her Orchard Cottage and told her that she was very disappointed with what she had done to *her* School. Mrs Webster replied that she had simply repaired the roof and put central heating in dormitories and bathrooms to keep the children warm. Mary Corbishley's response was: "*In my day, dear, Jesus kept us warm.*" She, Mrs Webster, was nonplussed.

Mrs Webster was concerned that Mary Corbishley intended to keep managing the School *her* way with no changes, so at one of the Governors' meetings she expressed her wish that Mary Corbishley be asked to allow her space and time to get to grips with her new job as Principal; she also expressed concern that having two Principals running the School would be confusing for the pupils and staff. The Governors accepted her assessment of the potential situation, and as a result Mary Corbishley withdrew and duly retired at the end of Spring Term in 1975.

Mrs Webster introduced changes to the teaching of deaf pupils in her charge. Rather than dispensing with phonics, she supplemented it by using "every ounce of residual hearing of every deaf child" with the help of individual and group hearing aids and concentrating on developing natural conversational English on an individual basis so as to enable the pupils to realise their full potential by the time they reached the age of 11 or 12, whereupon they left school for secondary education. Those with additional educational needs were allowed to stay on after the school leaving age after consultations with their parents, class teachers, local education authorities and head teachers of other schools.

Speech training with lipreading, language and vocabulary was introduced to the deaf child at an early age so that he or she was later able to develop self-expression skills with confidence (*as per School Prospectus, 1979*). This speech training was taught with the help of an overhead projector illuminating the written word along with its sound. Mrs Webster also brought in solid, tried and tested teaching methods she had earlier learnt and seen to work with success at

Woodford School. In maintaining the continuation of the same academic subjects as previously, she upheld the original aim of providing spiritual guidance with Scripture-based lessons where they were relevant; assemblies with prayers took place twice weekly.

The children at Mill Hall were either day pupils or weekly boarders; an addendum to the 1979 Prospectus dated September 1980 informed parents of potential pupils that: "… in response to the needs of some of our children we now offer full boarding in addition to weekly boarding". As a result, an increasing number of overseas pupils, particularly from Africa, entered Mill Hall and were offered opportunities to receive English aural/oral education.

Front cover of School Prospectus 1979
©Mill Hall OPA archives

The 1979 prospectus also explained the school's ethos: "Mill Hall School has a happy family atmosphere, having a devoted and caring staff of qualified teachers, including a speech specialist, plus classroom assistants … The teaching methods are based on the children's interests with emphasis on natural oral and written language … There is a carefully chosen library of suitable books for all ages and every classroom is well stocked with books and learning equipment. The West Sussex Mobile Library Service exchanges over 100 books three times a year and the older pupils are encouraged to make their own choice. The School has an excellent record of passes to Mary Hare Grammar School and also a record of high achievement in other secondary education establishments."

Mrs Webster believed that the true aims of oral education at Mill Hall were: "to forget oralism and replace it with normalism and one gets nearer to what we [the School] are trying to do. We try to turn our children into thoughtful human beings who can accept their handicap, and not to think they are poor little deaf things." (*Local paper, January 1978*) She did not permit sign language in the School in order to encourage the pupils to integrate with hearing people who normally speak and hear. "Sign language is taboo. We talk to them from the moment they arrive," she said. Where one or two pupils were unable to develop speech skills due to their inability to hear spoken English, they were permitted to miss speech lessons and concentrate *in lieu* on writing and reading and other academic lessons.

Sports were still being enjoyed; swimming lessons were taken at the Dolphin Centre in Haywards Heath, Sussex. Football, netball, rounders and country walks were continued to be enjoyed by the pupils. Leisure included dancing, shopping and annual Christmas shows.

Towards the end of 1974 members of Haywards Heath Round Table 95 (later merged with Hassocks and District 779) presented the School with a precast concrete 'Compton Strathmore' multi-purpose recreation block with insulation-lined walls and roof on a tiled in-situ concrete floor and foundations laid by the Round Table volunteers who raised £1,125 for the project. It was completed and the keys handed over in May 1975 by the Chairman with the expressed hope that "the building will give enjoyment to the deaf children while carrying out their indoor recreational activities." (*Unidentified local paper, May 1975*)

A new teacher, Mrs Avril Hardman, joined Mill Hall School in January 1975, having previously taught in a Secondary school, a Girls' Grammar School and two Primary schools mostly in the South for seventeen years. She came from Immingham, near Grimsby in North Lincolnshire and was educated at the Grammar School for Girls in Cleethorpes. Later she became a qualified teacher, having obtained her Certificate of Education at Homerton College in Cambridge.

It was in late 1974 when she decided upon a change of direction, seeking a new challenge. After having been shown an advertisement by a teaching colleague, she decided to take the plunge and applied for the post at Mill Hall. She was interviewed by Mary Corbishley, the retiring Principal, who commented on her clear speech and lip-patterns she considered essential for lipreading by her deaf children. Mary Corbishley was adept at lipreading. Avril Hardman was accepted and started her job in January 1975.

She qualified as a Teacher of the Deaf after in-service training for the BATOD Diploma Course and attending courses at Manchester University and at Walsall, taking her final examinations in Birmingham in 1979. However, following her husband's job move to Scotland, she taught at a Unit for Deaf Children at a Primary School in Dunfermline in Fife. She enjoyed a real pleasure of being involved in a different kind of teaching environment, finding the experience of great value. Upon the Hardmans' returning to the south in 1983, she, at the invitation from Mrs Helga Webster, re-joined Mill Hall and found herself teaching all subjects of the National Curriculum as well as Music which was an integral part of the time-table. It, the Music, became an important part of Morning Assemblies taking place once or twice weekly when the children sang the *Good Morning* song, the *Birthday* song and *"It's time to say Goodbye"* from the Nordoff-Robbins Song Book as well as modern hymns. [Ed: The Nordoff-Robbins Song Book is specially produced for music therapy for children and adults in need of expressing themselves through music to overcome their sense of isolation and vulnerability.]

Although she retired in 1994, she continued teaching Music part-time for one day a week at the request of Paul Simpson, the School's last Head, until 1996 when the School closed down.

Avril Hardman recalled many fond memories of her time at Mill Hall. She remembered one particular habit of the younger pupils which was to ask, "What for?" and "How old?" whenever visitors dropped in the classroom, fortunately causing much amusement rather than consternation! She told the author of how much she had enjoyed her time at the School, however challenging it had been, and she is particularly gratified that so many old pupils are still in touch after all this time.

It was soon after Mrs Webster's taking up her Principality that action began with a series of fund-raising events for a new classroom block to take in the increasing number of pupils. One of the Governors, Mr Michael Peacock, took on the daunting task, as Appeal Secretary, of launching an appeal to raise funds in 1975 and for the following three years he burned much midnight oil by writing to numerous businesses, charities, charitable trusts, clubs and other bodies and societies in addition to asking Magnus Magnusson, the presenter of BBC's Mastermind, to speak on BBC Radio 4 which he kindly did on Sunday 1st January 1978 at 8.45 in the morning. One of the first donations came from Sussex Barkers of Hove Variety Club who raised £2,500 in 1976.

Mr Peacock's daughter, Rachel, a former pupil at Mill Hall, recalled: "I remember the countless letters that arrived from all over the country with cheques and cash." Summer fêtes were organised with well-known personalities as guests of honour, one of whom in 1976 was Tony Hart of BBC television fame who drew cartoons of animals for 10p each for the fund. A Jubilee stone was built in the East wall during the construction period to celebrate the Queen's Silver Jubilee in 1977.

The Teaching Block Appeal Fund grew to a grand total of £70,000 by 1978 which was then used for the new classrooms. On 25th January 1978 the chairman of the National Westminster Bank, Mr R. Leigh-Pemberton, laid the foundation stone in the presence of many guests, among whom was Mary Corbishley.

Laying of the Foundation Stone by R. Leigh-Pemberton of
the National Westminster Bank January 1978
L to R. Mrs Connie Mager, Rachel Peacock, Mrs Helga Webster, Anne Mansell,
Jane Nabarro, Angela Kensitt, Eric Nielson, Robin Leigh-Pemberton
©*Image Courtesy of the Brighton and Hove Argus Archives; photograph on loan by Mrs Webster*

At the ceremony Mrs Webster thanked those present and reminded them: "I would particularly like to thank Miss Corbishley to whom we owe our existence, and the bank to whom we owe our survival." (*Unidentified local paper, January 1978*) The Bank had already arranged loans for the purchase of Mill HallOral School by the limited company, Mill Hall Oral School for the Deaf Ltd, and for the construction of the new classroom block. The block comprised five classrooms, cloakrooms, changing rooms, and dormitories; the plan was to adapt the old Mill Hall for additional sleeping accommodation in meeting the needs of an expanded pupil intake. The long handsome classroom block, completed at a total cost of £72,000, was constructed with brick walls, tiled roofs and a neat row of windows overlooking the school grounds.

On 12th September 1978 it was opened by a BBC personality, Richard Baker, OBE and named Peacocks in recognition of Mr Michael Peacock's unstinting and tireless efforts as Appeal Secretary who had raised the funds within the span of 2½ years, a personal triumph for his outstanding work. The audience witnessing the ceremony was composed of pupils, parents, governors, representatives of the LEAs, friends and those who gave donations to the fund; Mary Corbishley was likely to have been present as she would have been honoured to see another of her visions being realised. Mr Baker toured the new classrooms which were fitted out with "acoustic panelling, sound-deadening carpets, specially-made blackboards, group hearing aid equipment and an overhead projector to each classroom". (*printed article from unidentified source, September/October 1978*)

Peacocks Block. The Foundation Stone can be seen in the end wall.
©Photograph on loan by Jill Conquest

Foundation Stone (weather-beaten)   The Queen's Silver Jubilee Stone
©Ian M. Stewart, 2006 with owner's kind permission

George Mansell, Mrs Helga Webster, Richard Baker,
Rachel Peacock, Michael Peacock *©Mrs Helga Webster*

Early in 1978 there were 50 pupils of ages ranging mainly from 2½ to 11 or 12 with a few older ones, and a staff of 12 teachers, half of whom were qualified with two in training, in small classes designed to encourage homogenous groups of 5 or 6 children learning together. By the end of the year the total number increased to 70 as reported in *The Sunday People, November 26th*, a Sunday-only tabloid newspaper. Readers of '*Man of the People's Annual Appeal Fund*' donated £5,410 to Mill Hall. Also, the Burgess Hill Lions Club donated £1,000 for new gymnasium equipment.

In July of that year it was reported in *The Courier of Tunbridge Wells, Kent* that a local hearing school, Claremont School, as part of its annual policy of raising funds for charity, donated £1,000 to Mill Hall. The money was raised in a "sponsored swim by 3rd and 4th Year pupils with a combined distance of 33 miles." Mrs Webster received the cheque from Cyril Fletcher, a well-known comedian, at a presentation ceremony and thanked the children and told them their efforts would pay for a listening room and special equipment at the School. (*The Courier, 28th July 1978*) She also received many donations from various organisations including the East Sussex National Deaf Children's Society, which were used for continually improving facilities for the children.

Mrs Helga Webster receiving a new film projector
Mrs Webster with visitors in the classroom
©*Mary Hare Primary School archives, with kind permission*

Retrospectively, in May 1978, by order of the Secretary of State for Education and Science, Margaret Thatcher (before she became Prime Minister), there was issued a Report of the Committee of Enquiry into the Education of Handicapped Children and Young People under the chairmanship of Mrs (later Baroness) H. M. Warnock to review provisions for the education of deaf and other physically and mentally [then called] handicapped children with the aim of providing specialist provision and services in mainstream schools. The Report ran into 19 chapters and 1275 clauses outlining the history of Education Acts, investigating various forms of special education and suggesting proposals for inclusive integration of deaf and disabled children with learning difficulties.

The famous Warnock Report laid down recommendations which led to wide repercussions and implications for deaf children's education by mainstreaming them into special classes and separate units (Partially Hearing Units – PHUs) attached to LEA-maintained county schools, and which were embodied in the Education Act 1981. This Act required LEAs to fulfil their duty to secure special education for children with learning difficulties in accordance with their statements of assessment.

One notable recommendation in *Clause 3.25* was to abolish statutory categorisation of handicapped pupils and to re-name them as children with special educational needs (SEN), a new term used to avoid stigmatising deaf and other children with learning difficulties or disabilities. Attention was directed in the Report to the Education Act 1976 where under Section 10 the LEAs were to make arrangements to provide for "special educational treatment of all such pupils in county and voluntary schools, except where this was impracticable or incompatible with the efficient instruction in the schools or would involve unreasonable public expenditure, in which case special educational treatment *might* be provided in special schools …" (*Clauses 10(2) and (2A)*)

Later in the Report it was confirmed that this Section was on the Statute Book, thus having the effect of, subject to certain qualifications, placing deaf and handicapped pupils in England and Wales in ordinary schools for their integrated education, in preference to special schools. (*Clause 7.4*) The Report, nevertheless, pointed out that the three qualifying conditions set out in Section 10 (practicability, efficiency and cost) "are open to many interpretations". (*Clause 7.49*)

It would appear that the Education Acts 1976 and 1981 were likely to have a profound impact on Mill Hall Oral School nearly 20 years later as these Acts laid the first stepping stone towards closing down special schools for deaf children nationwide. Although Mary Corbishley had no time for politics of the game – apart from her arguments and disagreements with educational officials early in her career – one would wonder how she would react to the notion of her deaf pupils being given a new label *children with special educational needs* as she had always believed that deaf children had every right to a normal education which would equip them for the hearing world outside with independence and confidence. This official labelling might be compared with the earlier labelling of deaf children as "mentally defective or deficient", a term used in the 1930-40s against which Mary Corbishley fought for so many years.

For the next twenty years there were many changes of philosophy, ethos and policy shifting from segregationist education to all-inclusive education which were becoming more prevalent due to endlessly-changing Government policies and never-ending Acts based on numerous reports, inquiries, investigations, ideologies and initiatives reflecting equal and civil rights, equal opportunities, diversity and all-inclusive education in which politicians, activists and educationalists of all political persuasions were engrossed. Against this politically confusing background, Mill Hall continued in its steadfastness in providing natural aural/oral teaching for deaf children.

The School prospectus issued in 1979 stated the sources of finances for the administration of the School: "The School has no private source of funds, neither does it receive any grants. It is financed mainly from fees which are paid by the LEAs for the areas where the children come from, mostly West and East Sussex, but also Surrey, Hampshire, Kent and some of the London Boroughs as well as overseas. The fees cover the basic costs of running the School but charitable donations have played a vital part in making possible the many improvements carried out in the past ..."

In this context, it was after the Education Acts 1976 and 1981 became enforceable when special classes and Units for partially hearing children were set up in mainstream schools. Mrs Webster wrote [to the author]: "... there was much pressure to educate deaf children in Units in local schools. My own belief was that it was an ideal set-up for students who were making full use of their residual hearing, who had a grounding in the 3Rs who had good oral and communication skills, and who were well adjusted emotionally. Such pupils we were happy to see go into the outside world with success. However, we had many applicants, who without such a foundation, had failed miserably in the Unit system. The parents then had a battle Royal with their local education authorities to move their child to a more suitable educational setting. In most cases, the Governors agreed that we could accept such pupils, *sans fees*, whilst the battle raged. I was, of course, involved in these battles.

"On the other hand, we had many applications from Inner London Education Authority (ILEA). We had a reputation for dealing very successfully with "problem" children, and they would have gladly sent us more. However, I had no intention of turning Mill Hall into a school for the *maladjusted* deaf, so I kept them to less than 10%. In this way, the normal behaviour served as good role models and peer pressure to conform."

There was an incident at Mill Hall during the early years of 1980 when a video recorder was stolen as reported in the local paper: "Thieves have stolen a £450 video recorder used for teaching deaf children at a Sussex special school. The Sony Betamix machine was taken while pupils at Mill Hall School in Cuckfield were on holiday. Mrs Helga Webster, the Principal, said: "It was tremendous to find our only video recorder had disappeared. We used it to record TV programmes, including the subtitled BBC 2 news, and play them back for the children. It is an important part of their education." She appealed to the thieves to return the recorder. "We are lost without it," she added.

As reported in *The Evening Argus, 28th September 1983*, the Governors submitted to the Mid-Sussex District Council's Plans Sub-Committee for consideration a new project of easing the overcrowded boarding accommodation at Mill Hall by building three self-contained terraced units for 26 boarders in the school grounds. Mrs Webster explained the problem: "There is tremendous pressure on us from parents and education authorities to provide more boarding places. At the moment there isn't enough accommodation and a place does not become available until a pupil leaves. Because of this the teaching facilities are not being fully utilised." The result was deaf children being turned away because of lack of live-in facilities and there was a waiting period of up to ten months for potential boarding pupils.

In the Annual Report tabled by the Governors on 10th November 1983, it was stated that on 16th June 1983 the Department of Education and Science notified formal approval of the School under Section 11 (3a) of the Education Act (Children with SEN) 1981. This Act laid down further specific provisions for children with SEN. In the same report it was noted that the deficit for the year ending 31st August 1983 was due to "an unexpected reduction of pupils during the year, but since the accounting year the number of pupils increased for the Winter term." In common with other special schools, numbers of pupil intakes fluctuated from year to year, depending on their respective LEAs' education policy decisions.

After having served as Principal for ten years, Mrs Webster gave the Governors notice of her leaving school as she was moving out to Canada to live upon marriage to a Canadian in 1984 and, also, she felt the time had come for new blood and fresh ideas for the future of Mill Hall. She wrote (to the author): "Some of my happiest memories of Mill Hall are of the early days as Principal. There was a tremendous team spirit and camaraderie … a feeling that teachers, residential staff and parents were all working together, with ever present support from the Board of Governors." She went on to recall one incident. After the renovations had ended at the weekend before the Summer Term was due to begin, the teachers went in and rolled up their sleeves to shovel, sweep, scrub and dust over the weekend and, by Monday morning, the school was ready to receive the pupils.

Her place was then taken over by a young slim red-haired man of 32 with a caring nature, Malcolm Bown who was already teaching at Mary Hare Grammar School for the preceding four years. Malcolm Bown BA was born and grew up in Belfast, Northern Ireland; his mother, sister and future wife were all Teachers of the Deaf, and his father was also a teacher but not of the deaf. As a young man very keen on sports, he swam for Ireland from 1965 to 1968; he and his grammar school swimming club got involved in voluntary work with deaf children from the Jordanstown School in Belfast, which was when he first became interested in a teaching career with deaf children. Later, having graduated from Cambridge with a BA degree in Economics, he trained as a qualified specialist teacher of the deaf at Manchester University. (*Mill Hall Friends Newsletter No. 1,* 1989)

After four years at Mary Hare Grammar School he decided to move on from the Grammar School as he recalled in his e-mail letter to the author in May 2007 (*verbatim*): "I went to Mary Hare in September 1980, which after my first two teaching posts, seemed a little bit like landing in heaven! My job at MHGS was great for me, teaching Maths, Games and 'A' Level Economics and later taking over Careers; it was very varied and a brilliant environment to work in. I also got on well with the Head, Ken Pearce, whom I found to be a very stimulating person. I was quite happy at Mary Hare but also not worried about the prospect of going elsewhere; I did feel that I needed to leave MHGS and get

©Times Educational Supplement, 25th November 1983,
with kind permission of Mr Tony Shaw, Principal of MHGS (BHC)

more experience. David Braybrook [Head of Ovingdean Hall School, Brighton] suggested I apply for the Headship at Mill Hall which had already been advertised. (I hadn't really thought about it as it seemed too big a jump for me professionally). I did not feel comfortable about a late application but Ellen [Ed: Malcolm Bown's wife] took the bull by the horns and phoned Mrs Webster. As a result I got shortlisted very late in the day and got the job. That all happened very quickly and I went to Mill Hall in April 1984 …"

His leadership was to make a lasting impression on the school staff with his deep sense of dedication to his chosen career of teaching deaf children. A long-serving teacher, Mrs Mager, wrote on one occasion in May 1987: "I am fortunate in that I have been able to watch the school blossoming under Malcolm's guidance and in hearing the comments of visitors who all remark on the happy atmosphere and invariably want their children to be part of it. This has not come about by 'window-dressing'. Malcolm has a very profound understanding of children's needs and is constantly seeking ways to fulfil these needs educationally, emotionally, socially and aesthetically. I trust his judgement mainly because he believes in full consultation with everyone involved with the children and is prepared to admit when he is wrong. This may sound paradoxical, but what I am stressing is that his chief and only consideration is the complete all-round development of the children in his charge. The amount of work, both in and out of school hours, that he puts in to achieve this is phenomenal."

In his e-mail of 28th May 2007 to the author, he recalled that when he arrived at Mill Hall in 1984, there were 42 pupils, of whom approximately 10 mainly from overseas were privately placed. He did not realise that 13 of those pupils were already leaving in the summer of that year and with one new prospective pupil due in September the school had 30 pupils *"which was the limits of viability for a primary special school"*, said he, *"I realised quite quickly that the LEAs were not favourably disposed to the school, especially those in close proximity."* Before his arrival, it was found that privately placed pupils had the effect of overcoming the problem of diminishing placements from West Sussex, East Sussex and Kent LEAs. However, he was faced with the additional difficulties of private fee payments, inadequate early education and having to accommodate them full-board at the School rather than accepting weekly boarders whom he favoured.

For the first five years of his Principality, Malcolm Bown brought to Mill Hall many innovations. He introduced a new idea of different themes such as garage, jungle, circus and other fantasy ideas for the children's bedrooms "to reduce the young children's sense of loneliness traditionally associated with bedtime." (*School Prospectus, 1989*) Beds and furniture took upon the resemblance of cars, double-decker buses, petrol pumps, paddle steamers with portholes and, even, gypsy caravans; bed clothes were patterned with colourful climbing plants and jungle animals. Bathrooms took on the atmosphere of an underwater scene, a luminous Caribbean sea and a night-time scene.

Mill Hall School, 1984

L to R:

Front row: Troy Carter, Nicola de St Croix, Zarina Thobani, Chizoba Olejeme, Katie Hooker, Naomi Sheepwash, Andrew Hearn, Matthew Hearn, Alim Chandai, Philip Strutt

First row: (teachers) Mrs Connie Mager, Catherine Jones, Mrs Maureen Wood, Mr Groves, Mrs Avril Hardman, Malcolm Bown (Head), Clive Rees, Mrs Mary Bevans, Mrs Rebecca Clifford, Helen Simmonds

Second row: Chiamaka Olejeme, Martin Haynes, John Coppock, Emma House, Alison Leach, Emma Hancock, Carmen Carter, Kathryn Maynard, Matthew Hewitt, Mark Spearey, Katy Beeson

Third row: Neal Caws, Garry Simms, Thomas Page-Phillips, Paul Baker, Ross Dawes, Daffyd Jones, Leo Mansell, Phillip Barker(?), Rotimi Fashola, Richard Walker

Back row: Joanna Healey, Claire Gibson, Carrie-Ann Kuxhaus, Susan Pitt, Clare Mitchell, Joanna Tringham, Joanne Sargant

©Mill Hall Photograph on loan by Avril Hardman

1. Garage bedroom

2. Jungle bedroom
©Photographs 1 and 2 from 1989 School Prospectus by Ian M. Stewart

Original mural painting in Garage bedroom retained by present owners for its part in the school's history
©Ian M. Stewart, with owner's kind permission

As he was committed to the auditory oral education of deaf children, he was concerned to find that the audiology system was not up to standard and he checked all the group hearing aids with a hearing aid manufacturer and found almost all were non-functional, mainly due to low batteries in the teacher's microphone. He pointed out that: "This type of fault was very common then in all schools and units as routine testing of hearing aid equipment was not commonplace." It was apparent that the deaf children receiving auditory oral tuition at such a young age from 5 to 11 were not likely to be aware of this serious deficiency and probably never told their teachers! He introduced a new type of hearing aid, Phonic Ears, which was then thought to be the best available for the youngest pupils. For this he embarked on raising enough funds for equipping half of the pupils. Furthermore, in collaboration with manufacturers and suppliers, Malcolm Bown worked out a system of dramatically improving the monitoring of all personal and group hearing aids.

Nevertheless, he expressed his delight that his preceding Head, Mrs Webster, had appointed three young teachers of the deaf who were in tune and very much up to date with the auditory oral ideas and methods, which ensured the continuity of the School's good reputation and position. They were Cathy Jones, Helen Simmonds and Becky Clifford. He wished to record that he received invaluable support and advice from Mrs Mager, and that long-standing staff, such as Mrs Avril Hardman, Mrs Mary Bevans, were very supportive of his Principality.

At weekends foster families in Cuckfield looked after some of the overseas boarding pupils while weekly boarders went home. In 1986 a prefect system was initiated "where the older children would look after the younger ones and have responsibility at lunch time … We were told where to sit and everything differed from previously as we had new smaller tables." as Alison Leach, a former pupil, recalled.

In the summer of 1987 a special fund was set up to provide temporary funds for pupils whose applications for places at the School were being considered but not yet agreed to by the LEAs. The fund was registered with the Charity Commissioners as Mill Hall Scholarship Fund on 24th June 1987, the objects of which were to provide "support and assistance with the education of children at Mill Hall Oral School for the Deaf Ltd or eligible to attend the School".

The month of October 1987 was memorable for an unexpected 110-mph great storm which swept through the south-east of England, wreaking complete chaos, damage and flooding coupled with the felling and uprooting of thousands of trees. Mill Hall did not escape unscathed and sustained roof damage, incurring considerable costs, most of which were not accepted by the insurers, thereby having to be defrayed out of the school funds.

In December 1988, determined to rise up to the daunting challenge of meeting the never-ending need to keep the school funds healthy for not only the continuing work of redecorations, repairs and renovations of the school's fabric and its interiors, but also for renewals and repairs of hearing aid equipment, Malcolm Bown sent out to ex-pupils, parents and friends a letter of appeal for

"£250,000 required over the next four years which is a massive task, but we must have the best possible aids, attractive classrooms and sufficient teachers … This [significant contributions made by past pupils and friends to the School] indicates a tangible faith in what the school stands for and gratitude for Corby's past service." (*Letter of Appeal, 2nd December 1988*).

In the following year £85,000 was raised for the Appeal Fund as reported in the Board of Governors' Statement of Accounts for the year ending 31 August 1989.

Malcolm Bown continued with the underlying philosophy of aural/oral education and character build-up developed by the founder Principal, Mary Corbishley. The School's prospectus issued in 1989 affirmed (extracts *verbatim*): "Mill Hall is a junior special school which provides a natural aural education for between 45 and 50 children. The general approach emphasises the best possible use of each child's remaining hearing and the importance of normal conversational integration in developing natural spoken language.

"Mill Hall is committed to a wholly oral philosophy and all staff are involved in creating an environment where spoken language is real and relevant, both socially and educationally. The development of fluent spoken communication is seen as the key to academic advancement – in reading, writing and other curricular areas – and to eventual integration into hearing society.

"The philosophy in all areas of the school is based on creating active learning situations. Particular emphasis is placed on developing the conversation and language which arise naturally in such situations because they offer the pupils meaningful experience. Speech and articulation are not normally taught as formal lessons, but good spoken language is encouraged and developed as an integral part of all school activities …" One may be struck by the similarity of the original aims and visions set out in the 1939 prospectus for Cuckfield House Oral School and those in the 1989 prospectus for Mill Hall. Evidently, sign language was not used or encouraged in the School.

The 1989 prospectus stated that the majority of pupils at the School entered at the age of 7 or 8, having had earlier experience of mainstream schools or PHUs, in addition to other pupils transferred from special schools elsewhere. This new development was the result of the Education Acts 1976, 1981 (SEN) and 1988 (the National Curriculum) when there was a philosophical view that SEN pupils should be educated alongside their mainstream peers. The LEAs in need of making economies in the education budgets started closing down special schools for deaf children who were then dispersed to local mainstream

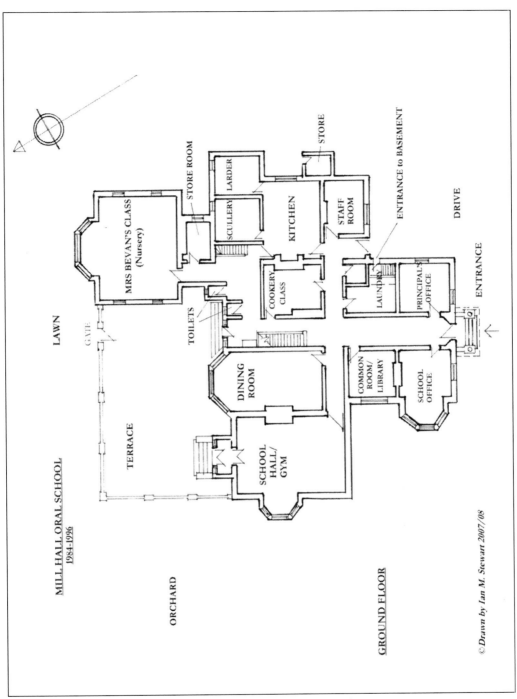

Mill Hall School - Ground Floor Plan
©Ian M. Stewart

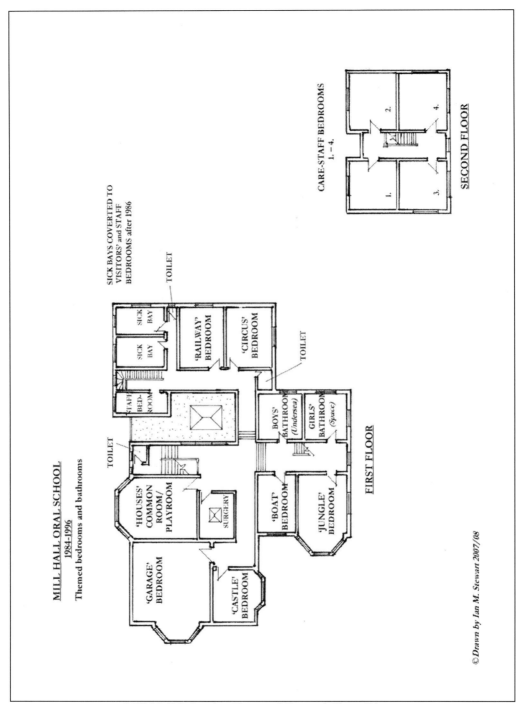

Mill Hall School – First and Second Floor Plans
©Ian M. Stewart

schools or PHUs in their local areas, in some cases of which, unfortunately, as a result their educational aims and needs were underachieved.

For the first two years of his Principality, numbers of pupils began to increase, most noticeably from a wider area; however, most of those pupils were placed at the later age of 8-9, in many cases, having received inadequate tuition at mainstream schools, and thus remained at Mill Hall for a comparatively short length of time, an average of three years. This caused a large turnover of pupils, one third of whom left annually resulting in difficulties of replacing them to keep Mill Hall economically viable. In addition, many parents asked for an additional year for their children whom they considered to be "academically and emotionally unprepared for secondary education, which was becoming more common". At the same time it proved difficult for Malcolm Bown to get the LEAs to agree to placements at Mill Hall. (*Malcolm Bown's e-mail, 28th May 2007 to the author*).

The School's curriculum, in order to meet future demands of the 21st century, was extensively progressed to cover many new subjects of science, art, craft design, information technology, computing, environmental studies and health and safety education. Library visits, educational trips, cycling proficiency training, swimming and horse-riding were all part of the pupils' learning process of becoming better informed, more confident and independent.

While music continued to be part of the school curriculum, as Avril Hardman recounted, a collection of instruments was gradually built up, bought with donations from parents of pupils and by very active fund-raising on the part of Mrs Helga Webster and Malcolm Bown. A keyboard, a set of four drums, hand-held tambours and tambourines, triangles, small cymbals or bells, a large gong, maracas and a number of ethnic rattles were assembled at the start. Chime bars of all sizes and tones, glockenspiels, a set of hand chimes and a set of reed horns resembling little trumpets were added later. A new upright piano provided accompaniment. Avril Hardman devised a visual score sheet using colour coded symbols for each type of instrument on a flipchart to enable the "orchestra" of attentive pupils to strike or blow on cue to achieve harmonised melodies selected from a range of classics and popular music – with the assistance of Jenny Baker, an excellent classroom assistant, who acted as the conductor, pointing at the chart to keep the players on time.

Avril Hardman explained to the author: "The instruments were also used for auditory training, the children learning to distinguish between high and low sounds or to identify which instrument was being played… these activities being seen as games at the beginning of each music session along with music, movement and singing. Rhythm and pitch were equally important as the children learned to listen to spoken phrases and names and then write down the rhythms accurately, understanding timing and pitch. A valuable aim of each music lesson was to encourage the children to concentrate in a group, working together in a harmonious and pleasurable environment."

Music class with Avril Hardman at piano, 1989
(L. to R.) **Sitting:** Matthew Robak, Victoria Paull, John Docker (chime bars)
Standing: Deepa Shastri (triangle), Chiamaka Olejeme (tambourine), Katy Beeson (tambour), Catherine Saunders, Roanna Simmonds, Matthew Hearn (reed horns)
©Photograph on loan by Avril Hardman

Two former pupils, Angela and Tracey Spielsinger told the author about their week-long intensive rehearsing the music for a recital for Princess Anne who visited the School in September 1991; the Princess was very impressed with the pupils' performance. Later at Christmas in 1993 the Mill Hall children competed against other schools at Crawley's shopping mall and won 1st Prize in the Schools' Music Competition.

Retrospectively, in 1986 a new block of two semi-detached boarding houses was erected and completed as independent units within the school's grounds on the east side to provide family accommodation under staff supervision for small groups of six or seven senior pupils who learnt home management skills on a day-to-day basis and who enjoyed independence and privacy in preparation for leaving school and moving onto secondary education.

The first *Mill Hall Friends' Newsletter No. 1*, issued in 1989, announced a new ambitious project outlining the main objects of the forthcoming £500,000 Appeal Fund (to celebrate the School's 50th Anniversary of its founding) for a new extension to the Peacocks classroom block. The vision of the future of Mill Hall was proclaimed *verbatim*:

"A small school, almost unknown in its neighbouring villages, has brought hope to deaf children and standards which have attracted national attention. Mill Hall School in Cuckfield had given some of the profoundly deaf children in the country a chance in life. For over 50 years it has been a place where a deaf child's dream of a normal life becomes a reality. Meaningless jumbles of sounds are gradually grafted into intelligible speech. Even the simplest attempts are nurtured as children painstakingly learn words and then sentences. Although an expensive and frustrating experience, it is highly rewarding for both teacher and pupil.

"Visitors immediately notice the happy atmosphere. It is this which allows words to be tested and communication to flourish. There's no fear of rejection at Mill Hall – everybody is encouraged to talk. The teachers' high standards have encouraged education authorities to send children from as far afield as Lincolnshire, Berkshire and the Channel Islands. A number of international children enrich school life.

"Now the Principal and teachers have agreed a plan to equip the school for the next century and to increase further the quality of teaching. New classrooms will mean a lower pupil/teacher ratio; better audiological equipment will facilitate hearing; and a new craft and design room and shop will give wider opportunities for creativity and recreation." An Appeal Committee was set up under the Chairmanship of Mrs Sylvia Smith to promote the Appeal and manage the Fund.

A series of fund-raising events was launched in 1990 with a BBC Radio Appeal by Sir Michael Hordern, a noted actor, followed by a Summer Fête organised by parents at the School, a planned sponsored mountain cycle ride over 14 mountains of the Welsh Peaks in Wales, which the Principal, a keen cyclist, gallantly looked forward to participating in, a Dinner held at the Lincoln's Inn Court in London (£100 per head) and a Fashion Show in London. But the sponsored mountain cycle run was cancelled due to the impossibility of obtaining insurance for the participants. On a hot July day Lavinia, Duchess of Norfolk, patron of the Appeal Fund, graciously cut the first turf to start the construction of the new extension.

Mary Corbishley at picnic with the children in the garden in 1987;
she told them a story of how she started the school 50 years previously in 1937.
Sitting with her clockwise: Joanna Healey, Luke Bond, Andrew Hearn, Alex Hurley,
Corinna Simmons, Fiona Mitchell, Alison Leach
©*Ian M. Stewart 2007, with Mary Hare Primary School's kind permission*

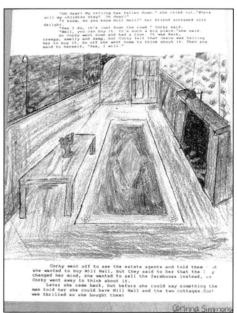

School Story Book created by Corinna Simmons, 1987
©*Ian M. Stewart 2007, with Mary Hare Primary School's kind permission*

Front cover of School Prospectus 1989
(Picture of Mill Hall Entrance drawn by a pupil, Angela Spielsinger)
©*Ian M. Stewart 2007*

Mill Hall School Friends' Newsletters Nos 1-5, 1989-1992
©*Ian M. Stewart 2007*

In the third Issue of *Mill Hall Friends' Newsletter No 3*, in 1990 encouraging news was announced that magnificent support had boosted the Fund to £450,000 and just £50,000 remained to be found.

The construction of the building commenced in September and was programmed for completion in the following March of 1991. The largest unit of the new extension was an Audiology Clinic which was envisaged to provide the best quality assessment of the deaf child's hearing loss and the most suitable and carefully tuned hearing aid to enable the deaf child to hear and understand – albeit to varying degrees – spoken English. This vision was intended to be realised after the opening of the Clinic – acclaimed in *Friends' Newsletter* as an unusual and pioneering development – when hearing aids would be more accurately, more effectively and more frequently monitored.

Mary Corbishley in her wheelchair at the turf-cutting ceremony,
talking to Mrs Sylvia Smith and Lavinia, the Duchess of Norfolk, July 1990
©Ian M. Stewart 2007, with Mary Hare Primary School's kind permision

As reported in the national tabloid press, two fund-raising fashion shows took place in September 1990. A top model flew in from New York to London to participate in the show free of charge; at a charity dinner at the Corn Exchange in Brighton, Sussex, a fashion parade took place in which a celebrated male television presenter modelled on the catwalk in a lilac lady's skirt and jacket to win a £1,500 auction bid. These two events raised £65,000 in total. Several other events were organised such as a Fayre in Guildford, a Donkey Derby and an Advent Concert at Nutley Parish church in Sussex. Some supporters ran in the London Marathon Run.

An Appeal Luncheon, organised by an Australian, Christopher Hume, one of the Appeal Committee members, attended by Freddie Truman, OBE (1931-2006), the well known and popular cricketer and bowler from Yorkshire, was held at the Copthorne Hotel (Gatwick) in Sussex on 1st March 1991, where several tables were sponsored by business people who raised what is believed to be approximately £10,000 for the Appeal fund.

At the end of Summer term 1991 Sir Winston Churchill School for the Deaf in Woodford was closed down, due to an unviable financial situation on account of the LEA-instigated reduction in the number of pupils. As a result 14 or 15 pupils of ages from 4 to 10 were dispersed to and admitted by Mill Hall, thereby leading to a record maximum of 59, resulting in making adaptations to accommodate this increase. The kitchen was enlarged and two extra temporary classrooms were provided. Malcolm Bown told the author that the School was very vibrant and maybe at its best in his tenure.

However, with the normal 1/3rd of the pupils leaving annually, the problem for Mill Hall was lack of recruitment which had become more difficult in 1991. At this point, Malcolm Bown made a very interesting observation: "Among them [Sir Winston Churchill pupils] were two or three of the most able deaf children I'd ever met in special schools, children of deaf parents who had been educated orally themselves. These children were extremely deaf, bilingual and highly literate and eloquent – very impressive indeed. I think the success of those children was primarily due to the input of their parents, who were highly educated themselves (many ex-MHGS) and had developed an incredible fund of language within their children before they ever went near a school. It is important to say also that I've met many equally able and literate children of hearing parents in mainstream schools, who have been educated using auditory oral methods." (*E-mail, July 2007 to the author*)

He and other teachers of the deaf and parents of deaf children felt that, although they strongly believed in integration in mainstream school education, special schools such as Ovingdean Hall and Mill Hall were still needed as a *safety net* for the minority of pupils who could not succeed in mainstream schools. He recorded: "The proof of that is that in 14 years between 1988 and 2002 I personally did 40+ SEN Tribunals and only lost one which we later won … the reason was very simply that we never took on cases where we believed that the pupil was correctly placed in mainstream and was doing well there, even if the parents wanted a special school. So our approach to lots of things was very different, but we were always on cordial terms." (*E-mail, June 2007 to the author*)

Later in 1991, after a four-month delay in the completion of the new wing construction postponing the original Opening Day, the red-letter day finally arrived on 13th September when the Peacocks Block's extension and Audiology Clinic were officially opened by HRH The Princess Royal who, escorted by Malcolm Bown, spent an hour touring the classrooms, meeting and chatting with the pupils, Governors and staff before unveiling a commemorative plaque. Then she watched and listened to some of the pupils' percussion performance of playing the music of *Edelweiss* from *The Sound of Music,* after which she had tea and a private conversation with Mary Corbishley in her Orchard Cottage. Before leaving the School, the Princess listened to a chorus of pupils singing *It's time to say Goodbye* on the back terrace in bidding their farewell to their royal visitor on a memorable day in brilliant sunshine.

It was reported in the local paper, *The Mid-Sussex Times*, January 1992 that the Vice-Lord Lieutenant of Sussex in his resplendent red and black uniform with a ceremonial sword, who escorted the Princess, admitted to having a lump in his throat while watching the pupils' percussion rendition of *Edelweiss.*

In her letter of thanks to Mill Hall, the Princess Royal expressed her deep impression of what she saw and experienced: "It was an uplifting experience to see the School and to witness some of the results that have been achieved by your dedicated staff. The Princess was particularly moved by the musical achievements of the pupils … Mr Bown and the staff have every reason to be proud of their accomplishments. She wishes to thank and congratulate everyone and to send her good wishes for the school's continuing success." Malcolm Bown's response to this historic event was that it was the highlight of Mill Hall's era as an Oral School for Deaf children, and also that it was the high spot of his time at Mill Hall.

One day in 1992, Mill Hall pupils themselves organised a coffee morning with cake stalls and a raffle and raised £381 for Save The Children, the Princess Royal's charity as a token of thanks for her interest in the School in the preceding September.

An unusual plan was announced in *Mill Hall Friends' Newsletter No. 5, 1992* to convert old dilapidated garages into a multi-purpose building with a new crèche for younger children to be offered to the local community of Cuckfield and its surrounding vicinity. Local school clubs and the community would use the new facility for their evening activities. The idea behind this project was to enrich the young deaf children's school life and to encourage them to mix with

ROYAL VISIT BY HRH THE PRINCESS ROYAL

13th September 1991

Princess Anne with Malcolm Bown
©Angela Spielsinger 1991

School chorus waiting to sing *Goodbye* to the Princess Royal
©Angela Spielsinger 1991

ROYAL VISIT BY HRH THE PRINCESS ROYAL *(Continued)*

New extension to Peacocks Block. The wall plaque unveiled by Princess Anne can be
discerned on the right of the entrance doors. On the right is the Old Summer House
believed to be erected in the 1930s
©Ian M. Stewart 2007, with Mary Hare Primary School's kind permission

Photographs taken from Selling Agents' brochure, 1996
©Ian M. Stewart 2007, with Mary Hare Primary School's kind permission

local hearing children and learn to speak at an earlier and more impressionable age. It was felt by Mill Hall staff that the "classroom can never substitute for learning to listen and speak in the most natural way possible – by playing with hearing children. Now local children can join the crèche, make friends and help deaf children talk!" How the oral education had moved on from Mary Corbishley's original philosophy of speech teaching of the 1930s onto Mrs Webster's free expression and then to Malcolm Bown's strong belief in young deaf children's ability to acquire natural talking and lipreading at primary age level 60 years later.

The *Mill Hall Friends' Newsletter No. 5* contained reports on many different activities and events in 1991 and 1992. A Children's Forum was formed and first met in May 1991 to "discuss the developments wanted by children and to choose grown-ups to participate in the next Forum. Minutes are kept by the children on their classroom computers and meetings are held monthly." Their first shopping list of changes gave an indication of their demands: a lunchtime club for computing, handwriting and sewing sessions, more team games against other schools such as ice hockey, prep work done at home and not in school, a heated indoors swimming pool and new playground equipment alongside a new football pitch. It was their initiation to pupils' power and democracy.

One Friday evening in June 1992 the School's grounds at Mill Hall were the venue for a 250-guest special fancy dress ball with a candle-lit supper as a fitting finale to the week of celebrating the 900th anniversary of the founding of the village of Cuckfield. In the Saxon times prior to the settlement of Kukefeld as it was then called, the favourite sport was hunting for deer and wild boar in the forest of Sussex which resulted in an open clearing or "*feld*", in which forest servants settled to preserve the ample supply of deer and boar. The clearing also was a haunt of cuckoos (*kuke*) thereby giving rise to the name of Kukefeld later changed to Cuckfield in 1091. (*Maisie Wright's A Chronicle of Cuckfield, 1991;* The Cuckfield Society's *This is Cuckfield, 1967*) Earlier on the same day of the ball, Mill Hall pupils put on a Variety Show of comedy, fantasy and "synchronised swimming" on the lawn.

In 1993, after a very eventful 9-year period as Principal of Mill Hall, Malcolm Bown decided to move onto fresh pastures and applied for and was appointed as Head of Ovingdean Hall School for the Deaf, a few miles east of Brighton in Sussex. During his tenure at Mill Hall he often lunched with Mary Corbishley who found in him another great friend and ally who shared the same philosophy of auditory/oral education for deaf children with her. In the ensuing four-month interim one of the teachers, Mrs J. Sewell-Rutter, stepped into the breach to continue with the running of the School until Mr Paul Simpson joined as the last Head of Mill Hall in 1994.

According to the Annual Statement of Accounts for the year ending 31st August 1993, the Governors wished to express their recognition of two stalwarts of the School – Mary Corbishley and Mrs Connie Mager, the long-serving teacher and Governor, by inviting them to become Vice-Presidents of Mill Hall, which they accepted.

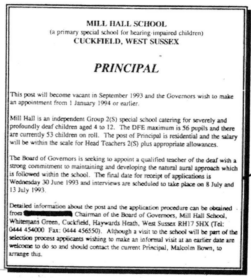

MILL HALL SCHOOL
(a primary special school for hearing-impaired children)
CUCKFIELD, WEST SUSSEX

PRINCIPAL

This post will become vacant in September 1993 and the Governors wish to make an appointment from 1 January 1994 or earlier.

Mill Hall is an independent Group 2(S) special school catering for severely and profoundly deaf children aged 4 to 12. The DFE maximum is 56 pupils and there are currently 53 children on roll. The post of Principal is residential and the salary will be within the scale for Head Teachers 2(S) plus appropriate allowances.

The Board of Governors is seeking to appoint a qualified teacher of the deaf with a strong commitment to maintaining and developing the natural aural approach which is followed within the school. The final date for receipt of applications is Wednesday 30 June 1993 and interviews are scheduled to take place on 8 July and 13 July 1993.

Detailed information about the post and the application procedure can be obtained from ████████████ Chairman of the Board of Governors, Mill Hall School, Whitemans Green, Cuckfield, Haywards Heath, West Sussex RH17 5HX (Tel: 0444 454000 Fax: 0444 456550). Although a visit to the school will be part of the selection process applicants wishing to make an informal visit at an earlier date are welcome to do so and should contact the current Principal, Malcolm Bown, to arrange this.

©Times Educational Supplement, 11ᵗʰ June 1993,
with kind permission of Mr Tony Shaw, Principal of MHGS (BHC)

Paul Simpson, MA (Oxon) in Classics and Modern Languages, took over the Headship in January 1994. He previously was Housemaster at Mary Hare Grammar School where his mentor was Mollie Mayes, the mother of Malcolm Bown, in 1984 -1987. He took the British Association of Teachers of the Deaf (BATOD) Diploma Course and qualified as a Teacher of the Deaf. At MHGS he was responsible for the pastoral care of approximately 95 boys in the boarding house as well as teaching French and "some English". After leaving the Grammar School, he worked as a peripatetic teacher in Leicestershire and then lectured on Teacher of the Deaf training courses in Birmingham, after which he moved to West Sussex to become Head of the Sensory Support Team

Winter Sports in France

Ski group in Montgenevre, the French Alps, 1991
©Ian M. Stewart 2007, with Mary Hare Primary School's kind permission

Having fun on ski practice slope in Risoul, the French Alps, 1992
©Ian M. Stewart 2007, with Mary Hare Primary School's kind permission

Mill Hall School, 1991

(L to R.)

Front row: Michael Clark, Tracey Spielsinger, Kafayat Badaru, Thomas Akers, Fergus England, Ross Edwards, Jamie Baillie, Jamie Doolan, Hamish Cooke, Sabira Yameen, Roy Kerr, Rowan Dixon, Coco Stone-Brown, Catherine Drew

First row: Luke Leyden, Sean Richards, Kris Meechan, Maha Shahid, Shawana Iftikhar, Damaris Cooke, Katherine Scase, Mary Pearman, Chloe Sharratt, Francesca Warren-Price, Lucy Clarke, Michael Roberts, John Scoufarides, Matthew Bateup, Darren Smith, Sonya Nye, Robert Childs

Second row: Brett Stewart, Fergus Cooke, Marcus Puccillo, Fozan Gulrez, Victoria Goodacre, Kirsty Brown, Katie Rumney, Angela Spielsinger, Yaa Mensah, Amanda Norris-Holgate, Aparna Koirala, Samantha Caiels, Qais al Badu, Gavin Lilley, Daniel Rumney, Thomas Beattie

Third row: Miss Pippa Dale (teacher), Mrs Bobby Freeland(classroom assistant), Bassim Baz, Eleni Botonaki, Alexandra Gargini, Lydia Docker, Rebecca Bailey, Karti Sundarlingoon, Mrs Linda Brierley (teacher), Ann (lady cleaner), Reese (classroom assistant), Mrs Jenny Baker (classroom assistant), Tracy (care staff)

Fourth row: Mrs Pat Francis (assistant cook), _____? (assistant cook), Mrs Phyl Metzner (cook), Mrs Sewell-Rutter (teacher), Mrs Erica Chapman (teacher), Mrs Meg Booker (teacher), Mrs Avril Hardman (music teacher), Mrs Mary ApSimon (art teacher), Mrs Mary Bevans (teacher), Jim Turnbull (gardener), Carol Barker (care staff), _____? (classroom assistant), 2 lady cleaners

Back row: Clive Rees (Deputy Head/audiologist), Adele (care staff), Alison (OOS), Patrick Swabe (part-time trainee teacher), Ilka Seeberger (care staff), David Couch (teacher), Natalie (classroom assistant), Fran (care staff/classroom assistant), Amanda (care staff), Malcolm Bown (Head), Sue Hepplewhite (Secretary/Head of OOS), Les Bailey (care staff), Mrs Debbie Stonley (P.E. instructor)

© *Photograph on loan by Jenny Baker*

OOS is out-of-school staff brought in the School to assist the in-house staff with various duties.

with the West Sussex County Council. Eventually, after interviews with the Governors and two external interviewers, he was appointed Head of Mill Hall School and remained there until its closure in August 1996.

The year 1994 saw the beginning of Mill Hall's crisis when, owing to the long-term effects of the Education Acts, 1976, 1981 (SEN) and 1988 (National Curriculum), local educational authorities nationwide were obliged or encouraged to make savings in school fee payments to special schools, one of them being Mill Hall, outside their respective catchment areas and restricting the pupils 'in county' by transferring them to local mainstream county schools. The inevitable result as envisaged by the Warnock Report of 1978 was a long process of closing down Mill Hall and other deaf schools. At the same time there grew a new approach by parents of deaf children towards an early start at school at the age of 2 up to 5. The parents found the idea of sending the children of that age range to a residential school so far away from home becoming less and less attractive.

During the ensuing years of 1994-1996 there was a noticeable decline in the number of pupils at Mill Hall as a large number of those who were dispersed there from Sir Winston Churchill School in 1991 had already reached their secondary age and so were transferred to Mary Hare Grammar School or Ovingdean Hall School and other schools as a natural process.

Receivable school fees had fallen from £715,000 to £553,000 alongside the respective running costs of £735,000 and £613,000 resulting in deficits of, respectively, £20,000 and £60,000. Despite continuing donations to the school funds and the success of the crèche, the situation became so serious that it became apparent to the Governors that unless they could attract more pupils the School would become "financially unviable." (*Governors' Annual Report for Year ending 31st August 1996*)

Paul Simpson organised an "Open Week" for parents and professionals in January 1995 to demonstrate the philosophy of natural auralism for profoundly deaf children in a specially-designed learning environment. The author paid a visit and during a conversation with Paul Simpson at lunch he was told the number of pupils was 44 comprising approximately 30 boys and 14 girls – a ratio of 2:1 – with twelve female and one male teachers at the time. He, the author, also dropped in to see two or three classes whom he had the special pleasure of telling he was a former pupil 50 years previously. He received excited responses from the bright pupils who were very competent in lipreading,

Photograph believed to be taken at the end of Open Day in *c.* 1990 with
Peacocks Block on the right.
©Photograph on loan by Jean Landriani

Aerial view of Mill Hall *c.* 1995
©Photograph on loan by Jenny Baker

School logo 1939-1996
©Original from Ian M. Stewart's collection

Mill Hall School 1994

(L. to R)

Front row: Roy Kerr, Tessa Boyd, Christine Woodward, Christopher Drew, Fergus England, Coco Stone-Brown, William Reynolds,, Ross Edwards, Victoria Draper, Thomas Akers , Hamish Cooke, Andrew Mayes, Harry Clasper, Jamie Doolan, Rowan Dixon

First row: Catherine Drew, Sabira Yameen, Jamie Baillie, Christopher Muldoon, Michael Clark, John Bishop, Robin Glover, Andrew Godber, Paul McTaggart, Giles Bowman, Oliver Mansfield, Sean Richards, Lucy White, Luke Leyden, Tracey Spielsinger, Daniel Rumney, Kris Meechan

Second row: Katie Rumney, Victoria Goodacre, Francesca Warren-Price, John Scoufarides, Matthew Bateup, Michael Roberts, Conor Downey, Chloe Sharratt, Damaris Cooke, Mary Pearman, Katherine Scase, Fozan Gulrez, Shawana Iftikhar, Rebecca Miller

Third row: Trisha (lady cleaner), Mrs Pat Francis (assistant cook), _____?, Mrs Avril Hardman (music teacher), _____? (classroom assistant), Ruth Underwood (classroom assistant), Mrs Erica Chapman (teacher), _____?, Helen Simmonds (teacher), Mrs Jenny Baker (classroom assistant), Mrs Debbie Stonley (P.E. instructor), Mrs Bobby Freeland (classroom assistant), Mrs Linda Brierly (teacher), Tracy (care staff), Mrs Jean Whybro (Bursar), Sarah (care staff), Mrs Sewell-Rutter (teacher)

Back row: Mrs Meg Booker (teacher), _____?, Christine Hart (classroom assistant), Sue Hepplewhite (Secretary/Head of OOS), Carol Barker (care staff), Paul Simpson (Head), _____? (assistant cook), Phyl and Anne (lady cleaners), Natalie (classroom assistant), Fran (care staff/classroom assistant), Les Bailey (care staff), David Couch (teacher), Clive Rees (Deputy Head/audiologist)

©*Mary Hare Primary School archives, with kind permission*

OOS is out-of-school staff brought in the School to assist the in-house staff with various duties.

listening to and understanding him – without the assistance of sign language – in keeping with the School's philosophy of natural aural principles.

In November 1995 Mary Corbishley MBE, the founder, passed away peacefully, and in her Will bequeathed her Orchard Cottage to the School.

The Governors' Annual Report for the Year ending 31st August 1996 stated: "Early in 1996, when it became clear that we would not have the resources to continue after the end of Summer Term [1996], the Governors had discussions with the Governors and Head of Mary Hare Grammar School, Newbury, to see if we could move the School to the Newbury area. The conclusion of these discussions was that Mary Hare would purchase property in Newbury, to be financed by the sale of our property, including Orchard Cottage in Cuckfield. All staff were offered jobs in Newbury and those who did not want to go were paid redundancy money.

"The main School building was sold for £625,000 during the year, Orchard Cottage for £130,000, and a small strip of land for £3,000. We envisage that, when everything is finalised, we shall have paid around £730,000 to Mary Hare including £37,000 from the donations account. In addition, the furniture, equipment and vehicles were donated to Mary Hare at their book value of £37,816. The Mary Hare Grammar School has spent £640,000 purchasing new premises and £450,000 preparing them for pupils."

Mary Hare Grammar School, formerly a Charitable Trust, had been incorporated as a Charity in July 1995 to fulfil the need for a corporate structure in order to "purchase land and buildings as part of the Mill Hall acquisition". (*MHGS e-mail to the author, May 2007*) Incidentally, the Mill Hall Scholarship Fund originally set up in 1987, having by then served its purpose, closed down and was de-registered at the Charity Commissioners on 9th February, 1996.

Previously, at an Extraordinary General Meeting of the Mill Hall Oral School for the Deaf Limited held on 17th July 1996, a special resolution was tabled that the Memorandum of Association of the Company (incorporated in 1972) be amended to replace the original wording of Clause 3 (a) of "To advance education by the provision and maintenance at Mill Hall, Cuckfield …. as conducted in such manner as to be eligible for approval as a Special School … within the Education Act 1944 …" with a new clause to read: "To promote and provide for the advancement of education of children and/or adults with hearing and other related disabilities in such manner as the Council of Management of the School shall decide … by the support of the work of the Mary Hare Grammar School for the Deaf …"

The Resolution was approved and passed, thereby facilitating a smooth transition from Mill Hall School in Cuckfield to new premises fully named "Mary Hare Primary School – Mill Hall" in Greenham Common, Newbury, Berkshire. One of the members of the staff at the Primary School explained to the author that the name Mill Hall was retained out of respect for and recognition of Mary Corbishley's founding of her School. Since then, the School was again renamed Mary Hare Primary School – under the new Group of Mary Hare Schools.

The news of Mill Hall School's closure and move to Newbury was widely received with shock, incredulity and sadness by former pupils, teachers, parents and friends who had contributed so much to the enduring success of the School which had become – in educational parlance – a centre of excellence as described by an ex-teacher who taught there for many years until her retirement in the late 1980s and who expressed her sadness in a private (unpublished) letter to a teacher (edited): "One would have to know the history of Mill Hall to realise the profound irony of what was being intended. [Ed: Mill Hall's closure] … Corby would turn in her grave if she knew what had happened to the little gem of a school that she founded. The school should still be in its wonderful purpose-built environment on the lovely site in Cuckfield. The way in which it was taken over … was not a happy one for Corby, Mrs Webster, Mr Bown and the dedicated staff who had upheld Corby's philosophy throughout the years."

Paul Simpson, in his e-mail letter *November 2005* to the author, wrote (edited): "I was not very much involved in that part of the transfer … The Governors dealt with the whole matter. My Headship was not long because of the rapid decline in numbers following the departure of a large number of the children who all reached the secondary age at the same time … This led to the decision to transfer to Mary Hare. Otherwise it was felt that the School would not have been viable. I met Miss Corbishley and am pleased that she died before learning of the plight of the School which would have no doubt caused her great distress."

Paul Simpson found himself in a difficult situation brought about by the fact that that shortly after his arrival the pupil population was drastically reduced by half as those of secondary age had to leave school. The School became much smaller and the staff had to be "rationalised" by redundancies, which was a very distressing time for all at Mill Hall. It had thus become clear to many involved that there was a lot of doubt about the economic viability of Mill Hall in the immediate future. The author in his e-mail in January 2006 to Paul Simpson (edited) raised a point:

Author: "There is the real question of why, generally speaking, there was a reduced intake of deaf pupils at special schools at the time (despite the Education Act 1944). It must have been a traumatic and saddening experience, seeing fewer pupils coming into your school, knowing what it all meant in terms of future education for deaf children. I have become more painfully aware of deep resentment and anger among the deaf community at the serious setback which is putting the deaf children at a disadvantage compared with the more fortunate hearing ones. What are your views on that?"

Paul Simpson: "In fact, the main problem was not *just* the general trend but a specific factor … Shortly after I arrived, Mill Hall's pupil population was reduced by about half at a stroke … It became clear that the school was not viable on such small numbers working in an independent way. Furthermore, it is clear that for children of that age, particularly following an oral approach, a residential school is not *always* ideal. Taking children away from their homes at such a young age is not acceptable to many parents. At secondary level it is a different matter. … I do not agree with the view you expressed that deaf children are necessarily being put at a disadvantage because fewer are going to special schools at primary level – it depends very much on the individual child. There is some excellent provision for profoundly deaf children in their local mainstream schools which works well, provided that they are adequately supported by qualified Teachers of the Deaf. It is true that many BSL-using deaf people feel that a residential special school is required but at primary level it is not necessarily the most desirable placement for the majority of deaf children under the age of 5." Nevertheless, it was generally felt that the arrangements where a large secondary school for the deaf, Mary Hare Grammar School, was able to take Mill Hall School under its wing for the remaining small number of pupils (fewer than 20) were the best solution.

Dr Ivan Tucker, the Principal of MHGS, appointed one of his teaching staff, Mrs Shirley Roberts, as the future Head of the new primary school; she went early in 1996 to Mill Hall to oversee and facilitate the School's move to Greenham Common where she took up the post of the first Headship.

After Mill Hall's closure, Paul Simpson became the secretary of the British Association of Teachers of the Deaf (BATOD), formerly the National College of Teachers of the Deaf.

The Governors' Report for the Year ending 31st August 1997 tabled on 4th May 1998 formally confirmed (*verbatim*):

"The decision had been made to close the School at Cuckfield with effect from 31 August 1996 and to move the remaining pupils to new premises to be purchased and run by Mary Hare Grammar School for the Deaf in Newbury. The Governors agreed with the Directors of Mary Hare that all the remaining assets of Mill Hall would be donated to Mary Hare to offset the cost of establishing the new school in Newbury which amounted to nearly £1.1 million.

"It is [a] matter of great sadness to the Board of Mill Hall that the School had to be closed. But it is with some pride that we were able to honour our obligations to deaf education by ensuring that our remaining accumulated assets have been properly invested in the reincarnation of Mill Hall School in Newbury under the stewardship of a much larger and financially stable charity. So far our trust has been well placed, the new school now has twenty three pupils with every prospect of it building to its capacity of around forty pupils."

It was ironic – life indeed is full of ironies – that after such an intensive period of continuously maintaining the high profile and reputation of Mill Hall's nursery and primary education for young deaf children with the help of generous donations and voluntary fund-raising, culminating in the new £70,000 Peacocks classroom block and its £500,000 extension and Audiology Clinic, the time had come for the regrettable enforced closure of the beloved School. It was generally felt that all the efforts by hard working Principals, Mary Corbishley, Mrs Helga Webster, Malcolm Bown and Paul Simpson and their dedicated staff and Governors might be in vain as Mill Hall's 50-year-long era came to an end on that august day of 31st August 1996. But the name *Mill Hall* still lives on to this day, engraved on the brass nameplate by the entrance door at the new Mary Hare Primary School in Greenham Common.

It was Mary Corbishley's expressed wish that upon her death her School at Mill Hall should be closed down as she did not desire it to be continued in her name thereafter, nor should it be continued in memory of her work; as a practical woman she considered her job done once she had gone. By a strange quirk of fate, after her death in November 1995, Mill Hall Oral School closed down nine months later in August 1996 …

Thus ended the era of Mill Hall Oral School for the Deaf as was known to and beloved by its founder, Mary Corbishley, for 50 years, though, mercifully, she never knew of its fate. One needs to look back to the day when she, after disagreement with her employer, Miss Mary Hare, walked out of Dene Hollow Oral School for the Deaf on the historic 10th of March 1937 to set up her own school in a bed-sitter in Hassocks, then an Oral School proper at Cuckfield House in Cuckfield in April or May 1939 and eventually at Mill Hall in January 1948, only for Mary Hare Grammar School, formerly known as Dene Hollow Oral School and named after its founder, Mary Hare in 1946, to enter and take over and re-locate Mill Hall School to Newbury and continue with oral-based primary education for deaf children nearly 60 years later.

It had come full circle ...

LAST HISTORIC GROUP PHOTOGRAPH taken in Summer 1996

(L to R)

Front Row: Nick Carter, Christine Woodward, Andrew Avery, Coco Stone-Brown; Toni-Jayne Ward, Phillip Webster, Ryan Goodwin, Danielle Mayo

First Row: Roy Kerr, John Bishop, Lewis Gerrity, Ross Edwards, Hamish Cooke, Thomas Akers, Victoria Draper, Rowan Dixon, Jamie Doolan, Christopher Muldoon, Lucy White, Conor Downey

Second Row: Mrs Christine Hart (classroom assistant), Tracey (care staff), Sabira Yameen, Lucy Jones, Tessa Boyd, Giles Bowman, Paul McTaggart, Mrs Jenny Baker (classroom assistant), Carol Michelle (classroom assistant), Clive Rees (Deputy Head/ Audiologist)

Third Row: Mrs Erika Chapman (teacher), Annie Hance (care staff), Mrs Meg Booker (teacher), Sarah (care staff), Alison Barry (care staff), Michelle (care staff), Mrs Pru Bourne (care staff), Sue Hepplewhite (Secretary/Head of OOS), David Couch (teacher), Alison (OOS)

Back Row: Leslie Bailey (care staff), Carol Barker (care staff), Sandra (domestic staff), Mrs Phyl Metzner (head cook), Sue Alexander (assistant cook), Mrs Pat Francis (assistant cook)

It is to be noted that the group photo of 1994 on page 200 shows 46 pupils (30 boys, 16 girls) compared with 24 pupils (15 boys, 9 girls) shown in this 1996 group photograph, which illustrates the drastic cutting down of the pupil intake due to the long-term impact of the 1978 Warnock Report and the LEAs' decision to transfer deaf children to their county mainstream schools for economic and political reasons.

LAST PHOTOGRAPHS OF MILL HALL ORAL SCHOOL in July
1996 taken two weeks before it was closed down for the last time

East elevation of Mill Hall
Fiona Mitchell in forecourt

Main Entrance porch

Main Entrance Hall

Main School Hall

©All photographs by Alison Leach, 1996

LAST PHOTOGRAPHS OF MILL HALL ORAL SCHOOL in July
1996 (*Continued*)

Old Corby's Staircase;
back door to garden

View of Peacock Block from the terrace
New extension and Summer House can be seen
at the far end

North-East panoramic view
from the tennis court

Fiona Mitchell by the tennis court

©*All photographs by Alison Leach, 1996*

With the author's special thanks to Alison Leach for her initiative of taking
these historic photographs upon her last visit to the School.

PRINCIPALS of MILL HALL ORAL SCHOOL for the Deaf
1948-1996

Mary S. Corbishley MBE
1948-1974

Mrs Helga Webster
1974-1984

Malcolm Bown
1984-1993

Paul Simpson
1994-1996

EPILOGUE

In September 1996 Mary Hare Primary School – Mill Hall in Greenham Common, Newbury, Berkshire was opened with the original thirteen pupils from Mill Hall School, Cuckfield, together with a few teachers under the first Head, Mrs Shirley Roberts. The new primary school was set up at Greenham Lodge, a Grade-II listed building built in the early 1880s in its 22 acres of grounds. After the Second World War Greenham Lodge was used as a club for the United States Air Force Officers based at Greenham Common Airbase from 1953 to 1992 when the property was vacated and stood empty for four years until 1996.

The Director of Mary Hare Schools, Dr Ivan Tucker, said: "It's a very tall order but we are working very hard to get the renovations achieved by September." (*Newbury Weekly News, May 1996*) It was envisaged that the pupils would increase to 45 boarders and day pupils aged 6-11. The whole of the operations of relocating the School from Cuckfield to Greenham Common was part of the £1.35 million rescue package, to which it was believed that a very substantial donation was made to offset the shortfall in the costs. The package also included the purchase of Greenham Lodge by Mary Hare School (MHS) from the Ministry of Defence.

Earlier in 1948 Greenham Lodge housed the first Jewish public school in Britain, Carmel College. (*Newbury Weekly News, May 1996*) Coincidentally, MHGS used to play football and cricket matches against the College in 1951-53 before the College moved out.

Although the news of the closure of Mill Hall School in Cuckfield was received with sadness, the people of Greenham welcomed the news of its move to the Lodge. One of Greenham councillors said: "We think this is absolutely great. Greenham residents are delighted." (*The Advertiser, Newbury, 21st June 1996*)

On 4th October 1997 the oak-panelled main hall at the Primary School was dedicated as Corby Hall in honour of the founder, Mary S. Corbishley MBE at a dedication ceremony at which the Vicar of Greenham Church, Mr John Clark, gave the blessing. A brass rectangular wall plaque was unveiled by Chris Rocket, an ex-Governor of Mill Hall Oral School, and Mrs Rocket in front of an audience of former pupils, ex-teachers, parents, Governors and the Director of Mary Hare Schools, Dr Ivan Tucker. Another ex-Governor, Mr Michael Peacock, was also present. A large photographic portrait of Mary S. Corbishley in its slim black frame was donated by the Mill Hall Old Pupils Association.

A year earlier in October 1996 Mill Hall was put up for sale for potential development. The old freehold property was advertised as a "substantial Edwardian residence extended and adapted for school use (with a Fire Certificate for its current use), together with a single-storey teaching block, a modern two-storey brick boarding house comprising a pair of semi-detached houses, a modern single storey nursery classroom and a modern two-storey Headmaster's house, all set in attractive grounds of approximately 1.36 hectares (4.6 acres), partly laid out with play equipment and two hard surface tennis courts." (*London Estate Agents, 1996*)

Plans for the development after sale were drawn up to divide the main building, Mill Hall, into three units with in-built dividing walls, one unit with six bedrooms on two upper storeys and a large reception room, one with three bedrooms and two large reception rooms and one with six bedrooms on two upper floors and two reception rooms. During renovations many original features were retained such as oak wall panelling and richly-ornamental fireplace in the Garden Room, black and red clay floor tiling in the passage to the kitchen (originally servants' quarters), ornate cornices and ceiling beams and wall panelling in the School Hall (after removal of acoustic panels), main staircase and balustrade and the large Victorian stained glass window to the landing. The present owner was telling the author: "It was when in 1997 we removed the hardboard encasing to the quality antique pine balustrade that we discovered the workmen's signatures and August 1955 written on the inside face of one of the hardboard panels." This work of enclosing the balustrade presumably was ordered by Mary Corbishley to secure the small young children's safety from accidental falling through between the balusters.

The Peacocks Block and its extension were converted into two detached homes, each with four bedrooms, two bathrooms and three reception rooms. The school grounds were partitioned with timber country fences or hedges into separate private gardens for each of the homes, some retaining period features such as the 1930s Summer House (since demolished in 2006 due to dry rot). (*Mid-Sussex Citizen's Property Plus, 28th October, 1996*) The tennis courts and bottom part of the original grounds were sold off to the adjoining farm. The Headmaster's house and semi-detached houses were separately sold.

Greenham Lodge
©*Ian M. Stewart, 2007*

Nameplate by the Entrance Porch

Primary School signboard

©*Ian M. Stewart, 2007*

Corby Hall memorial plaque
©*Ian M. Stewart, 2007, with Mary Hare Primary School's kind permission*

Dedication Portrait of Mary Corbishley MBE hung in Corby Hall
©Ian M. Stewart, 2007, with Mary Hare Primary School's kind permission

©David Vaughan, with grateful thanks

Epilogue

As all the eight separate homes are well within close proximity of each other on the same site, a special informal "Mill Hall commune" has sprung up, thereby maintaining mutual support and friendship providing communal benefits of eight families enjoying their independent way of life. An article appearing in the local paper, *The Middy, 28th May, 1998,* spelt it out: "Memories of Mill Hall School still echo round the old and well-loved building at Cuckfield – and the spirit is alive and well, thanks to the guardianship of eight families." Such spirit was still evident to the author who visited Mill Hall in the summer of 2007.

The adjoining detached house, Orchard Cottage, was separately available for sale. The neighbour at Mill Hall recalled to the author that the cottage had been standing empty for some time and the trees and shrubs were closing in around it. But after its sale it was demolished one Saturday morning in March or April 1998 to make way for a new much larger brick-built house eventually ready for occupation in the following year, 1999.

Thus ended the 50-year saga of Mill Hall Oral School for the Deaf from 1948 to 1998.

SELECTED SOURCES OF REFERENCE

(In alphabetical order)

Published Books

Appleton, Kate: *the first 60 years 1944-2004, National Deaf Children's Society* (2004)

Boyce, Anthony J. & Lavery, Elaine: *The Lady In Green – Biography of Miss Mary Hare 1865-1945* (pub. by British Deaf History Society, 1999) ISBN 1-902427-05-X

Boyce, Anthony J. & Lavery, Elaine: *Through Eyes Not Ears – A Brief History of Mary Grammar School for the Deaf 1946-1973* (pub. by BDHS, 2005) ISBN 1-902427-20-3

Clark's Mid-Sussex Directory for 1939

Corbishley, Mary S.: *Corby, Teacher of the Deaf for Fifty Years* (1980) ISBN 0 9506988 0 6

Encyclopaedia Britannica 1911 edition (Author's Collection)

Gannon, Jack R.: *Deaf Heritage – A Narrative History of Deaf America* (1981; 14th Ed. 2001) ISBN 0 913072 38 9

Gault, R.C.: *A History of Worcestershire Agriculture and Rural Evolution* (1939) (WRO)

Gregory, Susan; Knight, Pamela; McCracken, Wendy; Powers, Stephen; Watson, Linda: *Issues in Deaf Education* (1998) ISBN 1-85346-512-7 (RNID Library)

Horne, John: *Chipping Campden From the Grass Roots* (1982) (CCL)

Horne, John: *A Short Account of the Chipping Campden Grammar School* (1879) (CCL)

Hogwood, Marion: *The History of Cuckfield Baptist Chapel 1772-1984 (1984) (*WSRO*)*

Kelly's Directory for Sussex, 1938 (WSRO)

Kelly's Directories for Worcestershire, 1912-1940 (WRO)

Lloyd, Rev. R.H.: *Bredon Hill and its Villages,* 9th Ed. (1996)

McNeill, Ross: *Royal Air Force Coastal Command Losses of the Second World War, Vol. 1 – Aircraft and Crew Losses 1939-1941* (BHC)

Morton, Ann: *Education and the State from 1833,* PRO Publications, (1997) (NA)

Smith, Sheila: *Still Unique After All These Years – A History of Blanche Nevile School (formerly Tottenham School for the Deaf), 1895-1995* (1995) ISBN 0 9525444 0 7

Viner, David: *The North Cotswolds in Old Photographs* (1988) ISBN 0 86299 441 1 (CCL)

Warmington, Allan (editor): *Campden – A New History* by members of the CADHAS (2005) (CCL)

Published Books (*Continued*):
Ward, Joan: *Education in Cuckfield*, printed by West Sussex County Council (1981) (WSRO)
Wright, Maisie: *A Chronicle of Cuckfield, (1971, rep. 1991)* pub. under the auspices of Mid-Sussex Local History Group and the Cuckfield Museum Trust.

Other publications:
A. R. Treasure (MHGS Editor): *A Brief History/Register of Pupils' Entries 1946-1996*
British Deaf History Society's *Journal Vol. 9 Issue 2, December 2005*
Cuckfield House and Mill Hall School Prospectuses for 1939, 1979, 1989, 1992/3
Education Acts 1870-1988
Mid-Sussex Times
Mill Hall News Christmas 1959, Summer 1960, Spring 1961 and Spring 1962 (Author's collection)
Mill Hall Friends Newsletter Nos 1-5, 1989-1992 (Author's collection)
NCTD Constitution *c.* 1920: Rules 4, 9 & 15 (UBL)
RNID Library booklets: No. 483 – *The Government Hearing-Aid "Medresco"* (1948); No. 486 – *The Education of Deaf Children* (1953)
Teacher of the Deaf Journals 1925-1975 (NCTD/BATOD)
The Bluebird 1948-52 – MHGS magazine (Author's collection)
The Cuckfield Society's *This is Cuckfield*, 1967 (Ian Depledge's collection)
The Silent Messenger, South Africa, June 1959, June 1965, September 1970 (RNID Library)
NID's *The Silent World*, 1946-1949 (RNID Library)
The Times
The Times Educational Supplements
The Warnock Report: *The Committee of Enquiry Into the Education of Handicapped Children and Young People, 1978* (RNID Library)

Records, Reports, Documents:
Bricklehampton Parish Records 1890-1895 and 1942 (WRO)
Bricklehampton Public Elementary School Log Book 1910-1915 (WRO)
Censuses for 1841-1901 (FRC/WRO)
Cuckfield House/Mill Hall School Reports and Bills 1942-1963 (Rosemary Hackforth and Author's collections)
Land Tax Assessments for Bishampton, Bricklehampton and Comberton Parva 1898 -1916 (WRO)
Little Comberton Parish Records 1828-1917 (WRO)
Mill Hall Oral School for the Deaf Ltd's *Annual Reports and Statements of Accounts, 1972-1998* (Companies House, London)

Records, Reports, Documents (*Continued*):

Ministry of Education Circular 41 – *Handicapped Pupils and Medical Services Regulations, 1945*

Ministry of Education Circular 269 – *The School Health Service and Handicapped Pupils Regulations 1953*

Minute Book of St Michael & All Saints Church, Bricklehampton 1889-1893 (WRO)

Minute Book of St Peter Church, Little Comberton 1825-1894 (WRO)

Minute Book of the Board of Guardians for Pershore 1903-1913 (WRO)

Monumental Inscriptions for St Michael and All Saints Church, Bricklehampton (WRO)

Monumental Inscriptions for St Peter Church, Little Comberton (WRO)

Pershore Cottage Hospital's *Annual Report for year ending October 1911* (WRO County Hall)

Reece, Peter: *An Overview of Fulton School's History, August 2006* – Fulton School for the Deaf, Durban, Mozambique (formerly Natal)

Schutte, Carol: *Brief Biography of Miss J. B. Hancock, December 1984* – Fulton School for the Deaf, Durban, Mozambique (formerly Natal)

Letters:

Author's own handwritten letters to his parents from Cuckfield House and MHGS 1942-1953 (Author's collection)

J. B. Hancock's handwritten letters (copies) 1959 and 1964 (CID Archives)

Mary S.Corbishley's handwritten letters 1942-1944 and 1963 to parents of deaf pupils (Deirdre Taylor's and Author's collections)

Letter of Appeal, 2nd December 1988 from Malcolm Bown (Author's collection)

Letters of reference 1925-1937(typed copies from Catherine Penrice's collection)

Letters of reference 1935-1959 and 1965 from the Central Institute of the Deaf, St Louis, Missouri, USA (CID Archives)

Additional Selected References from Websites:

Britain 1906-1918. http://www.learningcurve.gov.uk/britain1906to1918/g5/background.htm

Cheshire: Bartholomew's Gazetteer of the British Isles 1887. http://www.fhsc.org.uk/genuki/chs/

Cuckfield churches. www.cuckfieldcompendium.co.uk

History of Chipping Campden. http://www.chipping-campden.net/history.html

History of the Central Institute for the Deaf in the USA. http://www.cid.wustl.edu/deaf%20education/CID%20History.htm

Poor Law Amendment Act, 1834. http://en/wikipedia.org/wiki/Poor_Law

Rubella. http://en.wikipedia.org/wiki/Rubella

Additional Selected References from Websites: (*Continued*)

The Canadian Army in the United Kingdom 1939-45. http://home.adelphia.net/~dryan67/orders/canadauk.html

The Pioneer 1949. www.royalpioneercorps.co.uk/rpc/history_main.1htm

Worcestershire: Bartholomew's Gazetteer of the British Isles 1887. http://www.genuki.gov.uk/big/eng/WOR

REGISTER OF PUPILS AT "THE HAYES", CUCKFIELD HOUSE & MILL HALL ORAL SCHOOLS 1937 – 1996

Note: *In the absence of adequate school records, the author has compiled all the pupils and their years as best as he could and is not responsible for any inaccuracies.*

"THE HAYES" in Hassocks, April 1937 – April 1939

1. Jean Baldry 1937-43
2. Catherine Hutchison 1937-43
3. David Kimbell 1937-51
4. Eleanor … ?
5. Hugh Mitchell 1937- ?
6. Colin Galbraith 1937 - ?
7. Simon … ?

CUCKFIELD HOUSE, April 1939 – December 1947

"Corby", p. 44: "January 1941 - …vacancies left by 34 evacuees … followed by 21 babies of two and a half years." p. 45 "… funny little school then had 17 pupils" in circa 1944 ; p. 46 - "… by the Autumn of 1947 thirty seven pupils were being taught at Cuckfield House."

Note: *The acronym MHGS indicated below is Mary Hare Grammar School, for which these pupils passed the Entrance Examination.*

8. Lorna Drillon 1940- ?
9. Gerda Drillon 1940- ?
10. Brian … ?
11. Peggy Laing 1940 (one term)
12. Brenda Tilley …?
13. Mary Hardy 1939- ?
14. June Hursey 1939- ?
15. Madeleine Reid 1941-43
16. Malcolm Reid 1941-43
17. Gabriel Saunders 1941-43
18. John Perrett 1941-45
19. Diana Whitby 1942-44
20. Ian Stewart 1942-46 MHGS
21. Rosalind Momber 1943-46 MHGS
22. Robert Riseley 1943-48
23. Michael Long 1943-51
24. Julia Crummy 1943-52
25. Susan Munt 1943-54 MHGS
26. Sarah Hutchinson 1943-55
27. Carol Sanderson 1943-58
28. Deirdre Millin 1944-45
29. Ann Down 1944-51
30. Patrick Chapman 1944-51
31. Patricia Johnson 1944-51
32. Julia Blakeway 1944-52
33. John Scott 1944-53 MHGS
34. Lois Raffery ?
35. Belinda Curling 1944-57
36. Jean Warburg 1944-57
37. Anne Bower 1944-57
38. Rosemary (Cherry) Mackenzie ? -1955 MHGS
39. Angela Batten 1945-56
40. Jennifer Bray 1946-52
41. Sally Woodhouse 1946-55
42. Elizabeth Mortimer 1946-58

CUCKFIELD HOUSE, April 1939 – December 1947 *(Continued)*

43. Margaret Murray 1947-57
44. Wendy Mears 1947-57
45. Wendie Holloway 1947-57

MILL HALL ORAL SCHOOL, January 1948 – Mary Corbishley's official retirement in April 1975

46. Sally Crouch 1948-58
47. Terry Prickett 1948-62
48. Helen Mackenzie 1948-63
49. Hilary Yarnton 1949-51
50. Angela Rosen 1949-61
51. Susan Hayward 1949- ?
52. Angela Gates 1949/51- ?
53. Eleanore Harms-Cooke 1950-51
54. Diana Butler 1950- ?
55. Elizabeth Seneff 1950-54
56. Lynda Fox 1950-64
57. Angela Bodenham 1950-64
58. Diane Rowe 1951-64
59. Helen Cunningham 1951-65
60. Sarah Allan 1951-66
61. Paula Norton 1952-66
62. Irene Roberts 1952-53
63. Eleanor Chapman 1952-59 MHGS
64. Rosemary Gilbey 1952-63
65. Judith Renshaw ? -1963 MHGS
66. Diane Purcell 1952-65
67. Veronica Armstrong 1952-66
68. Jill Jenner 1953-55
69. Dawn Moffatt 1953-62
70. Denela Platt 1953- ?
71. Gillian Richards 1954-62
72. Janet Easley 1954/55-65?
73. Joan Margeson 1954/55-65?
74. Helen Parr 1954-70
75. Julia Mathew 1955-65 MHGS
76. Susan Cox 1956-63
77. Janette Alexander 1956- ?
78. Alison Saunders-Davies 1956-65 MHGS
79. Shirin Nanji 1957 (short term)
80. Hazel Stevens ? -1964 MHGS
81. Susan Nash 1957-64 MHGS
82. Susan Marshall 1958-66
83. Linda Smith 1959-65
84. Ebrahim Saleh 1959-66 MHGS
85. Ian Depledge 1959-67 MHGS
86. Mary Underhay *c.*1959-68
87. Susan Carol Jones 1960-62
88. Ratan Vakeel 1960-63
89. Barbara Logan 1960-65
90. Margaret Redding 1960-?
91. Susan Stubbs 1960-68?
92. Mary Monk 1960-75
93. Fiona Damm *c.*1960/61- ?
94. Joan Schmidt *c.*1961- ?
95. Diane Merritt 1961-62?
96. Kevin Cave 1961-64.
97. Haridrani de Silva 1961-66?
98. Helen Hyslop 1961-66 ?
99. Carole J. Carter 1961-68
100. Susan Hooley 1961-68
101. Michael Hooley 1961-68
102. Margaret Finch 1961-70 MHGS
103. Janice Key ? -1971 MHGS
104. Linda Lewis 1962 - ?
105. Carolyn Maile ?1962-65
106. Penny Saunders-Davies 1962-70
107. Annette Turner 1963-65
108. Maia Nadler *c.*1963-66
109. Carey Mathew 1963-1968
110. Sandra Israel 1963-70 MHGS
111. Funda Gürel 1963-75
112. Bernadette McLoughlin 1964 -?

MILL HALL ORAL SCHOOL, January 1948 – Mary Corbishley's official retirement in April 1975 (*Continued*)

113. Catriona Johns 1965-72
114. Carol Allen ? -1972
115. Lesley Walker 1965-72 MHGS
116. Caroline Sanders 1965-75 MHGS
117. David Reynolds ? -1975   MHGS
118. Cathy Tippett 1966-69
119. Jacqueline Carcillo 1967-70
120. Sara Johnson 1967/8-71
121. Jayne Collins 1967-74
122. Jocelyn Simpson 1968-72 MHGS
123. Gillian Weeks 1968-73
124. Katherine Lewis ? -1974 MHGS
125. Rachel Godwin 1968-74
126. Karen Weeks 1968-75
127. Sarah Butler 1968-76
128. Hazel Binns ? -1976
129. Julian Atkinson ? -1976
130. Annabelle Bolingbroke-Kent 1969-77 MHGS
131. Marcus Diamond *c.*1970-78
132. Rachel Peacock 1970-78 MHGS
133. Annabelle Robinson 1971-81
134. Douglas Spooner 1972-80
135. Helen Lamond 1973-75 MHGS
136. Mark Woolven 1973-79
137. Yvonne Rankin 1973-late 80s
138. Richard Walker 1973-81
139. Celina Reed 1973-81 MHGS

MILL HALL ORAL SCHOOL, Mrs H. Webster 1974-1984

W1. Clifford Britton *c.*1974 -76 ?
W2. Richard McBrayne 1974-76
W3. Eric Nielson 1974-78 MHGS
W4. Anna Mansell 1974-80 MHGS
W5. Simon Kitcher 1974-82
W6. Suzanne Spooner 1974-83 MHGS
W7. Michelle Robertson 1974-83 MHGS
W8. Claire Hancock *c.*1974/5-1983 MHGS
W9. Emma Hancock *c.*1974/5-1985 MHGS
W10. Jane Nabarro 1975-79 MHGS
W11. Alexander Bull 1975-82 MHGS
W12. Christopher Smith 1975-1982 MHGS
W13. Alexander Boakes ? -1983 MHGS
W14. Daffyd Jones *c.*1975/6-84 MHGS
W15. Leo Mansell 1975-84 MHGS
W16. Douglas ……… (1976)
W17. Patrick ………. (1976)
W18. Matthew Hewitt 1975/6-86
W19. Angela Kensitt 1976-79 MHGS
W20. John Coppock 1977-85
W21. Nicolas Busk 1978- ?
W22. Niall Burke 1978-80
W23. Marcos Marchese 1978-82
W24. Rachel Caws 1978-82 MHGS
W25. Nadia Ali 1978-82 MHGS
W26. Thomas Page-Phillips 1978-84
W27. Muyiwa ….. *c.*1978-84
W28. Clare Mitchell 1978-84 MHGS
W29. Paul Baker *c.*1978-85
W30. Emma House *c.*1978-85 MHGS
W31. Richard Walker *c.*1978-86 ?
W32. Martin Haynes 1978-86
W33. Mark Spearey *c.*1978-86
W34. Alison Leach 1978-87 MHGS

MILL HALL ORAL SCHOOL, Mrs H. Webster 1974-1984 (*Continued*)

W35. Clare Smith 1979- ?

W36. Carmen Carter 1979-84

W37. Joanne Sargant ? -1985/86

W38. Neil Caws 1980-85 MHGS

W39. Debbie Carter 1980- ?

W40. Katie Hooker 1980-88

W41. Joanna Healey 1980-88

W42. Chiamaka Olejeme 1980-89

W43. Claire Gibson *c.*1981-86

W44. Ross Dawes *c.*1981- ?

W45. Fiona Mitchell 1981-87 MHGS

W46. Joanna Tringham 1982/3-86

W47. Susan Pitt *c.*1982- ?

W48. Garry Simms 1983-86

W49. Philip Barker? *c.*1983- ?

W50. Andrew Hearn 1983-88 MHGS

W51. Matthew Hearn 1983-89 MHGS

W52. Catherine Saunders 1983-89 MHGS

W53. Carrie-Ann Kuxhaus *c.*1984- ?

W54. Rotimi Fashola *c.*1984- ?

W55. Nanfua ……. ?

W56. Shiraz …………. ?

Note: Following pupils are not identified by their years 1965-84?

W57. Sally Barnacoat

W58. Jill Frankis

W59. Karen Elsey

W60. Laura Hiestand

W61. Christine Sands

W62. Leslie Turner

MILL HALL ORAL SCHOOL, Mr M. Bown, 1984-1993 : Mr P. Simpson, 1994-1996

B1. Kathryn Maynard 1984-87

B2. Kwame Afrik *c.*1984- ?

B3. Nicola de St Croix 1984- ?

B4. Alim Chandai 1984- ?

B5. Alexander Hurley 1984-88 MHGS

B6. Chizoba Olejeme 1984-88

B7. Naomi Sheepwash 1984- ?

B8. Katy Beeson 1984-88/89

B9. Zarina Thobani 1984-88/89

B10. Phillip Strutt 1984-89

B11. Troy Carter 1984-91

B12. Eleni Botonaki 1984-91

B13. Aparna Koirala 1984-93

B14. Timothy Burt 1985-86

B15. Corinna Simmons 1985-87 MHGS

B16. Janet Hickman 1985- ?

B17. Luke Bond 1985-88

B18. Catherine Cousins *c.*1985/6-88

B19. Alexander Fergus 1985-88

B20. Roanna Simmons 1985-89 MHGS

B21. Dornu Me …… *c.*1985-88/89

B22. Tina Nye 1985-90 MHGS

B23. Luke Taylor 1985-90

B24. Victoria Paull 1985-90 MHGS

B25. Matthew Robak 1985-90 MHGS

B26. Anthea Donker 1985-91

B27. Astara Marsden 1985-91

B28. Pieter de Heer 1985-91

B29. Ella Burke 1985-91

B30. Stuart Boakes 1986-87

B31. Zoe Kakolyris ? -1989

B32. Simon Miller 1986-90

MILL HALL ORAL SCHOOL, 1984-1993 : 1994-1996 (*Continued*)

B33. John Docker 1986-90 MHGS

B34. Karl Hammond 1986-91

B35. Sonya Nye 1986-92

B36. Samantha Caiels 1986-92 MHGS

B37. Jackson Bishop 1986- ?

B38. Robert Freeland 1986- ?

B39. Mark John Summers 1987- ?

B40. Evan Gibbs *c.*1987-90

B41. Brett Cheeseman 1987-90

B42. Lydia Docker 1987-92

B43. John M....... 1988/89 - ?

B44. Deepa Shastri 1988-90 MHGS

B45. Zoey Mason 1988-90

B46. Sarah Gilmour 1988-91

B47. Gregory Pierssene 1988-91 MHGS

B48. Alexander Cowen 1988-91 MHGS

B49. Angela Spielsinger 1988-92 MHGS

B50. Alexandra Gargini 1988-92

B51. Cheryl Bowyer 1988/89-92

B52. Brett Stewart 1988-92

B53. Yaa Mensah 1988-93

B54. Darren Smith 1988-94

B55. Victoria Goodacre 1988-94

B56. Reuben Clarke 1988- ?

B57. Aaron Turner 1989-90?

B58. Nathalie Abraham 1989-90

B59. Peter Lower 1989-90

B60. Nicky Cutajar 1989-91

B61. Michala Daly-Hadigan 1989-91 MHGS

B62. Laura Newman 1989-91

B63. Tanya Guy 1989-91

B64. Doran Scotson 1989-91

B65. Kirsty Brown 1989-91

B66. Robert Childs 1989-92 MHGS

B67. Rebecca Bailey 1989-92

B68. Amanda Norris-Holgate 1989-92

B69. Thomas Beattie 1989-92 MHGS

B70. Laura Dunkley 1989-92

B71. John Scoufarides 1989-94

B72. Francesca Warren-Price 1989-95

B73. Luke Leyden 1989-96

B74. Russell Cooke 1990-91 MHGS

B75. Karti Sundaralingham 1990-92 MHGS

B76. Lucy Clarke 1990-93 MHGS

B77. Gavin Lilley *c.*1990-93 MHGS

B78. Fergus Cooke 1990-93 MHGS

B79. Damaris Cooke 1990-94 MHGS

B80. Katherine Scase 1990-94

B81. Tracey Spielsinger 1990-95 MHGS

B82. Catherine Drew 1990-95 MHGS

B83. Roy Kerr 1990-96 MHGS

B84. Bassim Baz 1991-92 MHGS

B85. Kafayat Badaru 1991-92

B86. Marcus Fuccillo 1991-93

B87. Mary Pearman 1991-94

B88. Sean Richards 1991-1994 MHGS

B89. Maha Shahid 1991- ?

B90. Hilda Offrew ?

B91. Penny ...... ?

B92. Qais al Badu 1991- ?

B93. Matthew Bateup 1991-94

B94. Katie Rumney 1991-94

B95. Andrew Mayes ? -1994

B96. Harry Clasper ? -1994

B97. Michael Roberts 1991-94

B98. Shawana Iftikhar 1991-94

B99. Daniel Rumney 1991-94

MILL HALL ORAL SCHOOL, 1984-1993 : 1994-1996 (*Continued*)

B100. Fozan Gulrez 1991-94

B102. Andrew Godber 1991-95

B104. Robin Glover 1991-95 MHGS

B105. Jamie Baillie 1991-95

B107. Fergus England 1991-96

B108. Rowan Dixon 1991-96

B110. Thomas Akers 1991-96

B112. Michael Clark 1991-96 MHGS

B113. Sabira Yameen 1991-96 MHGS

B114. Paul McTaggart 1991-96

B116. Jamie Doolan 1991-96

B118. Nicholas Depledge 1992-93

B120. Rebecca Miller 1993-95

B122. *Christopher Drew 1993-96

B124. *Andrew Avery 1994-96

B126. *John Bishop 1994-96

B128. *Conor Downey 1994-96

B130. *Danielle Mayo 1994-96

B132. *Hamish Roberts ?1994 -96

B134. *Giles Bowman 1994-96

B136. Toni-Jayne Ward 1994-96

B101. Chloe Sharratt 1991-94

B103. Oliver Mansfield 1991-95

B106. Kris Meechan 1991-95

B109. Coco Stone-Brown 1991-96

B111. Ryan Godwin 1991-96

B115. *Ross Edwards 1991-96

B117. *Hamish Cooke 1991-96

B119. Christopher Muldoon 1992-96

B121. Lewis Gerrity 1993-96

B123. Christine Woodward 1994-?

B125. Lucy White 1994-96

B127. *Tessa Boyd 1994-96

B129. *Victoria Draper 1994-96

B131. *William Reynolds 1994-96

B133. *Lucy Jones 1994-96

B135. Nick Carter 1994-96

B137. Phillip Webster 1994-96

*MARY HARE PRIMARY SCHOOL – MILL HALL, Newbury in September 1996 [*Following pupils moved from Mill Hall to the Primary School in 1996*]

P1. *Ross Edwards 1996-98 MHGS

P3. *Hamish Cooke 1996-98 MHGS

P4. *Andrew Avery 1996-99

P5. *Christopher Drew 1996-99 MHGS

P6. *John Bishop 1996- ?

P8. *Conor Downey 1996- ?

P10. *Danielle Mayo 1996- ?

P12. *Hamish Roberts 1996-2001 MHGS

P13. *Giles Bowman 1996-2001 MHGS

P2.*Lucy Jones 1996-98 MHGS

P7. *Tessa Boyd 1996- ?

P9. *Victoria Draper 1996- ?

P11. *William Reynolds 1996- ?

Compiled by Ian M. Stewart: Updated May 2010